D1188337

Built for Use

Built for Use

Driving Profitability Through the User Experience

Karen Donoghue

McGraw-Hill

New York   Chicago   San Francisco   Lisbon   London
Madrid   Mexico City   Milan   New Delhi
San Juan   Seoul   Singapore   Sydney   Toronto

Library of Congress Cataloging-in-Publication Data

Donoghue, Karen.
    Built for use : driving profitability through the user experience / by Karen Donoghue.
       p. cm.
    Includes bibliographical references and index.
    ISBN 0-07-138304-2
    1. Customer services—Management. 2. Customer relations—Management.
  3. Consumer satisfaction. 4. Strategic planning. I. Title.

HF5415.5 .D655 2002
658.8'12—dc21
                                                         2001056215

Lycra® is a registered trademark of DuPont. Trellix and Trellix Web are registered trademarks. Web Gems is a registered trademark of Trellix Corporation.

McGraw-Hill

A Division of The McGraw-Hill Companies

Copyright © 2002 by Karen Donoghue. All rights reserved. Printed in the United States of America. Except as permitted under the United States Copyright Act of 1976, no part of this publication may be reproduced or distributed in any form or by any means, or stored in a data base or retrieval system, without the prior written permission of the publisher.

1 2 3 4 5 6 7 8 9 0 DOC/DOC 0 9 8 7 6 5 4 3 2

ISBN 0-07-138304-2

This book was set in Life by MM Design 2000, Inc.
Printed and bound by R. R. Donnelley & Sons Company.

McGraw-Hill books are available at special quantity discounts to use as premiums and sales promotions, or for use in corporate training programs. For more information, please write to the Director of Special Sales, Professional Publishing, McGraw-Hill, Two Penn Plaza, New York, NY 10121-2298. Or contact your local bookstore.

This book is printed on recycled, acid-free paper containing a minimum of 50% recycled, de-inked fiber.

For Mark and Max,
Mathilda Holzman and Muriel Cooper

contents

foreword

Michael Schrage

Co-director of the MIT Media Laboratory EMarkets Initiative
Author, *Serious Play*

Innovators innovate. Marketers market. Designers design. Salespeople sell. That's the organization given. The challenge is to align those arrays of skill, talent, and competence in formats that make sense to the organization and actually make money from the customer.

That's a hard problem. It's particularly hard to create alignment *not* because people don't care about customers and clients, but because nearly everyone has his or her own (legitimate) point of view about what should work. The Net makes it easy to embrace a hodgepodge of different POVs onsite. The result is the typical Web experience, something that looks as intuitively obvious and easy as riding a bicycle. You realize it's not so easy after you've fallen down, gotten kicked off, and gotten irritatingly lost for the third straight time in ten minutes.

We can talk about "leadership" and "customer-centricity" until the cows comes home and NASDAQ hits 5000 again, but we will be missing the key point that Karen Donoghue so artfully makes in this book. We create innovative user experiences by creating innovative metrics that challenge our creativity rather than force us into slavish compliance with inflexible requirements. We create value by having values—and having the courage and rigor to communicate these values in our designs.

If everyone has the same "customer-centric" concerns and comparable "customer-centric" metrics, we end up with the Web experience as a commodity. Don't get me wrong: Commodities can be wonderful things. Some of my best friends are commodities. You can even make money selling commodities. But don't think for a moment that you can build a unique brand character or a unique customer relationship if the experience you provide looks and feels like that of everyone else. We create value-added experiences through differentiation, not commoditization. The interplay between the standard and the unique is absolutely critical, and this is a theme that Karen comes back to again and again. It matters.

Sure, the book has terrific anecdotes and case studies. Yes, it has the crisply expressed and well-prioritized checklists. But what matters most to me in this text is that there is a design sensibility that is rigorously tested and measured against expectations. The recommendations here are the beginning of the design dialogues, not their conclusion. What makes this work is the design integrity that insists we have to measure even the qualitative and touchie-feelie stuff that designers aren't supposed to want to measure.

The reality, of course, is that the marketplace is the ultimate arbiter of the (economic) effectiveness of our designs and experiences. That said, you want to go to market where the metrics and heuristics you're using make it easier for you to get the *best* out of your colleagues and customers rather than get in the way. By respecting the hard realities of the design process, Karen has made it an order of magnitude easier for organizations to craft compelling design realities of their own.

So is the problem of creating compelling Web experiences effectively "solved"? Of course not. In fact, this book creates a brand new problem for its readers: Do they have the guts—not the creativity, the guts—to hold themselves accountable for the quality of their design collaboration? The readers who do will be transformed; the readers who don't, won't, or can't will have to live with the understanding of what they're missing—and what their customers are missing.

preface

The View Toward the Future

The trends covered in this book suggest that companies must address the issue of how to deliver an equilibrium of value—for the firm and for customers—through the user experience. Trends in technology, medicine, and science are moving toward a scale that is smaller than a human being. Indeed, DNA sequencing, stem-cell research on embryos, and nanotechnology that enables the design of microelectronics in a test tube are happening daily—but we still need to keep focused on the human being who is having the experience with technology. The human-scale experience will remain critical even as we resolve to ever-smaller scales of technology.

In my work as a strategic planner, I am asked to design many types of user experiences. I may be working with the Victoria & Albert Museum in London to design an experience architecture to deliver the collection of British art and design for a multilingual audience using new kinds of technology. Or I might be asked to design a new equities trading system for Fidelity Investments. Regardless of what I am asked to design, my initial approach is always the same, and I begin by asking the following questions:

- Who is the end user?
- What's the value proposition of the experience?
- What is the best experience that will deliver value to the user?
- What are the measures of success in the experience?

This book is not meant to stifle innovation or to prevent innovators from coming up with novel experiences. It's meant to help guide strategic planning and development toward the goal of delivering a return on investment, something we all sorely need in this post-dotcom era. Not all good user experiences are designed to satisfy a business case. Some user experiences—Napster, for example—are highly successful user experiences that don't necessarily produce a return on investment (ROI). The measure of success depends on the intended goal.

I wrote this book to answer many of the questions about user experiences that executives and practitioners have asked of me in the past few years. I have often found it difficult to explain to people at parties, or to prospective clients, exactly what it is that I do. I hope this book will help.

With that, let's begin to analyze why user experiences are important to business and should be tied more closely to profitability.

 Amidst the turbulence of the market, successful firms still understand that regardless of the technologies used, the ultimate end users are people, who don't evolve as rapidly as technology.

acknowledgments

The experience of writing this book was like participating in a moveable feast of ideas. Thank you all, it is a privilege to know and work with all of you.

Peter K. Bennett of State Street Global Advisors, thank you for your vision and for allowing me to work on such innovative experience architectures.

Thank you Michelle Williams at McGraw-Hill, Wagner at Waterside, and Susan Clarey and Janice Race at McGraw-Hill.

Thanks also to Nicholas Negroponte, Michael Schrage, and Mike Hawley of the MIT Media Laboratory.

Thanks also to:

Dan Bricklin from Trellix Corporation, whose encouragement at the outset helped shape my thinking on this topic

Jeffrey Feldgoise of Fidelity Investments

Hans Peter Brondmo of Netcentives

Ronna Tanenbaum of Alexa Internet

Christina Pandapas

Hollie Schmidt of Lifting Mind

Peter Schmidt of Lifting Mind

Ryan Gorer

Erik Heels

Joseph Paradiso, Ph.D., of the MIT Media Laboratory

Demetra, Kevin, and Liam McDonough

Maryam Mohit at Amazon.com, and Madeline Zech

Sam Joffe and Tom Blackader of FitSense

James Currier of Emode.com

Jennifer Gabler and Bill Blundon of Extraprise

Deborah Frieze

Frank M. Days of MediaPearls

Mark D. Halliday of MediaPearls

John McClain of State Street Global Advisors

Pattie Maes of Open Ratings

Teresa Esser

Steve Woit

Kathryn Blair

William Buckland and Keith Macbeath

Tim Jackson

Stephanie Houde

Christopher Gant

Paul O. Perry

Ron Perkins of Design Perspectives

Alan Schell, Ph.D.

John Choe

Dan Workman of Oracle

Kathy DeVivo

Mike Gonnerman

John Frank and Doug Brenhouse of MetaCarta

Jim Logan of Gotuit Media

Iang Jeon of Pioneer Investments

Charlie and Joan Call

Glen Urban of MIT Sloan School

Joost P. Bonsen of MIT Sloan School

Dianne Goldin at MIT

Gil Roeder

Marylin Hafner

Eric Sall

Barry Horwitz

Amanda Powers and Yonald Chery, Patrick Purcell

Hyun-A Park and Jacob Friis

Kevin Brooks of the Motorola Human Interface Lab

Tom Tullis, Ph.D., of the Fidelity Investments Human Interface Design group at the Fidelity Center for Applied Technology (FCAT) within Fidelity Investments Systems Company (FISC)

Philippe Stessel and Gail Smith

Rene Holl, Alison Harris, and Art Mellor

Maureen and Bill Wrinn

Randy Souza and Paul Sonderegger of Forrester Research

Don DePalma

Rusty Szurek

Charles Dao

Francois Gadenne

Henry Lieberman of the MIT Media Lab

Matt Molloy and Bob Preble of Trellix Corporation

Noubar Afeyan of NewcoGen

Trish Fleming of the MIT Enterprise Forum of Cambridge

Ben Howell Davis

Sudhir and Ed at Angstrom Medica, Inc.

Alison Fields

Albina, Bob, and Elizabeth

introduction

Despite the recent collapse of many dot-coms, the Internet has quietly established itself as a vital customer-relationship channel. Amazon.com created a new experience for buying books and consumer goods online, Yahoo! Finance allows market enthusiasts to get up-to-the-minute stock quotes and track their portfolios. PowerStreet Pro™ empowers Fidelity Investments customers to trade equities online, and eBay enables the world's biggest secondary market. In the business-to-business (B2B) world, Google now powers some of the most popular search engines. The ability of these and many other businesses to quickly amass a large and loyal audience relies in large part on the attention they've paid to a key discipline: *the user experience.*

Successful user experiences deliver a firm's value proposition— the brand promise—to customers in the most effective and appropriate way. Usability is now linked to revenues—and profits—as never before: If a customer can't engage in the full brand experience because of usability issues, the value proposition is diminished in the customer's mind.

The term *user experience* is complex. In the narrow sense, it describes the electronically mediated customer relationship and its enabling mechanisms, which include the physical user interface and the engagement and interaction processes as well as the feedback system. In the broadest sense, the term *user experience* encompasses the behaviors and attitudes of end users and their incentives to actually use the system—something that can demand change management in B2B environments. Satisfying end users' needs so that they change their behaviors and actually want to use the experience is critical to success. Without these fundamentals in place, great user experiences have no hope of wide adoption. To be successful, user experiences must deliver an equilibrium of value for both firms and users, working in the service of building trust, satisfying user goals, and enabling the successful completion of tasks while driving profitability at the same time.

> Successful user experiences deliver a firm's value proposition—the brand promise—to customers in the most effective and appropriate way.
>
> Usability is now linked to revenues—and profits—as never before: If customers can't engage in the full brand experience because of usability issues, the value proposition is diminished in the customer's mind.

The user experience is now a major part of the value of any firm that uses the Internet as a distribution channel, and it will continue to play an important role in the increasingly networked world. The "hard" metrics used to measure online success—buyer conversion rate, unique visitors, return visitors, session duration, percentage of abandoned shopping carts, and so on—are all critically dependent on the "soft" discipline of user experience. Consider, for example, where Amazon.com would be without the "1-Click" buy feature or what the opportunity cost would be of a lost customer who can easily jump to a competitive site on the Web. We can now begin to value the user experience by considering that it affects the answers to these strategic questions: What is the value of a lost customer? What is the lifelong value of a return customer? What is the relationship of customer acquisition to the overall business model?

In the next few years, user experiences will play an increasingly important role in B2B commerce relationships, facilitating dynamic and on-the-fly ebusiness relationships among business partners participating in real-time business transactions. Firms that are electronically easy to do business with will gain competitive advantage. Those that fail to architect their enterprise systems and integration efforts around the needs of end users will fail to see a return on their massive investments. As more face-to-face interactions are disappearing, the user experience will emerge as a crucial part of the intangible value of firms—and a new source of intellectual property (IP) as relationships matter more than physical assets.

Amidst the turbulence of the market, successful firms still understand that regardless of the technologies used, the ultimate end users are people, who don't evolve as rapidly as technology. The user experience offered to a visitor to a Web site or to a corporate employee using an enterprise portal is the start—or the continuation—of a customer relationship, with significant long-term value. Just as a haughty clerk can chase away a shopper in a store, a frustrating or inconsistent user experience online can be just as damaging.

Successfully leveraging the Internet requires that companies develop customer experiences that satisfy customers and drive profitability. Yet customers still have bad experiences online: bad navigation, irrelevant search results, unclear directions on how to purchase, lousy customer service, all resulting in low levels of retention and a lack of trust. Imagine that a bad user experience is represented as a person: now imagine that at every step that person thwarted your progress, made offensive remarks, and acted inconsistently. Would you want to associate with that person again? Never.

The user experience is the new vehicle for conducting customer relationships online: It will become an even more critical competitive advantage for establishing and maintaining market share in the future as more business revenue flows through increasingly transactional experiences inherent in ubiquitous computing. As such, user experiences must now effectively blend the needs of users into an experience that drives business profitability—and be tethered to business results. Companies must focus on delivering core functionality and a user experience that will deliver short-term results—without all the fancy bells and whistles—and evolve to larger scale user experiences as the business supports them. The user experience is a large part of the brand proposition—often, it *is* the brand—and it must now deliver one relationship, consistently, regardless of channel. The release of Microsoft's XP platform illustrates that the industry is beginning to view the experience with software as an encompassing environment, beyond just the user interface or the underlying technology.

An Overview of *Built for Use*

This book addresses the need for user experiences to be better designed for the ultimate end user—the customer—and to be more closely tied to business profitability in the future. It also covers strategic issues, tactical advice, and best practices on how to incorporate user-centric practices into the culture of the firm.

This book is for marketing executives and managers to read and pass to the development teams with whom they collaborate. This book is also a handbook for those involved in the actual process of strategic planning for the user experience—the information architecture, experience strategy, creative design, product development, and so on—who need to have a thorough understanding about the "why" behind the process of development. The best practices suggested throughout will be useful for management to use as guidelines and recommendations to be shared among multidisciplinary development teams.

This book is intended to provide a new framework and language for developing useful and valued electronically mediated experiences, regardless of context. The medium is shifting: We are speeding toward an even more constrained design environment than the Web—the wireless Web and ubiquity. Despite that development, holding user-centric concepts as a core part of the strategy won't change; instead it will become even more important. And for the first time we have a body of knowledge and some useful methodologies that can be carried over into the new contexts that will be used to deliver new kinds of commerce experiences in the future.

Provided in the pages that follow is a framework to catalyze thinking for marketers who must develop online customer experiences. Many of the practices suggested throughout have been used successfully with clients such as State Street Corporation, Fidelity Investments, and Trellix Corporation, who have developed user experiences that blend profitability with usability. Insights from interviews with senior executives at firms such as Amazon.com and eMode are also included.

The Internet has elevated the importance of the user experience to the strategic level, because of its immediate effect on profitability and the heightened expectations of customers. Customers now expect user experiences to be easy to learn and easy to use and to consistently deliver value. Going forward, firms must implement strategic and effective customer-centric design to make the critical difference in success—arguably between life and death, or at minimum between limited use and broader adoption. Quality of user experience will also be a crucial success factor in growing B2B ecommerce and in the acceptance of corporate portals. The big winners in the ebusiness arena will be those that understand the value of the user experience and practice customer-centric design. Based on our research in writing this book, firms that place the quality of user experience at the center of their user experience strategy share these characteristics:

1. A customer-centric culture driven by senior management, focused obsessively on being "of service" to customers, and whose user experiences successfully deliver an elegant equilibrium between satisfying customers' goals and those of the firm.
2. Rigorous practices, as derived from traditional product development blended with the best practices methods learned from the dot-com era.

3. A strong learning culture, where team members are encouraged to continually add to their knowledge, learning new technologies and design techniques and how to apply them to solve business challenges.

4. Open communication and a respectful interchange among multi-disciplinary teams—comprised of members from business strategy, technology development, and creative design—who have distinct goals, work processes, and metrics for success.

5. Shared metrics across the enterprise, so that each distinct group understands its contribution to overall user experience and its impact on business success, as well as continual measurement and refinement.

6. Profitability as a driving component of the design and development process.

This book is separated into three sections. The first section lays a framework for executives to understand why user experience is of strategic importance and should be more closely tied to profitability. The second section is more practical and suggests processes for planning, designing, and building successful user experiences. The third section casts a look—both near and far—into the future of user experience, and it offers insight into how the design and development of user experiences will evolve as technology and the business landscape evolves.

Part One:
The Case for the Customer Experience

Part One of *Built for Use* covers the strategic implications of delivering user experiences that compromise business success. The bursting of the dot-com bubble showed us that creating great customer experiences on the Internet is too expensive to deliver short-term profitability. Chapter 1 argues that firms need to employ better planning processes to determine a suitable ROI for the short term, tied to benefits in dollar amounts. They also need to put in place a framework to incrementally evolve to a longer-term relationship and satisfy the long-term ROI over time.

Chapter 2 gives a list of critical user-experience issues for marketers to consider. For executives who want to glean the top-line strategic issues in this book, reading this chapter will deliver a large portion of the value proposition of this book.

Chapter 3 presents a discussion of why trust is the linchpin of developing successful relationships in the networked world, and why it will increase in importance in the future. Guidelines for developing trusted user experiences are given. As user experiences must continually work in the service of building trust relationships with customers, and increasingly among business partners as more B2B commerce is conducted electronically, trust is key to successful user experiences. New forms of negotiated trust, among devices that will move seamlessly among local wireless networks, will become necessary as user experiences become increasingly transparent and ubiquitous.

Part Two:
Strategic Experience Envisioning

Part Two of *Built for Use* covers best practices for planning, designing, and building valued user experiences. Beginning in Chapter 4 with an argument for why it's important to capture the right customer requirements at the outset as informed by the business case and competitive landscape, the subsequent stages of architecture and design, technical evaluation and execution are covered in detail (see Figure I-1). The cultural and political issues of developing usercentric experiences are covered, as well as why the skill sets of the team members are important to consider when building a team.

The importance of information architecture, and its effect on the user experience, is discussed in Chapter 5, as well as the necessary cultural conditions to develop and retain this kind of talent. This chapter shows why information architecture and user-experience design are difficult and demanding crafts. With the advent of the

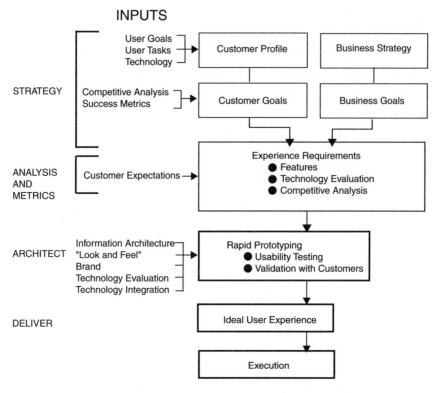

INPUTS

Figure I-1. A strategic lifecycle for designing business-relevant user experiences is covered in detail in this book. The strategic planning process uses business and customer goals/requirements as inputs and covers areas such as competitive analysis, branding, information architecture, "look and feel," rapid prototyping, and technology development.

Web as a medium of commerce, they can have huge impact on business profitability.

This book argues strongly for more rigorous architecture in the design of user experiences. Like the best technology architectures, user experiences must be architected for scalability, to be able to evolve as the business model changes and the user population expands and evolves. For business, good bones matter more than skin when architecting user experiences. This section also follows the technology evaluation and architecture phase through to launch, keeping focused on the need to deliver the intended experience.

Chapter 7 presents a discussion about the necessary change management that must occur for successful user experiences to become part of the ongoing culture of a firm. The Internet casts a harsh light on inconsistent business processes and badly integrated systems. Firms that are not working to integrate their preexisting information systems and back-end systems will be revealed to be only paying lip service to the notion of "customer-centrism." As more face-to-face interactions are disappearing, the user experience will emerge as a crucial part of the "intangible value" of firms—and a new source of IP (intellectual property) as relationships matter more than physical assets. Companies will need to be better able to capture and translate the user experience into intellectual property. A new approach to treating user experiences as intangible assets with real value, and protectible intellectual property, is covered.

 The user experience is a crucial part of the "intangible value" of a firm, a new source of intellectual property that will grow in importance as customer relationships matter more than physical assets.

Part Three: The Future

Part Three takes a look into the future of user experiences. As the next decade will bring new business models that leverage the Internet to create customer experiences that are global, mobile, and transactional, and increasingly invisible, there will be a demand for new and innovative thinking about design and the human-machine interface.

Ubiquitous experiences will demand more rigorous experience design than the flimsy ones that often were delivered during the dot-com age. The wireless Web will never deliver a return on investment unless companies get the user experience right: An underlying intelligence in the infrastructure, appropriateness, and contextually aware sensing and relevance of information are key.

Future value will be delivered more and more through transactional experiences that aren't visible, demanding new forms of negotiated trust, better translation of customer requirements into useful experiences, and a supreme mastery of an "invisible and ubiquitous" medium. User experiences such as TellMe—a telephone-based service that allows consumers to search for local information using empathetic voice recognition over the phone—indicate the future of transactional experiences. To deliver value, technology will have to work in the service of delivering an increasing amount of value to people while at the same time demanding less of them.

part one

the case for the customer experience

the gap between what customers want online and what they get

Company RetireCo has just launched a new online retirement planning site, complete with educational and account information, up-to-the-minute market data, and news. The business model relies on usage and customer loyalty to drive profitability. After a costly marketing campaign, the site is attracting plenty of traffic. The usage logs indicate thousands of users are arriving at the home page daily and . . . leaving. Why? What went wrong?

User experiences that fail to deliver value to customers compromise business success. This gap—between what customers want online and what they get—is costing firms money. It is due to businesses failing to craft user experiences that build and strengthen relationships with customers. Before launching the site, RetireCo never bothered to ask its prospective customers about their goals for an online retirement planning service. Since many users were novice Internet users, they needed more help in understanding how to initiate and complete the registration process. Early adopters, however, had no difficulty registering but felt underserved by a lack of "power user" features.

During the Internet boom, companies spent millions of dollars creating user experiences that did not deliver a return on investment. And consulting firms justified the costs in the "hype of the moment." In the post-Internet era, firms still need to leverage the Web to build customer relationships, yet they can't waste valuable resources to do so. Now, user-experience strategy must better link firms' profitability goals and business success to the usability and usefulness of their electronically mediated experiences—and ultimately be held to longer-term accountability. A new model for planning and developing user experiences is needed, one that enables managers to deliver on short-term return on investment (ROI) goals yet at the same time establish the "experience framework" for creating long-term returns.

In the short term, a bad user experience immediately impacts profits. A customer who picks up the phone to call customer support in the midst of a frustrating online transaction now costs the firm approximately $80 in customer service costs for a transaction that should have cost pennies online. Or, as in the RetireCo example, customers couldn't even figure out how to engage with the site upon first experiencing it, never mind taking the first steps in building a relationship.

In the long term, the user experience is a critical component of building a sustainable competitive advantage online, because it now impacts the effectiveness of relationship building.[1] This in turn impacts buyer conversion and retention—the more critical measures of success online. Developing these experiences demands a new aggregation of skills called *experience relationship design*—a complex collaboration among marketing, technology, design, and product management. Each department of an enterprise has different goals, processes, and metrics for success. Marketers speak of success in terms of "retention and loyalty" and "maximizing returns on channel investment." Designers speak of "engagement" and "empathy for the user." Engineers either only want to build "cool technology" or else don't want to risk using the latest technology because of maintenance challenges. Perhaps paradoxically, the direct-sales force does not want the online channel to succeed because it cuts into their returns and diminishes their control over the customer relationship.

Ultimately, these competing agendas must coalesce into an experience that delivers value to the ultimate end user—the customer. Success for the end user means *extreme usability*: an experience that makes it easy to complete goals and accomplish tasks with a minimum of friction. Yet these user-focused measures of success don't address the business objectives of the firm,[2] which typically guide the strategic planning process. Successful user experiences deliver an equilibrium of value for the customer and value for the firm; they provide an experience that ultimately drives profitability. This book sets out to provide an actionable framework to enable experience owners to plan and develop user experience strategies to develop more effective relationships online, and to enhance profitability.

The term *user experience* describes the customer relationship and its enabling mechanisms (see Figure 1-1), which include the physi-

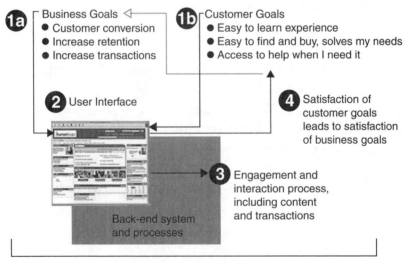

the User Experience

Figure 1-1. The user experience encompasses the entire electronically mediated customer experience, driven by the (1a) business goals and (1b) customer goals, (2) the physical user interface, (3) the engagement and interaction processes that communicate with the back-end system, and the feedback system. Successful user experiences (4) satisfy customer goals and drive profitability.

cal user interface, the engagement and interaction processes, and the feedback system. At a broader level, the user experience also encompasses the behaviors of end users and the change management required to drive adoption and usage. To be successful, user experiences must work to build trust, satisfy user goals, and enable the successful completion of tasks while driving profitability at the same time.

These electronic customer relationships can take many forms, depending on the type of business involved:

- A retail ecommerce experience, such as Amazon.com
- A product or application experience, such as Fidelity PowerStreet Pro™, an online retail trading system
- A customer relationship management channel, such as a private customer extranet
- A marketing channel, such as a Web site that serves as electronic collateral

Each of these relationships demands a specific and unique experience, one that empowers users to satisfy their goals and complete their tasks. Though the user interface for a business-to-business (B2B) exchange may look different than a retail auction site such as eBay, both deliver a similar experience-value proposition of access to liquidity, rapid price discovery, and the ability to transact. The key difference among these experiences is that the end users for each are radically different, requiring an interface that delivers product features and functionality in a way that delivers a uniquely good experience for each type of end user.

These differences demand that those responsible for the success of the user experience in terms of furthering the company's goals really "get" user experience. These "experience owners"—product managements or marketing people—must understand:

- How the user experience and user interface features satisfy customer goals

- How the strengths and limitations underlying technology enhance/hinder the user experience
- How usability impacts the bottom line—profitability

Many marketers are now the new "owners" of the user experience. Successful and profitable experiences will result from managers who have mastered the medium, who understand the impact that usability has on the bottom line, and who can communicate this to their development teams.

Build the Experience That Customers Want, the First Time Around

Identifying and understanding what customers want online can help companies plan and develop successful Internet customer experiences that drive revenue and profitability. But first, firms must determine a way to rapidly capture that knowledge and turn it into an actionable plan that will drive the design of the experience and contribute to business success (a point that is surprisingly overlooked far too often). Firms must plan user experiences with the end goal—the ultimate customer relationship—in mind, and work toward realizing that goal.

RetireCo could have avoided the failure of the site by taking a prototype with several key screens to customers early in the development process. It could have asked them to comment on what was and wasn't useful and what they wanted in the experience. It would have found that RetireCo's users wanted fast and easy access to enrollment, and they did not want to engage in more than a few clicks to find it. RetireCo would have also learned that many of the users—novices, as opposed to early adopters—needed proactive help in completing the enrollment form. Nothing causes attrition faster than a bad site experience, and the worst time to find out that an experience is not working is after the site has been launched.

More than ever, a large part of a firm's value rests in intangibles such as relationships with its customers. The degree to which these relationships are electronically mediated will increase and span multiple channels as customers determine where, when, and how they want to interact with a company.[3] For example, a customer might initiate a transaction over the phone in the morning, update the order via a wireless device in the afternoon, and check the status of the order online at home on a desktop computer in the evening. Successful firms will maximize the value of these *"ubiquitous user experiences"* across channels, minimizing friction for the customer and maximizing return on investments in retention-building strategies that deliver consistency and enhance the customer relationship. The customer will see only one relationship with the firm—the channel will be transparent. Electronic Customer Relationship Management (eCRM) is the integration of all sales, service, and marketing processes across all channels and is powered by ebusiness software applications. The successful execution of eCRM—recognized by analysts as strategically important to information technology (IT) investments over the next several years[4]—will enable firms to gather and develop a detailed behavioral history of the customer relationship. This, in turn, will help firms better understand their ongoing conversation with customers, allowing them to create the best possible experiences within each channel and among channels. Ultimately, this effort will drive profitability, because firms will be better equipped to predict and deliver the personalized experiences that customers want.

We'll begin with an analysis of why good user experiences create business value and propose a process for capturing the business drivers for a user experience strategy.

The online experience is the most engaging and intimate experience of a brand, where all of the rules of branding apply.

—*David Tames, Media Technology Consultant*

The Value of the Customer Experience

Customers now expect to choose among several channels for conducting a relationship with a company. As the online channel is becoming a more increasingly transactional one, the user experience has more impact on the relationship. In a sense, its value is comparable to that of a distribution channel. The resources that Barnes & Noble dedicates to developing and maintaining its retail stores indicates how it values the distribution experience. With a long history as a retail bookseller, Barnes & Noble's deep understanding of customer behavior and needs forms the basis of a knowledge bank that it uses to evolve the brick-and-mortar customer experience. Starbucks has also placed much value on the customer experience, which has been carefully designed to drive retention and loyalty through an environment and experience that is valued by customers and distinctly associated with the Starbucks brand. Part of what Starbucks customers value is consistency in the experience. Regardless of how many times a customer returns for another latte, or whether he or she visits another Starbucks location, the experience delivers consistency.

Online customer experiences must be more carefully developed than brick-and-mortar ones, because customers who go online can more easily escape to competitors. Yet often, online experiences are not better designed nor are they as successful as brick-and-mortar ones, although both measure their success by the same metrics of loyalty and retention. Bad user experiences lead directly to attrition, and they have adverse effects on retention and relationship building. Yet it seems as though many of the real-world principles of customer service have been disregarded in the design of online experiences, despite a great deal of preaching. And who owns this issue now? Increasingly, it's becoming a customer-relationship issue. So, does marketing now own the user experience?

It probably does—and it will continue to do so in the future. Yet the user experience cuts across many sections of the organization: Its development is the result of a complex, negotiated ownership among marketing, technology, operations, business development, and product design. Ultimately one executive has to own the experience to drive the process and guarantee best practices and the best experience for the customer.

User Experiences: Incremental and Evolutionary Design Is Key

Building great online experiences is costly. The millions of dollars spent on Web strategies in the last several years is evidence of this fact. And, it's unclear if firms ever see a return on their investment. Recently, Stanford Business School's Mohan Venkatachalam, and Shivaram Rajgopal and Sureth Katha of the University of Washington examined the relationship between marketing strategies and financial ones at ecommerce firms. In their study they used online quality evaluations of Web sites generated by a rating service[5] to identify forty-seven Web sites that deliver a superior online consumer experience. The service rated aspects of the customer experience such as the ease of navigation, customer confidence, product selection, virtual-community building, and price leadership and used those ratings to produce quality scores for Web sites. The measurement of shareholder value was based on price-to-sales ratio, a common measurement tool of ecommerce firms. The researchers discovered that, on average, for every 1 percent increase in the customer experience quality, there was a 1.66 percent increase in traffic to the site and a 0.84 percent increase in revenues. All of this speaks well for enhancing the online experience to better serve customers, yet it illustrates how building a great experience is a costly venture. Looking at profits, the researchers found that a 1 percent increase in the quality score was associated with almost the same increase in operating expenses and a 2 percent decrease in net income. They determined that the short-term benefits were dubious, and it was only those aspects of the user experience that drove customer relationship building that actually produced the potential for any long-term competitive advantage. Competitive advantages, such as ease of use or price, are quickly imitated by competitors. In the results of the research, investors showed no confidence that building a superior online experience provided a long-term competitive advantage.

Indeed, it is true that designing good user experiences is costly, but optimizing costs is only part of the equation. In the long run, developing a good user experience is a wise investment for a firm because it impacts critical components of building successful customer relationships—the ultimate basis of long-term shareholder value. Yet it takes time to see these long-term results, so companies must therefore define both short- and long-term ROI goals for the user experience and design incrementally by continually testing and making refinements and enhancements. "Firms should not be measuring the benefits and the cost incurred in the same period," says experience strategist Deborah Frieze, former chief experience officer and co-founder of Zefer Corporation, "because the benefits are going to come out two or three quarters down the road." Customers are still going to demand good experiences, but they don't need the "blockbuster" experiences that firms had been building throughout the dot-com mania. They were too expensive to ever deliver a return. To satisfy short-term needs, firms should develop user experiences that are "good enough" to deliver on short-term business goals and satisfy customers (as measured against specific dollar benefits) with an experience framework in place that will enable "experience evolutions" toward continually enhancing relationships. The short-term experience architecture, if developed with enough rigor and foresight, can be part of an additive effect that results in long-term returns.

As more people become savvier online consumers, they will begin to demand good experiences—forcing an efficiency in the "experience marketplace"—and firms will be under added pressure to deliver competitively good experiences. Why should a customer have a great online experience at a retail shopping site and a lousy one at a retail bank site? The goal for firms will be to balance the business case against what the customer needs to see value in the relationship.

The Stanford research of Mohan Venkatachalam and colleagues used a valuation model—namely price-to-sales ratio—to measure market value of pure-play Internet firms. But this argument would hold only if the valuations that the market assigned to these firms were indeed realistic. Does anyone actually think that the stock market had any idea of what it was doing when it valued Internet stocks? But the important aspect of the research—namely, comparing the quality of the customer experience to the ultimate hard metrics of shareholder value—is a very interesting concept and may serve as a model for the way firms will value intangible assets in the future.

User Experiences Should Be Just "Good Enough"

Nobody would argue that the financials at ecommerce firms, especially the price-to-sales ratio, would reflect a rational market. But this metric of value is reflecting the market's perception that pure-play Internet companies don't have a long-term competitive advantage when it comes to the overall quality of the customer experience. What is the bottom line? Firms still need to develop user experiences that are "good enough" to deliver a short-term ROI. Yet they should also spend accordingly on putting in place the right framework for building longer-term relationships with customers by developing scalable user experience. Firms don't have to go overboard and create the equivalent of online blockbuster movies or magnificent works of art. The value is in the perception of the experience, the fulfillment of value, and in the delivery of what the customer wants in the way he or she wants it. "Good enough" means good enough to produce both long- and short-term shareholder value. Achieving this value means concentrating on the aspects of the user experience that directly impact revenues and profits, such as the ability to help customers initiate and complete online transactions.

Think about your own travels online. While using an ecommerce site, you've probably:

- Ended an ecommerce transaction when you've been asked to enter your credit card number before you know your total cost and shipping cost
- Become lost on the way to the checkout screen and dumped your shopping cart in frustration
- Been unable to add an extra item on the way to checking out without abandoning the transaction
- Received an "Error 404: File Not Found" message during a transaction—and not known how to proceed
- Been denied access to a popular ecommerce site or been presented with a "This site is now shutting down due to server errors" message

It is amazing that all of these experiences still happen at ecommerce sites. In some cases, they are the result of technical difficulties that reflect the infrastructure of the Web. For example, issues such as the "Error 404: File Not Found" can't be controlled by the site designer because the problem lies in the external environment of the Web, which was not designed to handle errors gracefully. But bad navigation design for the shopping experience is an example of something that is easy to fix in the user experience. There's no excuse for it. Being able to add an extra item to a shopping basket is something that people do in the real world all the time, but it's been overlooked in the design of online systems. This experience is particularly noteworthy, as it has a direct impact on revenue.

Though the amount of frustration users will endure in order to use a site could arguably be an indication of its perceived value, customers certainly don't deserve these poor online experiences. They diminish the opportunity to build relationships with customers, and they lead directly to attrition by driving your customers directly into the arms of your competitors. Customers would never tolerate these bad experiences in brick-and-mortar stores. Imagine being told that the shop you were in was shutting down immediately and you were being forcibly ejected out the front door. Or picture a store that places a trip wire at the customer's knee level just as he reaches the cash register. How long would that store remain in business? By failing to provide the best online customer experience, firms are missing out on opportunities to develop and deepen relationships with customers, and losing chances to build trust, the cornerstone of any relationship. So, if online experiences are so important, why is it so difficult to develop good ones?

Part of the challenge to developing a good Web site is that sites are developed for technical platforms and delivery channels that are evolving rapidly and not very stable. Unlike customer experience in the brick-and-mortar world that use well-understood materials such as glass, wood, and concrete, customer experiences online are developed in an environment that rests on an ever-shifting set of unstable building blocks. There are no rules, no best practices, and no established body of knowledge of what to do and what not to do. Like pioneer architects in the mid-1800s who attempted to use a then-new material called steel to design bridges, we are searching for some rules of tensile strength, malleability, and a reliable framework in which to develop and enhance customer relationships through the Internet. And that environment is still evolving, because as ubiquitous computing moves into the mainstream it will again require new knowledge and practices as customer relationships are built in an increasingly invisible and transactional environment.

As the Internet is used to connect more appliances and devices, and as user experiences become increasingly networked and mobile, there may be no visual experience at all. These invisible-but-ubiquitous experiences will be even more challenging to design, because they will need to build trust without many of the usual cues that customers expect to have available. Experience designers of the future will need skills that combine knowledge about multiple channels and types of input—such as voice or gesture—with more experiential elements such as empathy for the end user. The ultimate environment in which these experiences are delivered may be more transactional—and potentially more impoverished—than the Web we know today. Think about how excruciating it is for someone to enter a Web site Uniform Resource Locator (URL) into a Wireless Application

Protocol (WAP)–enabled cell phone. Requiring the user to enter a special "mode" to enter letters and special characters means that typing in "http://" alone can take over two minutes—a bad design with even worse usability. Consider 3G, a new third-generation communications infrastructure designed to deliver information to handheld wireless devices at high speeds. To deliver on the business case, 3G will require designs that blend usability with usefulness and appropriateness and a new form of experience design that exploits the strengths of the medium to make the tasks easier for users. Ultimately, keeping users' goals and tasks as the central drivers is key to developing successful experiences in these new media and will help produce the return on investment for infrastructure to support such a mobile service.[6]

The best methods for planning a user-experience strategy are rigorous enough to enable a firm to establish a beachhead for the user experience yet remain flexible enough to accommodate evolution in technology or business models. Like architects who specialize in designing skyscrapers in San Francisco, customer-experience architects must be mindful of shifting tectonics and adjust accordingly with some flexibility and scalability in their designs. Evolving and scaling a design is far easier than having to rearchitect and redesign after launch—an often time-consuming and costly endeavor.[7] And, the dynamics of today's marketplaces demand the ability to change rapidly. Think about the rapid shift of businesses out of business-to-consumer (B2C) and into B2B business models? If the user-experience strategy is well planned, with a rigorous architecture in place that revolves around the needs and tasks of users, the experience framework can evolve along with the business strategy.

ROI Model for the User Experience

ROI is a means for calculating payback, to determine when an investment will pay for itself. In terms of an IT project, the inputs to determine ROI include the project cost, expected financial benefits, and time horizon when those benefits will be realized by the organization These benefits can be in the form of cost reductions, revenue growth, or both. The benefits may take years to appear, or they can be evident in months.

For a simple approximation of an ROI model for the user experience, start by quantifying the benefits in dollar amounts and discounting the value into today's dollars. Calculate the net present value (NPV) of each specific benefit using

- The dollar amount of the benefit
- Length of time until the benefit is realized
- The relevant interest rate (i.e., cost of capital/return on equity) for the particular business for the same length of time

The interest rate used should reflect the opportunity cost of not investing the project cost funds in other areas of the business. After calculating the NPV, subtract the cost of the project from the future benefit and divide this number by the cost of the project. The result is a percentage, positive or negative, that can be used to quantify the benefits of engaging in a user-experience project.

Let's look at an example. A U.S.-based consulting firm wants to grow its practice and leverage the Web site to increase their client base and enhance mind share among prospects. The ROI model would look like this:

Cost of developing enhanced site: $500,000

Measurable benefit to firm:

New leads that originate from site and become clients— $2 million expected to be generated at end of one year of use of the site. This would be verified by asking new customers how they found out about the firm and by tracking emails requesting follow-up information that originate through the site.

The ROI calculation for this benefit would look like the following:

1. Calculate the NPV of the benefit in today's dollars, based on the time horizon of n and an opportunity cost ("interest") of k:

Net present value of benefit =
future value of benefit $\times$ $(n)/(1+k)^n$

n is the number of time periods—in this case we will use 1.

If the interest rate were 10 percent, then the benefits for our example above would be:

Net present value of benefit = $2M/(1 + 0.10)= $1,818,181

This is the present value of a future amount to be received n periods from now, assuming an opportunity cost of k (interest rate to be used/ROE/cost of capital).

2. Subtract the incremental costs for development and divide by the costs:

ROI = (Net present value of benefit − cost) / cost

For our example, this would look like:

ROI = ($1,818,181 − $500,000) / $500,000 = 2.64

This means that the user-experience enhancement will produce a 264 percent return on investment that can be measured—a very good return.

This method can also be used for calculating the return on adding functionality—such as personalization or comparing multiple options for development. (See Figure 2-1.)

Developing User Experiences Is an Iterative Process

User-experience strategy involves a large amount of planning, a deep understanding of the business, and knowledge of customers' expectations. It also requires an understanding of the technical environment—its strengths and limitations—and the impact and importance of good design. Many clients express trepidation at having to take the leap of defining a user experience in such a swiftly evolving medium. They hesitate at having to outline an architecture when their businesses are evolving so rapidly. Worse yet, they worry about having to rearchitect, which is a challenging and painful process.

Developing a successful user experience is not simple. Success comes from an iterative, learning approach that uses observation, testing, adjustment, and refinement as part of the process—not unlike that of the seasoned merchandiser in the retail world. It's only after trying an approach, seeing how customers react, and then adjusting and enhancing it that user experiences will evolve to deliver ongoing value. Coupling behavioral metrics with qualitative methods is the best way to get the appropriate data to enhance the user experience.

To develop a successful online customer experience strategy means blending the needs of the customer with the firm's business goals—creating an elegant equilibrium between value for the firm and value for customers. Consider Amazon.com, the Internet's largest retail store, widely considered to provide a successful customer experience. Amazon has created a valued experience for its customers by paying obsessive attention to the details of the customer interaction. It allows Amazon's customers to accomplish their goals while, at the same time, encouraging more business by engaging the user in a respectful conversation that builds with each return visit to the site. This extends to the actual user interface: Amazon's "1-Click" Buy enables a customer to select a product and place a secure order using only one click of the mouse. It does this by storing the customer's preferred credit card and shipping method. This mechanism provides a clever means of establishing Amazon's value proposition in the customer's mind—delivering efficiency and ease-of-use while at the same time driving transactions. In using the Web as a real-time testbed for deter-mining usefulness, Amazon routinely tests two distinct user experi-ences in real time with customers—and then kills off the less suc-cessful one—often making decisions within a matter of hours of ini-tiating the tests. It's clear that Amazon lives and breathes ease-of-use and customer-centrism as a basic principle of their business philoso-phy, and it shows in the online customer experience.

Great user experiences can enhance the brand experience. Consider the experience a recent customer had after purchasing items online at Staples.com. She chose the express delivery, com-pleted her transaction, and then remembered she would not be home the next day to sign for the delivery. An email to customer support resulted in a nearly immediate response—she suspects via autoresponder—which explained that she should visit a specific URL to download and print a form to sign and tape to her door. This form would allow the express delivery service to leave the package without first obtaining a signature. This example of proactivity in the user experience illustrates that good design makes provisions for the kinds of goals and tasks that users have, in a variety of situations. The inherent value in the transaction—the assistance that solved the problem immediately—really impressed the customer. That Staples.com had taken the time to think through a customer issue such as this and developed an appropriate reaction enhanced the brand proposition in her mind.

The Value of the Lost Customer

To understand the business importance of the online customer experience, consider the value of the lost customer. In 1998, 42 percent of users abandoned an online transaction for traditional channels,[8] and a recent Shop.org survey suggests that this fact is still true. So more than one-third of the customers abandoned an online transaction; many of them instead picked up the phone to call the firm. Considering the cost of the typical phone call to customer support (ranging from $5 to $80), an online transaction that costs less than a dollar is an attractive savings that is directly impacted by the online user experience.

On the Web, business success metrics are impacted by the user experience, the new vehicle for building customer relationships. Over the last few years, analysts and companies invented new metrics to describe performance of ecommerce firms that had little to do with profit. Some of these new metrics included conversion rate (the ratio of buyers to shoppers), degree of engagement and time spent on the site, look-to-buy ratios, mindshare, and other more financial metrics such as retention rate.[9] The measures of success will undoubtedly change in the next few years as firms continue to build customer relationships online, but some of the earlier metrics of the Internet economy that are surviving include the number of unique users, the revenue per user, and the revenue per page view.

Marketing Needs Better Analytical "Chops": Let's Apply Some Science

The user experience is now offering a real-time testbed where science and measurement—and a different kind of market research—come into play. This "real-time product design" will demand strong analytical skills of marketers who will own the user experience and will need to understand how to interpret and analyze data captured from users to rapidly test a concept and adapt it in real time, if it is not working. Firms must define rigorous metrics for analyzing performance of their online experiences and, putting egos aside, quickly choose the experience that is delivering the best results. By viewing an ecommerce effort, not as a marketing effort, but as a long-term relationship effort, marketers should be saying "let's apply some science" to the process.

Relationship metrics are directly and immediately impacted by the user experience and easy to measure. Financial metrics are also impacted, the effect just takes time to measure. At their core, both of these kinds of metrics are really measuring the opportunity to build a relationship and the building of trust online. Trusted relationships lead to more loyal customers—and to more transactions. This in turn increases the value of the online customer experience.

Another way to value the online customer experience is to consider gains in efficiency and productivity. Let's examine the business goals behind the Web strategy for a large financial services firm:

1. Convert browsers to customers and increase client base
2. Deepen customer relationships and increase retention rate
3. Increase productivity inside the firm

To satisfy the first business goal, a large proportion of visits should lead to users taking action to initiate a relationship with the firm. For prospects, this might mean emailing to request a brochure or a follow-up call with a customer-service agent. For customers, this might mean increasing the depth of relationship with the firm by purchasing more products or services. The experience should deliver opportunities for these transactions to occur in contextually relevant ways and with prompts that call the user to action. The ease of completing these actions is important to satisfying this business goal. Measuring the efficiency of the experience in satisfying the business goals is straightforward with site analysis tools: If a large number of site visitors never return or visit only the home page and then leave, or the "Request a Brochure" page is never requested, then the experience is failing. Most important, the business goals will not be satisfied. Figure 1-2 displays a matrix that relates business goals to desired actions on the part of the user.

To address the second goal of increased retention, the experience must be compelling and deliver enough value to cause customers to return and place more trust in the firm over time. To meet this goal

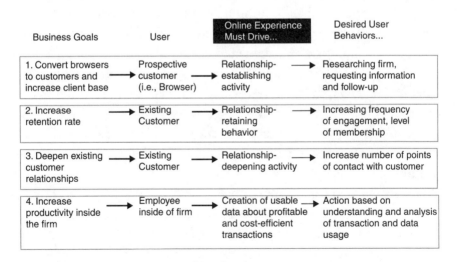

Business Goals	User	Online Experience Must Drive...	Desired User Behaviors...
1. Convert browsers to customers and increase client base	Prospective customer (i.e., Browser)	Relationship-establishing activity	Researching firm, requesting information and follow-up
2. Increase retention rate	Existing Customer	Relationship-retaining behavior	Increasing frequency of engagement, level of membership
3. Deepen existing customer relationships	Existing Customer	Relationship-deepening activity	Increase number of points of contact with customer
4. Increase productivity inside the firm	Employee inside of firm	Creation of usable data about profitable and cost-efficient transactions	Action based on understanding and analysis of transaction and data usage

Figure 1-2. The online experience must deliver value to all user segments to drive desired actions and behaviors, all driven by business goals.

requires a thorough understanding of what value users are seeking and the kind of experience through which they want it delivered. If customers value speed, efficiency, and rapid access to business-relevant information, then the experience must deliver business value in a manner that meets these experience requirements. Similar to building relationships in the real world, this goal requires the experience to consistently deliver value—on aspects such as appropriateness and usefulness—so that over time a level of trust and comfort is developed.

A good example of this kind of targeted, useful experience is shown in the private client extranets that State Street Global Advisors (SSgA), an asset-management firm, offers to its institutional clients (See "Trust Relationship Driving User-Experience Process: State Street Global Advisers" in Chapter 3.) These clients—such as pension managers who manage multibillion-dollar funds—have access to a custom extranet experience at a site called Client Corner that delivers account information, alerts from relationship managers, and custom presentations specifically created for the customer. Speed, efficiency, and utility are important to this customer segment—in surveys, these customers mentioned that they wanted this information and nothing more—and this customer data drove the design of the experience. The interface was developed to minimize clicks and maximize the value of the information for each session so that the user feels comfortable about using the site more frequently and engages in more services with the site. Peter K. Bennett, principal and strategist at SSgA, describes a notion of an "Experience Ledger" as a driving concept behind the Client Corner site: "Every experience with the site should add a check mark in the credit column of the user's experience ledger."

To meet the third business goal, increased internal productivity, firms should drive site experiences to artfully employ user-experience mechanisms that create value for their customers. In the spirit of Amazon's 1-Click buy, developing user-interface mechanisms that create a win-win situation for customers and for the firm can help drive internal productivity and efficiency.

Some real-world work processes lend themselves to online experiences that deliver huge efficiencies, both for the firm and for customers. Let's take an administrative example, such as the process of updating customer addresses for a firm in which the sales force functions as relationship managers. Imagine a real-world work process that requires this task to be done during business hours or only via fax. Customers must wait to hear back from the relationship manager to make sure the request has been serviced. Faxes sent after hours—or to a rep that happens to be out for the day—might be delayed. Worse yet, they could be lost.

Now imagine an easy-to-complete online address update request form. The online form, developed with step-by-step instructions, is an example of an efficiency for which the Web is perfect: enabling a "win" for customers by allowing them to easily complete the form and send in the update at their own convenience, any time of the day or night. Customers receive immediate feedback that the update has been received. The firm sees an increase in productivity, since reps no longer need to take time on the phone to take address-change information. And, because the customer is entering the information, the potential risk of keying error is greatly reduced.

The importance of a good customer experience becomes apparent in this example because ease-of-completion is the pivotal aspect of the user experience that enables both the customer and the firm to derive benefit. Ease of completion is critical. Without this, the value of the experience is degraded. As with the shopping cart that won't let the user add another item before checkout, the effect on the bottom line is immediate. If the form is difficult to complete or confusing, there's no value delivered if the transaction cannot be completed. Instead, the customer picks up the phone, and a transaction that should have cost pennies (see Figure 1-3) now costs the firm up to $80.

Figure 1-4 shows the ideal efficiency curves for this situation. As the number of online address-change requests increase, the number of phone calls for the same request should decrease. To see both curves increase would mean a serious flaw in the user experience: It

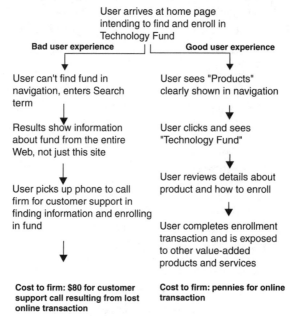

Figure 1-3. The left side of the flow diagram illustrates how a bad user experience can cost the firm as much as $80 on a transaction that should be generating revenue instead.

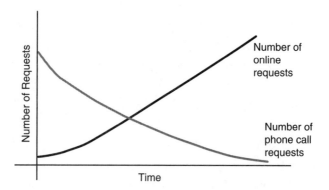

Figure 1-4. The ideal curves for enhanced efficiency: Efficiencies are increased as the number of phone call requests for address updates decreases and online requests increases.

would indicate that users are attempting to complete the transaction, and upon being unable to do so, are picking up the phone for customer support.

The Ultimate Success Measurements Are Financial

Over time the ultimate measures of online success will be hard financial metrics such as retention rate, number of new customers, and growth of wallet share. Though there have been many "soft" metrics proposed by analysts over the last few years, ultimately it will be the financial metrics that matter in calculating the value of companies. Online customer relationships are unique in that the financial or "hard" metrics for measuring value are outputs that depend on "soft" metrics as inputs, such as the perceived value of the experience, the degree of engagement, and time per page.

Encouraging an ongoing, deepening relationship is the way to win and retain customers. The value to the firm is in the retention of customers (return customers are the key to profitability), so firms should concentrate on the retention aspects of their online customer experience. Compare the cost of improving the loyalty-enhancing factors of the site experience such as developing better navigation, personalization, and overall usability with the cost of increasing the advertising budget to double the number of site visitors. The former is a long-term investment that can turn a $200,000 one-time cost into a definite retention-increasing experience that can grow the customer base over time. The latter is a short-term enhancement that demands an increasingly larger advertising budget to grow the customer base.

Retention is a metric that is easy to measure but difficult to get right in the design of the experience. Retention is really measuring the results of an ongoing process of developing a relationship with the customer over time: the rate and degree to which customers engage and evolve a relationship with a site over time, and the rate and degree to which they cede control in the experience. The user experience at My Yahoo!—Yahoo's own version of a personalized Web site—delivers well on both of these metrics by enabling users to quickly experience the value of personalization. With only one click from the Yahoo! home page, users gain access to a personal site that subtly encourages further personalization. There is no friction in the process, no lengthy registration page featuring inappropriate personal questions (e.g., "When is your birthday?"). Instead, the experience delivers rapid exposure to the value proposition of better, faster access to relevant information, and a subtle push to deepen the relationship by offering examples of other personalized sites (e.g., "The Entertainment Fan" and "The Sports Enthusiast") that are just one click away.

Usability is one aspect of the overall online customer experience that has an immense effect on retention, but the term has only recently worked its way into the vernacular and processes of online design. It has been difficult, if not impossible, to assign best practices for usability issues such as navigation, searching and finding, and brand representation. The availability of new authoring tools coupled with the highly visual nature of the Web has enabled design culture to influence Web design, but often there is a conflict between the goals of creative designers (visually stunning), technologists (technical innovation), and end users (effectiveness and usability). To drive the customer experience, the entire team should understand the business case behind the design, how it will be expressed in the user experience, and how its success will be measured. Across the entire organization, using shared metrics—which map financial metrics to customer-relationship metrics—to guide the design of the user experience is good practice.

The Ideal User Experience

Analyze what makes a user experience successful and apply the same thinking at the outset of a Web strategy. Consider Yahoo! Finance, one of the most successful financial portals. For Yahoo!, the business model behind this site is driven by advertising revenue, which means that the site's business offers aggregated content and searching, and targeted advertising for their direct customers, the advertisers. Yahoo! Finance's value proposition to its direct customers includes highly targeted traffic (or "eyeballs") of end users. The business goals include acquiring end users and retaining them (see Figure 1-5), which strengthens Yahoo! Finance's offering to its customers (again, the advertisers).

Consider the goals of the end users of this site, typically online investors who are technically savvy early adopters. They want lightning-fast access to content that they value, such as stock quotes and market feeds. For these users, the value is expressed by the measure of speed, efficiency, and no-frills rapid access to financial content.

Yahoo! Finance - a successful user experience

Business Goals:
- Premier online financial portal
- Revenue from advertising
- Customer acquisition
- Customer retention & engagement

End User Goals:
- Efficient access to stock quotes, news feeds
- Fast download of info, no waiting for download
- High-volume, rich content
- Easy to navigate
- Personalize to my needs and interests

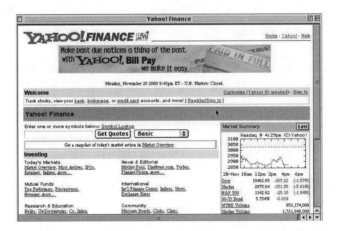

Figure 1-5. Yahoo! Finance Business/Customer/End User goals for success.

(Reproduced with permission of Yahoo! Inc © 2000 by Yahoo! Inc. YAHOO! and the YAHOO!

logo are trademarks of Yahoo! Inc.)

Richness in the experience is the volume, quality, and real-time aspects of the content, not the visual style. Utility is what counts. In a sense, the brand proposition is simply efficient access to relevant content. And Yahoo! Finance delivers concrete value to the user— the ability to aggregate and monitor stocks in a portfolio, and the ability to easily track this portfolio over time. While users are engaged in this activity they are exposed to advertisements, but the ads are delivered in the exchange of value to the user.

Consider again the business goals, which are acquisition and retention. Yahoo! Finance has extremely loyal users who engage with the site throughout the day, every day. The behaviors being exhibited by users (easily measurable using site-analysis tools) are answering the business goals of the site perfectly; at the same time they are delivering an experience that end users value. This perfect equilibrium is necessary in a successful user-experience strategy: a marriage between value for the firm and value for users as articulated through the user experience. This equilibrium has allowed Yahoo! Finance to become the standard of success for financial portals, both from the business and end-user perspectives. It's an engine for delivering value to both its advertising customers and end users, providing an experience that results in satisfied customers and increased customer activity, which satisfies the success metric of retention.

Since customer acquisition is expensive,[10] it makes sense to put effort and resources into developing retention aspects of an online experience, and the ability to enhance relationships with repeat customers. As illustrated in the earlier example about spending on loyalty-enhancing factors of the site experience versus investing in advertising, strategies to increase retention and decrease attrition in the online customer experience help satisfy the business goals of any firm. Understanding customers' values, attitudes, expectations, and behaviors at the outset of any Web strategy helps satisfy the business in the way that Yahoo! Finance has done. The analysis of user behaviors doesn't end with the site's launch, it only begins. A deep understanding of the clickstream—the measurable actions of users in the online environment—should be one of the drivers of user-experience refinements to continually enhance the overall quality of the customer experience.

Driving the Customer Experience Strategy with the Business Case

Most successful online experiences are driven by a strong business model and a strong value proposition for the customer. While there are examples of successful experiences—Napster, for one—that are driven by technological innovation, they don't necessarily include strong business models. Successful customer-experience strategy evolves most efficiently when driven by a rigorous business model, clearly defined value proposition for customers, and a strong revenue model.

Good user-experience strategy resembles best practices for some methods of market research and product development, following a typical life cycle for Web development (see Figure 1-6). The process can sometimes take weeks, even months, to get through just the

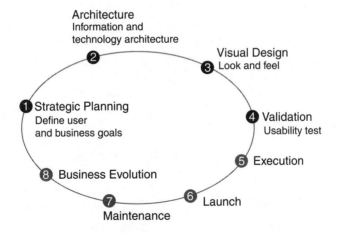

Figure 1-6. Life cycle of web development, with user-experience life cycle indicated in gray.

strategy phase, incorporating traditional market-research techniques and best practices from software design and usability. Here is a suggested method to accelerate this phase and to help firms determine a general model of what their site experience should entail. The following also includes known tactics that can help accelerate the process of gathering knowledge about what customers expect in an online experience and a plan for catalyzing the development process, in order to reduce time to launch without compromising quality.

Assemble the Owner Executives

At the outset, gathering all executives who will own or impact any part of the online customer experience enables each to have input into the strategy. Owners may come from among executives, marketing, information technology, customer-relationship management, and content management. Include owners who may have strong influence on the Web strategy later on in the life cycle. In some industries, such as financial services, the executives who represent legal and compliance are an important part of the customer-experience strategy team and should be included at the outset to prevent any bottlenecks later in the cycle.

Define the Mission Statement and the Business Goals

Defining the mission of the overall user experience is a good exercise to start the strategic planning process. Articulating a statement as simple as "to create the premier online experience for consumer retirement planning" helps the team begin to brainstorm and to catalyze around a simple, common vision for the site.

After the mission is defined, the next step is to articulate the business goals and what your target customers value in an online experience.

Answering these questions about your business goals begins the process:

- What are the business goals for the firm?
- Who are the customers, by segment? (Are they novices, early adopters? Are they consumers with a clear idea of what they are looking for? Are they business managers with a need for efficiency and business relevance?)

- What is the firm's online value proposition for its customers? (Are you making their lives easier and more efficient? How is this online experience enhancing task flow and easing some of the administrative tasks users need to complete for their job?) For example, State Street Global Advisors, the asset-management firm mentioned previously, has developed several private extranets. One of them focuses on the pension/investment consultant community. The experience is designed to provide easy access to investment product information and research along with the ability to view investment performance information of shared clients. This saves time by aggregating both activities (product evaluation and client service) into one interface.
- From a business perspective, what is the intent of the firm's user experience?
- What are the short-term ROI goals for the user experience as defined by dollar benefits? In other words, what benefits must the firm see immediately for the expense of developing the user experience? What will be the long-term ROI goals?
- What is the impact of the brand on the user experience?
- What are competitors offering in their customer experiences, and have they made compromises that might offer an opportunity?

Beginning with the business goals allows the team to understand the drivers that must be satisfied in order for the experience to be successful. Now let's proceed to consider the needs of customers, and what they expect in an online experience.

Understanding Customers

Understanding what customers value is the next step in understanding how to create an online customer experience using an *economy of clicks*. Simply put, this means developing the most robust, engaging experience in the fewest number of clicks and striving to make each and every click enhance the brand proposition in the customer's mind.

One click can provide a valuable experience. Creating a transparent experience is key, where the value is in the overall experience and not in the mechanics of the user interface. Amazon.com delivers huge value to the user and to Amazon through its 1-Click buy mechanism.

A list of what customers value in an online experience would look like a list of what they would expect in a real-word relationship with a firm, including:

- Ease of use
- Convenience and efficiency (e.g., the ability to complete a task more quickly and more effectively through the online channel)
- Respect in the relationship (e.g., respectful behavior toward the privacy of the user, and an experience that addresses the user in a tone and language he or she can understand)
- A solution to customer's frustration and help as they need it
- Concrete value, in the form of information and/or entertainment that is tangible (e.g., the Yahoo! Finance portfolio of stocks)

Ease of use is crucial and involves issues of navigation and transaction completion, which are vital to relationship building in the customer experience. Bad user experiences typically result in users feeling lost, unsure of how to proceed, and so frustrated that they leave a transaction before completing it.

Users also want convenience and efficiency, and they want it delivered in ways that are specific to the type of experience they require to complete their tasks. For retail shoppers, this means searching for product, price discovery, and availability. For online traders, this means lightning-fast access to the information and knowledge they need to complete a trade, and fast, secure trading.

Respect in a relationship can be manifested in many ways, including tone and language. Customers want to be addressed in a language and tone that makes sense for them. If they are novice users, they don't want technical jargon or detailed cryptic messages about how to use the site. When things go wrong, they don't want to know what a "404 Error" means, nor do they want to attempt to decipher the technical jargon of the error message. Many of the big ecommerce sites don't pay enough attention to this. How do you feel when you have to put in your credit card number before you're told your total? It's not the best way to build trust with a customer.

Elegant Equilibrium

A successful user experience creates an elegant equilibrium between delivering value for customers and value for the firm. This equilibrium is necessary for success because customers won't value an experience that only delivers value for the firm. A site that aggressively pushes its products, constantly upselling customers with unwanted email in the absence of delivering any value soon becomes harassing. Likewise, an experience that serves only the customer is not beneficial, as it does not necessarily create revenue. Consider Napster, an online experience that was hugely popular but lacked a viable business model. Recall the success of the Yahoo! Finance example discussed earlier, and how valued the site is among its loyal users. The site exemplifies an *ideal user experience*: perfectly meshing what customers want in an experience that at the same time creates business value.

Initiating the user-experience strategy by clearly articulating the business goals is the first step in driving the process effectively. The next step is to clearly define what customers want and define the right measures of success, discussed in detail in Chapters 4 through 7. The following chapter offers a sort of "Top 9 Highly Effective User-Experience Strategies" to clarify the mission-critical set of strategies that marketers need to understand to effectively orchestrate online experiences.

nine things a marketer
needs to know about
user-experience strategy

"How do I exploit this ever-evolving environment
to create a valued experience for my customers?"

Think of the experience of drinking espresso. Rich flavor that delivers an immediate catalyzing effect in a rapid-fire format. Here we present the mission-critical, key concepts of user-experience strategy in espresso format—fast, concentrated, immediately useful.

While we can't solve all of the business challenges, the knowledge presented in this chapter explains the key concepts that underlie the development of successful user experiences. Customer-experience owners can use this framework as a checklist at the outset of their strategic-planning process and as a basis for organizing brainstorming sessions to drive a Web strategy. Like the espresso, it's fast and concentrated. More detailed discussion about these areas are included in later chapters in the book.

The best way to approach the strategic-planning process for user experience is as a business case—with a plan for how the experience will satisfy the market and drive profitability, and a strong plan for execution. With a strong strategy, defensible value proposition, and robust execution, the likelihood of success is increased. Such an approach should address the following strategic issues:

- The user experience is the vehicle for building relationships online and transacting commerce to maximize profitability.
- Retention is a measure of success, which is critically dependent on the user experience.
- Usability directly impacts retention and experience engagement.
- Opportunity cost is correlated to the user experience, a competitive advantage on the Web.
- Next-generation user experiences will deliver more personalized, more useful, and proactive experiences to a wider range of customers.
- Marketing is now responsible for revenue and will own the user experience. This situation will demand new skills for architecting, driving the process, and measuring success.

I. Capture What Customers Expect in the User Experience

When it comes to creating a "best practices" prototyping culture . . . the rules of the game appear to be shifting. To succeed today, the prototype can't be seen as the property of the engineers, designers, or marketers—it has to be seen and treated as community property. And the most important member of that community must be the customer.

From *Serious Play* by Michael Schrage[1]

Successful user experiences begin with a clear vision of the end in mind: What will the ultimate user value in the experience? What are the qualitative aspects of the experience that will delight customers? What are the quantitative aspects that will answer their needs and allow them to complete tasks in the most efficient manner? How can the user experience answer needs such as "I want the experience to be as easy as finding the books I want on Amazon.com" and enable efficiencies like "I need to see the price in one click; I can't waste my time looking for it"?

The best way to gather this kind of rich data is to ask your customers what they think. Showing customers a prototype of a user experience will help you to gauge their reaction and gather critical input early in the process, which will enable you to narrow the scope of possibilities and evolve the design toward the optimal solution. Ten thousand dollars spent early in the design process to validate a prototype with customers is money well spent if it prevents a $1 million investment in an unusable user experience. It can also flag critical gaps between customers' expectations and what the user experience will deliver and help you to correct the course quickly. For example, using tactics like customization and personalization to drive retention can be a big risk if customers expect that in exchange for their personal information they will receive better service—and the firm fails to deliver because of issues like a lack of integration. Issues like these can be dealt with, if flagged early.

Studies show that most products are successful if the voice of the user is incorporated early in the process[2] and, as evidenced by the successful lightning-fast development process of Microsoft's Internet Explorer 3.0, a working version is placed in the hands of customers at the earliest possible opportunity.[3] This factor will continue to be a critical one in the success of more transactional and ubiquitous user experiences—experiences that customers cannot necessarily see and feel. Validation of such experiences must be done early in the design process to ensure usability and usefulness.

Narrowing Design Choices Earlier

A successful customer model includes prioritization of what customers expect in the experience. For example, it should address the commonly expressed need: "More than anything, I want to be able to trade easily, from every screen." One of the most successful aspects of the development of Fidelity Investments' PowerStreet Pro™ trading site was that customer feedback was incorporated while the product was in its embryonic stages—within a few hours of the first prototypes being developed. Early decisions about critical aspects of navigation—traders demanding "security-centric" navigation and the ability to trade from any screen—were surprises to the design team until customers asked for these elements of the experience in reaction to the first prototypes they saw. This kind of rapid feedback process can help narrow the options early in the design process and help ensure that the user experience is satisfying the target audience.

Coupled with pre-existing customer knowledge and quantitative data such as transaction history, these inputs should form the basis of an accurate model of how the user experience needs to be designed to ensure that it delivers the right experience.

Leveraging pre-existing models of behavior in the brick-and-mortar firms helps establish the model of behavior for the electronic experience. How to design the next-generation online bank? Clearly define customers' goals and behaviors while they engage in banking activities in the real world. Find out what they value highly in experiential terms for the online counterpart to the brick-and-mortar experience. Observe their daily behavior in their natural environments to determine their goals and tasks. These observations of usage and behavior should influence the design of the experience, and form the core components around which revenue-generating opportunities will be woven.

Sharing this customer intelligence rapidly throughout the enterprise and among different owner groups helps the process keep moving. Circulate the customer model to owner groups such as product development, marketing, and the technology team for their feedback and reactions. Often, after a day of brainstorming, rough notes and sketches can be posted to the corporate intranet for sharing and feedback among the different groups. Iterations of prototypes are posted on the intranet as well, to be shared among the different groups who are involved. A prototype provides a visual talking piece, which is especially useful for owners who won't actively participate unless they can see how the experience is going to impact them. It helps catalyze discussion among these distinct groups, accelerating the process.

Carefully capturing the expectations of customers in the planning stages can help keep a user experience from compromising the business strategy. An example of such an impediment is a site that delivers a rich experience on one platform but, as the business evolves to include new delivery channels, fails to deliver equivalence of experience on another. Currently, industry is struggling with quality issues relating to evolving experiences from the Web to handheld and wireless devices: Surfing the Web using a cell phone is a painful experience, as evidenced by the numerous key modes needed to just input the "http:" part of a URL. So, before planning a personal digital assistant (PDA) or cell phone user experience, it's important to look at whether the experience will deliver enough value to the user on the device to satisfy the business goals. If not, then the product or service is probably not worth pursuing.

The entire team must keep the customer's environment in mind as the experience evolves, and the team must understand the revenue implications for compromising on delivery. The ultimate owner of the experience—the product manager or marketing manager—must drive the process through to execution with the target audience always in mind. An ecommerce site architected for creating community among fans of a broadcast television show looked great when demonstrated on the T1 line at the major ad agency that designed the site. But somewhere in the process, the target user's profile got lost. When asked about the platform and connection of the target users— in this case women and girls ages 14 to 36—the answer, that the speed of the typical receiving modem was 56 kilobytes per second, meant the creative team had to go back to the drawing board. They were not happy. Otherwise, trying to deliver the design-intensive information over the connection would have been like pushing a Thanksgiving turkey through a straw—an experience that no consumer would relish.

2. Link Usability and Profitability: Metrics for Success and Ease of Use

The success measures for business:

- Revenue
- Retention

The success measures for end users:

- Ease of use in completing transactions and satisfying goals
- A solution to their frustration

Empowered customers want an experience that delivers value—and on their terms. Success means achieving goals and completing tasks with a minimum of pain, a maximum of efficiency. Site owners measure success in terms of channel efficiency, on the return on investment. So while business goals guide the development of site experiences, the success metrics for the experience measure totally different aspects such as ease of use and degree of engagement.

This mismatch of measurements of success must change so that what constitutes success for customers aligns with what constitutes success for the business.[4] Nowadays, nonfinancial metrics are suspect. Ultimately, will the only metrics that matter be the financial ones that all companies were held to before the Internet economy? Probably, but they'll probably now reflect more process than pure financial results. Most likely there will be both process and results metrics, and the former will be as important as the latter.

Business success can mean a range of things: It can mean monetizing the user experience so that it delivers optimal revenue opportunity. It can mean a relationship-furthering experience, which leads to an enhanced relationship for both prospects and customers. Prospects feel compelled to contact the firm and ask for more information. Customers engage at a deeper level, by signing up for added services for their pre-existing account. The success metrics for the user experience are connected to the business metrics, yet they demand a new set of softer metrics that reflect the quality of relationships.

New metrics will be needed to map usability to profitability. Customer-centric firms such as Emode.com, a firm that has over 9 million registered users who visit the site to take personality tests, continually measure the aspects of the user experience that impact their business. Emode.com does so using 16 different variables—and they do it every week. As part of this model, they measure what people are doing, determine where in the site they are going, and analyze users' responses to new features as they are added. This kind of rigorous model and measurement is the only way to know if the user experience is doing what it's supposed to do.

Gathering and analyzing both qualitative and quantitative data about users' experience—from the first site visit throughout the entire customer life cycle—will become the means for proving that user experiences are delivering utility and value. Some of this data gathering is done by hand—analyzing log files and tracking user activities and behaviors—but new tools to automate and enhance the measurement and analysis are now becoming available. Firms such as Vividence, a software and services company, are already working on these kinds of customer-experience measurements and developing software tools to help understand what is—and isn't—working in the user experience. For example, Vividence's software products capture and analyze behavioral data from vast numbers of customers on the Web. Coupled with the capture of qualitative data (captured through users' annotations on the actual screen and thoughts about the user experience), these rich data provide new insight into how to make enhancements that improve profitability.

Measuring success of the user experience is a combination of science and art. It involves using the hard metrics (such as revenue and number of new accounts) and the soft ones (such as conversion rate, look-to-buy ratios, degree of engagement, or the number of unique visitors). "The value is in the aggregation of several methods of measurement," says usability consultant Chauncey Wilson, "and you need to convert them to ROI. At one firm we noticed 20 percent of the usability problems came from error messages, so we redesigned the error system and were able to reduce it by 30 percent. To do this required us to analyze the monthly expenditures on error handling—reviewing the usage logs and monthly budgets from technical support—and we had to convert this into ROI. It's really difficult to do this." He notes that the process takes time: "After setting up the metrics it can take months to have a few answers." Analysis demands an ongoing process of measuring and adjusting the experience to continue delivering the best value, the best experience, on an ongoing basis.

A way to think about ROI for different user-experience options is to develop a subjective measure—a scale such as 0 (Very Bad) to 5 (Excellent)—that ranks both the quantifiable and the subjective benefits of each option (Figure 2-1). For example, if a company wants to develop an enhanced user experience for a new ecommerce site, it must compare the two options (version A in column 1 and version B in column 2) for specific benefits—such as increasing the number of accounts. Comparing the aggregate rankings and assessing costs offer a way to determine the best design approach.

	Version A of User Experience (Transactional and Personalization)	Version B of User Experience (Transactional and no Personalization)
Quantifiable Benefits		
1. Number of new accounts or conversion rate	4	3
2. Ratio of new sales to budget spent for development	5	2
Subjective Benefits		
1. Expand mindshare among customers and prospects	3	3
2. Be recognized as a leader in the competitive landscape	3	1
TOTAL	15	9

Subjective Measure: Scale of 0 to 5

```
    0        1         2         3         4         5
    +--------+---------+---------+---------+---------+
 Very Bad   Bad   Acceptable   Good   Very Good   Excellent
```

Figure 2-1. A subjective measure can be used to aggregate and rank user-experience development options.

Defining a model for success in the user experience begins by defining success metrics for the business drivers and marrying them to the relationship success metrics. Consider an example of planning a brokerage Web site. We can list each business driver and a corresponding success metric as shown in Table 2-1.

These are easy metrics to define, and they are easy to quantify. We can also define a measurement of success for the end user's goals. Again, referring to our example of the brokerage site, we can see the end user's goals in relation to customer success metrics in Table 2-2.

For the end user, the trade transaction drives business success for the customer, the brokerage firm: The more successful trades the end user (the trader) executes, the closer he gets to achieving his goals of efficiency. At the same time, this activity satisfies the business goals.

Business Goals	Success Metrics
Increase revenue	Revenue amount over time
Gain efficiencies	Increase in trade transactions/throughput Increase in quality of trades
Decrease risk	Decrease in trade execution errors

Table 2-1. Business goals and corresponding success metrics.

End-User Goals	Success Metrics
Help me to be better or more effectives in my daily work-related tasks.	Number of successful, error-free trades completed
Help me to look better to my boss and coworkers.	Increased profile among colleagues Team members viewing you as an expert
Save my time.	More tasks completed during workday
Enhance my life.	Accelerated career goals
Add value without forcing me to change my behaviors.	Speed and ease with which expertise with user experience is gained

Table 2-2. Customer goals and corresponding success metrics.

For the brokerage site, the trade is the *atomic unit of revenue generation* in the user experience and should be considered mission-critical in terms of usability: Trade initiations and completions have to be easy to initiate and lightning-fast to complete.

Develop a model that correlates financial metrics to relationship metrics—as measured through the performance of the user experience. In our example above, the brokerage firm should use a model of the variables that characterize business success—the number of successful trades executed, or the number of abandoned trades—and continually measure them to make sure that the numbers are going in the right direction.

Best Practice

Define a model for user-experience success that blends the relationship metrics with financial ones, and put in place processes to continually monitor them as part of ongoing analysis and refinement.

3. Good Bones Are More Important Than Good Skin: Architect for Navigability and Scalability

The Internet economy placed great value on the concept of the network effect. This was often a test of a business model's viability by venture capitalists. This ability to exploit the network effectively meant that as the network of users grew, the value of the network also grew.[5]

But the network effect could only be achieved if the business model could achieve scale. Scalability was seen as a measure of how likely the technology—and the business—could accommodate explosive growth and usage required to achieve the returns that investors and acquiring companies were looking for.

Scalability put pressure on technology architecture and, by extension, on the user experience. It meant that as network traffic grew exponentially, the technology architecture had to accommodate the increase gracefully, and that it had to be transparent to the end user. Scaling to hundreds of thousands or even millions of users meant that the user experience could not degrade in any way lest the business be compromised.

Having moved beyond the technical scalability issue, user-experience architects are now under pressure to deliver a form of evolutionary extensibility. This means that user experiences must be architected to accommodate the following:

- *Changing business goals.* The goals of business are constantly changing. For example, a user experience that was stand-alone now might be private-labeled, or a new business product might demand a new navigation system.
- *Evolving customer relationships.* Customers become more expert and demand more functionality.
- *Changing needs and goals of more and varied users.* Evolving from a B2B model to a B2C one means that more customers are novices.
- *The evolution of technical platforms.* With changes and improvements in technology the user experience can evolve to exploit new strengths in the technology.

Information architecture—the strategic "blueprint" for the user experience—should blend business goals into a structural framework that satisfies users' goals and allows them to effectively complete their tasks (see Figure 2-2). Yet designing information architecture is like designing a house to be built on quicksand: It can be challenging because it is done in a highly dynamic environment. In some cases, this need for evolution has resulted in information architecture that can accommodate changes and updates after the first release. Or perhaps what was needed was a more complex or content-laden navigation scheme. Like a well-designed yet small "starter" home, though, the overall structure can gracefully accommodate new additions as the needs of the owners change. In other cases, this need for evolution has necessitated user experiences that exhibited *proactive personalization*: the same architecture accommodating

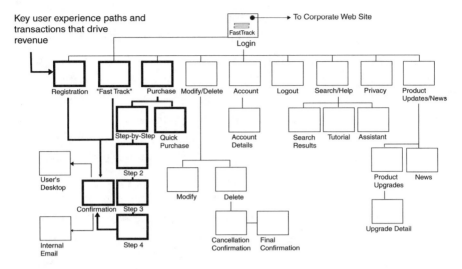

Figure 2-2. An example information architecture (IA) for an ecommerce Web site, showing key tasks, paths, and transactions that drive revenue.

many users but, through technologies such as collaborative filtering, now delivering content that is dynamic and specific to the unique user.

The following is a good example of how architecture can affect extensibility: A large global firm developed a user experience that was highly graphical, including all of the navigational elements that were rendered as graphical text. The site used frames to delineate the navigation areas from the content. These architectural decisions affected the firm's ability to scale the experience easily. Why? In order to add new elements to the navigation or to update existing ones, the firm had to bring in the external consultant at a high cost. As the business evolved, it wanted to offer clients published research and whitepapers on the site, but it was difficult to do so with a design that utilized frames. Clients receiving an email update that a report was ready were unable to visit a page directly by clicking on the link. This inability to access information easily required a complete rearchitecture of the site, a lengthy and costly process. The foregoing scenario illustrates why it is much easier to develop scalable architecture the first time than to try to retrofit new choices into a unscalable framework.

All of this speaks to the need for rigorous information architecture that can achieve scale, and accommodate a wider, more varied audience or an evolution to other platforms and devices. As site experiences become more technically complex, because they are serving more varied audiences across channels, the central organizing principals must remain based around the goals and tasks of users. Navigation must always be working to help users effectively complete tasks and, at the same time, satisfy business goals. The navigational scheme used by the portal Yahoo! Finance achieves this by only presenting tabs that are relevant for the stage of the relationship, a form of dynamic navigation that will become more relevant and important for next-generation sites. These user experiences will deliver a more proactive, personalized experience that will result in more value for less work on the part of the user.

Thought of in metaphorical terms, the user experience is like a human body. The information architecture represents the skeleton. The content is the muscle and flesh. The graphical treatment is the outer layer, the skin. Adding more flesh can only happen to a point; after that, the skeleton will collapse under the weight of the muscle and flesh it is trying to support. The usage patterns of customers is the blood—the flow of clicks as users engage in and navigate through the user experience. A healthy user experience has adequate blood supply to all of the most important areas, with no atrophy.

The information architecture forms the blueprint for the user experience. Embedded within that architecture should be the business goals and strategies, which are projected onto a framework that delivers an engaging experience. Achieving evolutionary scalability means that the information architecture is flexible and extensible enough to accommodate future enhancements without the need for rearchitecture. The best architectures use a system to superimpose the current architecture with those of the future—using greyed-out text or visual slots—to show the current experience, and how the next phases will impact the information architecture.

Developing the information architecture can be among the most difficult phases in the strategic process. Companies often don't understand the need to be careful in this stage. They may try to rush the process or use unseasoned talent without the adequate expertise to understand how the architecture impacts the overall design or answers the business goals. Mistakes in the architectural phase can result in fundamental flaws in the user experience. For example, bad architecture can impact navigation, which will directly affect usability. The information architect has to balance empathy for the user with the business goals to deliver a successful experience. A common mistake is to use an architecture with a framework based around the organization of the company and not around the tasks that users need to have a good experience. Often, too, an architecture design is too rigid to accommodate new customer segments. Like a brittle tree, it cannot support the addition of more branches, lest it collapse.

Mistakes in the architecture-development phase result in the need to rearchitect later on, which is a costly and time-consuming process. It's the user-experience equivalent of doing structural engineering on your home as opposed to minor cosmetic enhancements.

4. Make the First-Use Case Frictionless

More than any other point in the customer relationship, the very first exposure the customer has to the user experience can make or break the success of the product or service. Like a first date, the initial experience can lead to a furthering of relationship (that is, to more dates) or to a quick departure (the frosty "goodnight").

In our client work, many of the user experiences we see that are failing do so because they fail the "first-use" case. Those experiences frustrate customers and drive them away on the initial visit to the site. The effects on the business metrics are immediate, because without passing the first-use experience, users can't do the following:

1. They can't immediately perceive the value proposition through their initial exposure to the user experience.
2. They can't engage and begin a relationship. If it's not clear the first time why they should sign up or how they can access their

accounts, users can't register for the service or access their accounts later on.

3. They can't see a reason to maintain the relationship. Customer retention is immediately affected—negatively.

In the example at the beginning of Chapter 1, the RetireCo site experience would have been more successful if the first-use case was satisfied. If users arriving at the site the first time were given the option to choose a "How Do I Set Up My Retirement Account?" choice, many of the users would have not "jumped channel" and called the 800 help number in confusion.

Some common first-use mistakes include the following:

- Site architectures reflect corporate organization's goals and needs, not the users'.
- Navigation that prevents progress, such as unclearly labeled choices that require users to "guess" at where links will take them.
- Language or tone that is irrelevant or inappropriate for user segments.
- There is no easy means to initiate transactions.
- Proactivity is not woven into the experience, and prompting is lacking.

Some of the best first-use practices are the following:

- Navigation that addresses the goals of all user segments, and facilitates progress. For example, a QuickJump menu on the first screen might answer users' common questions—such as "How do I learn about mutual funds?"—but at the same time provide a structured query that quickly helps the user establish a point of view and a relationship with the site.
- User-experience mechanisms help present the site's value proposition in an easy-to-digest format. Streaming-media presentations might be used, as they do at State Street Global Advisors.

- The demonstration process is clear and easy to follow with tips and alerts about what can go wrong in the process.
- Initial experiences are personalized based on knowledge about the user. For example, through use of cookie technology, a user could be presented with personalized information, specific to that user, as they do at Amazon.com.

For firms whose Web site is the channel through which the product or service will be delivered, the most important experience is the initial one. A retail banking portal whose first screen differs depending on whether the customer navigated from the bank's brokerage partner site or directly from the public home page is a good example of a custom first-use case designed to deliver a segment-appropriate experience. High-net-worth customers, for example, might not want the same experience as retail banking customers.

First-use problems typically appear in several ways:

- Usage logs indicate that users are arriving at the home page and leaving without clicking anywhere else.
- Users choose the Search item upon visiting the site and search for obvious terms such as products or services.
- Users first visit the home page and than jump channel, pick up the phone, and complain.
- Users complain about not being able to find their way around from the home page.

Answering the following questions will help to pinpoint issues with first use:

- Do users arrive at the site and not know how to proceed?
- Do users arrive at the site, navigate only to a shallow level, and then leave?
- Is the first use helping users to segment themselves onto the proper paths of the site?
- Do users feel compelled to engage with the site after the first use?
- Do they understand the value proposition of the site?

- Are products and services introduced in the appropriate way? Is there too much sales and marketing being pushed into the face of the user?

To be successful, the first-use case should always rapidly establish the brand proposition in the user's mind and lead the user toward furthering of the relationship, introducing the products and services using the appropriate presentation. Anything else adds risk that the user will never return.

5. Thread Ease of Use Throughout the Experience

Ease of use should be embedded in the DNA of the user experience and intrinsic to its development process. It should be present in every atomic action in the experience, in each and every click. Each click should add value, and add positively to the cumulative experience over time.

This goal is not always easy to accomplish. Think about what makes some of the best experiences in the real world and you'll understand that they are developed in a way that is both holistic and systemic at the same time. Disney World is an environment where entertainment and suspension of disbelief are maintained through the entire experience. Drop a paper cup on the ground and a smiling Disney character walks by and—in a single graceful gesture designed to maintain the suspension of disbelief—the cup is swept away. User experiences should strive to be this proactive, transparent, and useful.

My husband and I recently went into a furniture store to buy a mattress. As we had our toddler with us, we knew that we had only a brief window of time to do our research and make a decision. While we tried out several of the mattresses, a clown emerged from behind the store's counter, gradually made his way over to where we were, and silently kept our son amused with balloon animals and magic tricks until we had made our decision. Then, as we began to close the deal with the salesperson, the clown quietly sauntered off.

Without demanding any proactivity on my part, the shopping experience delivered value that was critical to my being able to complete my task, and the people involved intuited my needs and goals without my having to articulate them. For the furniture store, it was a critical part of delivering the value, of consummating the deal. It was something that was implicitly understood in the way the experience was architected—not forced or artificial, but translucent, as though it was a natural part of the experience narrative. Needless to say, we became intensely loyal customers almost immediately, and we have remained so. And we tell all of our friends with children to shop there.

Ease of use will become even more critical to the design of next-generation online experiences, because consumers will demand more proactivity but not necessarily more interactivity—they will want more value for less work. Ease of use won't necessarily be reflected in the point of contact, or interface, between the customer and the experience. It will instead be inherent in the DNA of the design, and threaded throughout the experience and will happen appropriately, in context. Like the Staples.com site that simply knew that a signed form would allow the deliveries to be made tomorrow regardless if anyone would be home. Like the alert delivered on a cell phone that a flight—which was booked online—is delayed two hours. You get the mission-critical information you need at the location you need, and you don't have to "hunt and peck" through a Web site.

Like the clown who appears exactly when you need him, the experience will know what you need before you do.

6. Execution: To Outsource or Not

After all of the strategic planning is finished—the user experience validated with target customers, the technology architecture defined—it's time to execute. It's a risky time. All of the planning and design and prototyping must result in a finished product that delivers value for customers, maintains the vision for the customer experience, and drives the business toward its goals.

Yet the process for delivering the final design now can range from a totally outsourced solution to one that is done totally in-house. Add some very interesting hybrids that fall somewhere in between, integrating some of the internal resources in a firm with those from the outside, and you have several options to choose from. Some are more risky than others, others more beneficial than others.

Why is flexibility to outsource this important? In the last few years, the gold rush mentality caused many firms to rush toward Web strategies and partnering schemes that were not optimal, did not satisfy the business case, and were not managed with the goal of providing the best customer experience in mind. It was mind-boggling to see the number of bad experiences that plagued the 1999 holiday ecommerce season, where many sites offered experiences that looked and felt like they were constructed with little or no regard for what users were trying to accomplish. Executing badly meant that customers were underserved and the business compromised.

Under pressure to define and execute their 1999 Web strategies with limited time and in-house talent, companies adopted outsourcing as a typical solution in the 1998–2000 time frame. A thriving market evolved around this need: The ecommerce integrators (eCIs), offering total outsourcing, began refusing clients and increasing their minimum engagements up past $1 million per project. These firms offered critical talent and resources at a time when large institutions, dot-coms, and other companies found it impossible to successfully plan, execute, and launch new Internet products in the time frames that were demanded by market pressures and investors. Yet costs for doing the work were overpriced. A typical response my company heard during this period when potential clients inquired about availability: "If this is not at least a million-dollar project, we shouldn't continue the conversation." Indeed.

During this time, designers held certain power. There were not enough of them to do the work that was pouring in. "If they became unhappy, they would leave," says one ecommerce integrator project manager. Often, because neither the client nor the business development team members understood the design process, designers were often the most bitter members of the team. Because their work process was not well understood, they often became the bottleneck for the completion of projects.

What many clients found during this time was that the integrators—unable to find bodies rapidly enough to staff their projects—were putting junior people onto projects that were far beyond their abilities. As a result, many ecommerce sites were designed, executed, and delivered by people who were unqualified, unsure of the medium, and inexperienced when it came to designing user-centered experiences. For many designers, usability was a dirty word, one to which they paid lip service but privately ignored as they felt it constrained their creativity. The risks for using inexperienced integrators were many: In cases in which integrators delivered suboptimal solutions, the client would be forced to pay more to fix the problem. Bad design choices would result in astronomical fees to update unusable sites. In all, the wrong choices, made with the wrong intent, compromised the value that companies were delivering online.

The takeaway? Regardless of what model you employ, make sure to own the customer experience. Don't rely on an external team to understand what it means to create the best experience for your customers; they don't know your business to the extent that you do. As Philippe Stessel, user experience practice lead for Plural, Inc., an ebusiness consulting and development firm, notes: "It's important to balance the team between creating dazzling design and business relevant design. Everything we do should further our clients' business goals by meeting and exceeding the goals of the user. Many of our clients are major financial institutions. Of course they want their sites to be well-designed, but every design choice is tied to a business goal and bringing value to their customers." Assemble a team with senior members who have user-experience *experience*. Write the contract to assure that these seasoned team members are actively involved in the project and have the appropriate skills, training, and background. And make usability the central tenant. Ask to see consultants' practices and methods, and ask about their usability expertise: Ask what challenges they have overcome by implementing usability testing and how they incorporate it into their practices. Demand that usability be part of the process and practice, not something that is left for the end of the process.

Consultants walk out the door at the end of their engagement and take their expertise with them. Help your internal team become a learning organization so that the best practices and methods of the top eCIs and other consulting firms will influence the way your enterprise works in the future. Companies are now attempting to build internal competencies that blend some of the expertise of eCIs with the deep domain or industry-specific knowledge within the firm.

Ultimately, the execution phase is going to impact the business and customers, so it's important to do it right, learn from the process and people involved, and retain the critical process knowledge in your organization.

7. When Things Go Wrong: Fixing Broken User Experiences

User experiences now have more business impact than ever before: Bad experiences will cause attrition, which is easily measurable. Now that the business success metrics include retention, there's added pressure to deliver a consistently good experience.

Usability, a term long submerged in the technology development process, has suddenly become strategic. CEOs, marketing executives, business development managers, technology architects—all use the term *usability*, and *ease of use* as part of their everyday vocabulary because usability now affects customer relationships, which affects the bottom line.

So, user experiences must now deliver relevant business value. When the user experience fails, customers are underserved. Users can't do what they need to do to satisfy their goals, the customer relationship suffers, and the business suffers. This sad fact was once articulated to a marketing team by a marketing vice president who, when queried about why he believed something was wrong with his online service, responded: *"The dog does not hunt."*

In this particular case, the site experience needed to promote a very complex set of business services and product offerings, and the business goals included increasing leads through the site and retaining current customers. Yet bad navigability was preventing access to business-critical information: Users weren't exactly sure what they were looking for, and the organization of the navigation prevented them from easily figuring it out or making progress as they tried to complete their tasks. The names of the categories did not accurately reflect the content within each section, and the navigation was set up around the organization of the firm—as opposed to around the tasks and goals of the user. Usability was an issue: Hovering over a navigation choice resulted in a rollover display of the underlying choices. Yet when the user attempted to move the mouse to click on them, the choices disappeared as soon as the user moved out of the original choice.

Most important, this site was failing the first-use case. On first glance, users could not figure out where or how to start, and they were sitting confused and irritated. But the attractive graphical rendering belied the true problem: The site had great skin but bad bones.

Unlike bad design of a paper brochure or collateral—where bad usability would be irritating but not fatal—bad design of the user experience in an online environment can produce a far worse effect: attrition. Users leave because the cost of switching is low.

The marketing team was desperate to do something, and fast. The dog "had to be able to hunt."

The best approach in a case like this is to first establish the scope and degree of the problem (see Figure 2-3). Again, using the bones-and-skin metaphor, the first step is to do triage: Feel for broken bones, and check for a pulse. One of the fastest ways to know something is wrong is to check the log files specifically for the error logs. It's easy to see what actions users have taken that have resulted in errors—and attrition.

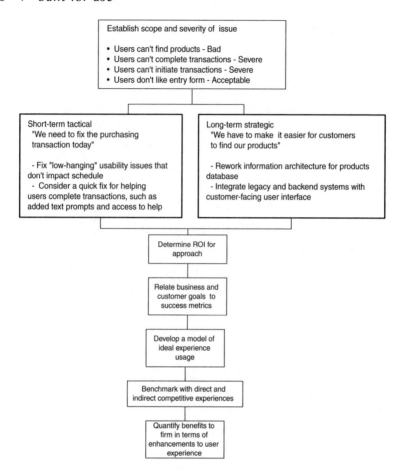

Figure 2-3. An approach for fixing a broken user experience.

Segmenting user experiences into the following categories is the first step toward setting the strategy on how to best approach fixing them:

- The site is dead, the user experience has no pulse.
- The site is alive, has a weak pulse, but is in the I.C.U. (Intensive Care Unit).
- The site is alive, and it is experiencing minor cosmetic discomfort.

Define all of the issues that are preventing user success: Users can't initiate or complete transactions. They are complaining about being lost. They can't figure out how to customize. Then define the business goals again and show how the site is failing in regard to them. Rank the business goals according to what is most business-critical. Decide what aspects of the experience you can live with, and those that you can't. Is it possible to develop a "Top 10" list of "Low Hanging Usability Issues"—issues that can be fixed quickly and with little or no impact on the development schedule but which deliver big wins for making the user experience better and more useful?

In the case mentioned above, the navigation was the one area that needed immediate attention, because it was having an immediate negative impact on the business.

The next step is to determine the best approach to fixing the problem, weighing the customer needs and the business requirements:

- Short-term tactical (Fix the user experience *today!*)
- Longer-term strategic (Fix the user experience for the *future*)

Determine the return on investment for each approach. How will developing the short-term approach have immediate and measurable business impact, and what will the costs be? Is the experience so bad that no amount of cosmetic enhancement will salvage the business proposition? Can we take the 80/20 cut and get 80 percent of the benefits by only doing 20 percent of the work?

For the ecommerce client in the navigation problem mentioned previously, revenue was low because a key transaction was too complex to successfully complete—users kept falling off the "path to purchase." This transaction was the *atomic unit of revenue generation*, so fixing meant that the 80/20 cut would be satisfied, at least for the immediate term. Fixing this one transaction path in the user experience—making it easier to initiate and complete using clearer and more proactive prompts—meant that the major business drivers were met. The costs to do the enhancements were minimal, and they delivered huge payback as soon as the site was relaunched. It was a short-term approach that had enormous value for the user and for the business.

To establish what the critical issues are, be sure to consider what the process will be. Issues such as navigation—where users are confused as to how to proceed, routinely get lost, and become frustrated—often require a long-term approach, with the result usually being a redefining of the information architecture. Rearchitecting a site is definitely a long-term approach. You may choose to run a usability test to establish the cause of the issues, and then execute a redesign.

Be sure to clearly consider the business goals and the user goals and do the following:

- Relate business and customer goals to success metrics (for example, increase enrollment and easier access to enrollment; the metric is an increase in successful enrollment transactions completed)
- Develop a model of ideal site usage and behaviors
- Benchmark with direct and indirect competitors
- Quantify enhancements in productivity, efficiency, decreases in risk and errors

Crucial to this process is the initial establishment of scope and severity of problem. And if everything isn't broken, make sure the original strengths are maintained in new design and don't get thrown away. Often when a new team starts, or when an external eCI is brought in, the first response is to throw the entire design away and start from scratch. But if customers have expressed a strong affinity for components of the existing user experience, or if they have given you feedback about how easy it is to initiate and complete transactions, then it's important to make sure that these points of value remain in the new design.

To prevent the issue of a bad user experience from recurring again, ensure that the customer experience is owned by a team inside the firm. Charge an internal task force aggregated from all owner groups with keeping the experience business-relevant and customer-focused. Get ongoing and informal external validation from target customers. One way to do this is by regularly conducting small-scale usability tests as a matter of course every month. Ensure ongoing success by assigning metrics results that this team is responsible for delivering to the organization at regular intervals.

This team can also maintain a database of competitive user experiences that represent the best practices for that particular product or service. Studying competitors is an important part of defining what the competitive advantages of a product's user experience might be. Conducting usability tests on competitive sites is a good way to learn what does and does not work, and what makes these competitive user experiences successful. From this, look for opportunities to better serve customers through the user experience, a source of competitive advantage that will be increasingly important as more consumers purchase products and use services online and in a wireless, networked environment.

8. Channel Integration: Harmonize the Brand Experience Across Channels and Environments

The Internet casts an intense and revealing light on any company's business practices and as a result will expose any inconsistency that exists across customer channels. Getting timely, high-value information into the hands of a customer via the Internet can cause more harm than good if it exposes a lack of integration with the company's other channels.

—William Blundon, writing in *Extraprise Report: Only the Ubiquitous Will Survive,* June 2000

For many firms, the electronic user experience represents only one touch point for a customer. Other channels such as telephone, paper, and brick-and-mortar also represent user experiences that reflect corporate brand. One of the biggest challenges for firms is to maintain a single, seamless relationship with the customer and "experience equivalence" of brand across channels.

While planning a user experience strategy, it's important to consider the electronic experience in the context of the other channels: How will it maintain and enhance the brand equity of your company during every customer interaction? How will you measure this? What will you do if it fails? A great Web site experience is diminished in the customer's mind if, when he makes a call to the support line, the representative answering the phone is rude. So, too, would the impression of a fabulous catalog with beautiful photographs and high-quality paper be diminished if it led a prospect to visit the Web site—and every catalog page had been scanned in and a navigation bar had been carelessly slapped onto the screen. Excruciatingly long wait times for downloading, coupled with a lack of searching, means the customer will go back to the paper catalog and never visit the site again. There's an inconsistency in the brand experience based on the channel.

Maintaining brand equity across channels is difficult, and it demands an integrated infrastructure that can support it. A customer can now access information about a firm's products, pricing, and availability through the Internet; often she knows more about the company than the customer support person on the phone. Waiting on the phone for the support person to bring up account information, then waiting even longer while he or she accesses more details that are often not up to date, gives the customer a lopsided brand experience. The phone experience fails if it doesn't accurately reflect the immediacy and accuracy of the online experience, where account information is instantly available. When browsing for something online, then deciding to call and order instead, I begin to perceive the organization as not being technically astute if they can't match up the prices that their internal salespeople see with the prices I have seen on the site.

A good way to think about a strategy for channel harmonization is to aim for "experience equivalence" across channels. Customers should have an experience that delivers value in a manner that is appropriate for the channel, which allows them to feel like they have a single relationship with a firm. This effort requires that the metrics that satisfy the brand promise be satisfied in a manner appropriate for each channel and customer segment. This can only happen with a commitment by management for the appropriate investment in infrastructure and integration to make customer-centric experience design possible. It also requires that the channel experiences not be owned by different team members who never talk to each other—for example, a Web master who owns the Web and a voice response unit (VRU) manager who owns the phone channel. A single person, or more likely a team, should own the cross-channel experience.

Let's consider a corporate 401(k) program. If the value proposition for the customer is easy and fast access to 401(k) account information and a wide selection of funds and services, then experience equivalence on the phone means that the user can access the critical points of value and complete tasks using an amount of effort not hugely disproportionate to doing these tasks online. It means that account access happens with a single click and the keying in of the account number and password. And it also means that there are rapid tracks to often-used activities, and not too many choices at each level so you don't have to take notes on what the choices are. There's no brand harmony between a great Web site experience and a phone experience that resembles Voice Jail.

9. Next-Generation User Experiences: Invisible Ubiquity and Transactional Intelligence

More and diverse types of customers are using the Web for transactions—seniors, teenagers, women, global users, the affluent—and this diversity will only continue to increase. As such, this new audience will demand new user experiences that satisfy their needs and help them complete transactions more effectively, offering a higher degree of proactivity and more guidance and advice than the site experiences of today typically deliver. So too will the early adopters who have been using the Web for years, such as mobile knowledge workers, begin to have higher expectations for their networked experiences. They often lead the evolution.

Developers of next-generation experiences will have to work harder and in new ways to build trust and deepen customer relationships, because important aspects for trust building such as visual cues will be removed. Aspects of the user experience such as navigation and task completion will have more impact on building relationships. Customers will value the experience—and hence the brand—by execution, efficiency, and appropriateness. To effectively design these highly intelligent and transactional experiences will require deep knowledge of design, technology, cognitive science, and a high degree of empathy for what the customer needs—both to be understood and to understand what to do.

Just as the advent of the Web as a medium for creating experiences spawned new tools for authoring, new tools for designing for ubiquity will emerge that blend relevant behaviors with context. Plural Inc.'s Philippe Stessel believes this development will challenge designers in new ways: "Understanding what makes a good user experience is like having good manners. Once you understand the principles behind them, you can apply those principles to any given situation." Designing ubiquitous experiences will be like teaching manners to another person, something that happens by observing contextually appropriate behavior. Firms such as TellMe, which allows callers to access information, businesses, and services over the Internet by speaking into a telephone receiver, are pioneering a form of customer experience that approaches this kind of appropriateness, threading empathy and customer perspective into the experience as a strategy for building loyalty. TellMe's service will respond to a caller from New York looking for local sports scores with "The Yankees lost a tough one to the Indians" instead of the harsher "The Indians beat the Yankees."[6] The user experience will be an increasingly important part of building competitive advantages that impact the speed and rate at which relationships—and loyalty—can be developed with customers.

Successful user experiences in the future will exhibit qualities such as transactional intelligence, which means that the machine can facilitate the completion of the transaction for the user without demanding much interaction. Think back to the Staples.com example in Chapter 1 and how the user experience proactively solved the problem of a customer not home to sign for delivery by offering a form to sign and tape to the door. This kind of proactivity and utility in experiences will become commonplace—and expected—by consumers in the next few years.

The conflict between creating rich experiences—and those that deliver utility—will continue. But rich experiences will no longer mean visual ones, as they have on the Web. Wireless and handheld devices provide a new challenge that goes beyond the wired Web: Create an experience that delivers the kinds of information and intelligence that mobile customers need in an even more constrained environment. Yet designers chafe at the notion of creating experiences in such an impoverished medium; it has all the subtlety and nuance of the old MS-DOS menuing interfaces. But those designers are missing the point: There's a great opportunity to design new kinds of experiences that transcend platforms. The value is in the transaction and the delivery of appropriate information through the appropriate channel, not necessarily the visuals.

And like using an E-ZPass to pay for drive-through fast food, it may be it's the utility, speed, and mobility in the experience that will deliver the value.

building trust through
the user experience

Two knowledge workers beaming their contact information to each
other via their Palm Pilots is a transaction that demands a simple form of
negotiated trust. My Palm Pilot must trust that yours will share only
relevant contact information and store it in the appropriate place.
In the future, when a mobile knowledge worker flies to a new city to
do business, the mobile device she carries will be "live"—as opposed to
"dead." Live devices will be wireless, and "on" when appropriate and dead
devices will require downloading of updated information. The live device
will know how to negotiate and form trust relationships "on the fly" with
every device and appliance it encounters. For example, on the plane it
will scout out favorite shops and services. In the cab on the way to the
hotel, it will secure reservations and a good table at the highly rated
French restaurant that the cab passes. Arriving at the hotel, it will move
seamlessly in and out of local wireless networks it encounters—first, the
hotel's network, and then the temporary network for the conference that
is being held there this week—all the while gracefully negotiating relationships that will add value for the knowledge worker. When the knowledge worker steps into the ballroom where a CEO is giving a keynote
address, the device will transparently become part of a peer-to-peer network that allows it access to the presentation that the CEO is giving,
complete with his live hand-drawn annotations. Comments from audience
members will beam around the room, shared by all. "He isn't addressing
the profitability issue head on, he's avoiding the question" comments one
person. "His tie doesn't match his suit" says another.

Webster's Collegiate definition of trust describes a complex concept, spanning the emotional as well as intellectual, and producing both active and passive results. The emotional component describes the feeling of trust: assured anticipation and confident hope. The intellectual component is based on performance over time that confirms trust: "assured reliance on the character, ability, strength, or truth of someone or something." The active result is confidence in the relationship. The passive result is an absence of worry about risk.

But *Webster's* definition is primarily describing trust among people. What if there's no person involved in building the trust relationship with a customer, only a machine? Or what if two machines are involved? How does my Palm Pilot build trust with yours? What does the machine have to accomplish to successfully negotiate and maintain trust?

Successful user experiences work toward building trust relationships with customers that translate into loyalty. By satisfying the requirements for building trust between two people, these experiences produce both active and passive results that can ultimately be measured by financial metrics. Successful ecommerce firms consider trust to be core to the online customer relationship. The user experience must "convey the feeling of looking into someone's eyes to establish trust," says Maryam Mohit, vice president of site development at Amazon.com, and "strive to consistently do things that are really useful. Anticipating customers' concerns, and demonstrating this over and over, shows that you really care about them." Not an easy task when the means for communicating with the machine still rest in the click of the cold button of a mouse.

This chapter covers why trust underlies successful user experiences and how it can impact customer relationships now and in the future. As ubiquitous computing—mobile wireless devices and appliances all seamlessly connected to the Net—allows for shared experiences mediated through mobile devices and appliances, trust will continue to be important in the design of user experiences in the future but will be more difficult to build and maintain in more constrained environments.

Trust will be built on dimensions of the experience like relevance and appropriateness. Fulfillment of transactions, and the frictionless mechanics of delivery, will be critical to building trust. How will users be able to trust an experience that they cannot see? In the ubiquitously networked world, boundaries of ownership of physical objects will begin to fade. As shown in the example of the knowledge worker and her mobile wireless device, at the opening of this chapter, transactions among devices will require a model of trust that enables machines to negotiate and consummate transactions on behalf of humans.

Trust models, therefore, must be able to scale from the current desktop computing model to accommodate ubiquitous user experiences. Multi-channel transactions will demand a new way of designing user experiences that build trust. New business models and marketplaces will rest upon a new invisible-but-pervasive model of trust that builds a single, seamless customer relationship across channels, built through the delivery of effective and appropriate transactions that utilize many modes of communication. Beyond the right business models, we'll need the right infrastructure and appropriate intelligence to be in place for customers to see value in these "invisible experiences"—welcoming back many of the classical problems from artificial intelligence, such as attempting to allow computers to reason, learn, and engage in natural modes of human communication. The machine will have to determine first what trustworthy behavior is appropriate and then how to behave in that way toward the end user.

The paragraphs that follow analyze how successful firms currently employ strategies to continually enhance trust in the user experience. They also propose a model for developing and measuring trust in a networked environment for current and future ubiquitous user experiences.

Trust Is the Linchpin in Online Relationships

Trust is the linchpin for creating successful customer relationships online. One well-publicized online privacy violation can erode public confidence in ecommerce sites and cause them to be viewed as untrustworthy. Remember when bankrupt Toysmart.com tried to sell personal customer information collected on the company's Web site?

An entire industry is being built on creating trust for enabling online B2B markets to flourish online. "B2B marketplaces have failed because of trust," says Dr. Pattie Maes, co-founder and director at Open Ratings in Boston, a firm that is working to establish trust in B2B trading scenarios. "If you need a supplier, you want a preferred relationship—you want to know how that supplier performs on a range of parameters like on-time delivery, quality of service, etcetera." Along with other firms like BizRate, which is working to develop trust in the consumer marketplaces, Open Ratings is building ratings systems to enable participants to trust that B2B marketplaces are secure and fair. As more strategic business partnerships are built on the fly, Maes thinks this system will help in establishing trust online, because it allows trading partners to "manage the right expectations. They have more complete information on which to make their partnering and trading decisions. Says Dr. Maes. "You can still do business, but you have the right expectations."

Beyond overall trust in the Internet itself, customers expect experiences at specific sites to be trustworthy. The current high rate of shopping-cart abandonment,[1] however, indicates that aspects of this requirement aren't being satisfied. Many sites thus miss the opportunity to better serve customers during this pivotal point in the furthering of the relationship. A trip wire at the knee of the customer at the checkout counter—with credit card in hand—is not the way to build trust.

Trust-building components span the entire user experience. They are present in the appearance of the site, the engagement experience, the fulfillment of promises, and the satisfaction of external standards such as third-party seals of privacy approval. Surprisingly though, results of testing trust in user experiences indicate that users don't necessarily rely on seals of approval to establish trust.[2] Like banner ads, trust seals may eventually become invisible to users. Pressure is thereby put on the channel, and the user experience, to deliver the best relationship and to work to build the trust relationship with customers at all times, at every opportunity. Pressure is also put on those who ultimately own the user experience—typically, senior marketing executives. They have to have the technical skills to quantitatively assess the effectiveness of the user experience and to understand how aspects of it are affecting loyalty and trust among customers. Senior marketers really have to understand the value of the user experience in order for firms to create truly trusted online experiences.

Simple aspects of the user experience can subtly undermine trust. Requiring that a customer enter a credit card number before displaying the total cost is one example. Not being asked to confirm a transaction before the amount is charged to a credit card is another. These experiences undermine trust because they do not conduct the appropriate dialog that the customer wants them to. Conversely, being aware of the concerns that customers have and proactively addressing them can also enhance trust. In the early days of ecommerce, Amazon.com understood and addressed the anxiety that customers felt about buying online. "Adding something to shopping cart was a new idea," says Maryam Mohit of Amazon.com, "so we addressed that concern by enhancing the 'Buy' button with a notation that reads, 'Don't worry, you can always remove it later.' . . . We knew customers were new to the Web, and we were straightforward about addressing their concerns." (See Figure 3-1.) User-experience mechanisms such as this can help to build trust in subtle ways. To be successful and drive business value, these efforts must constitute part of a holistic approach to building trust at every opportunity in the user experience.

Building trust with customers is the basis of creating long-term business value, and the online user experience is a part of the value for firms that do business online. Yet it takes a commitment and a culture that recognizes the importance of the user experience to the business strategy. Recall the discussion in Chapter 1 about the Stanford Business School researchers who found that developing a great customer experience is too expensive to deliver any short-term

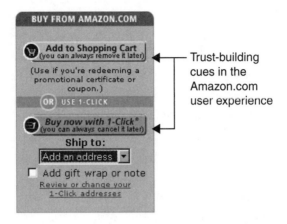

Figure 3-1. Example of early trust building mechanism in Amazon.com user experience. Amazon.com understood and addressed the anxiety that customers felt about buying online. User-experience mechanisms such as this can help to build trust in subtle ways.

shareholder value.[3] The bottom line is that aspects of the user experience that directly impact trust building are the most critical, and they should benefit from the focus and resources of the organization. If a firm only has resources to update one aspect of the online experience, it should focus on strategies and tactics that are devoted to building trust.

The User Experience Impacts Trust

If trust is the currency of the Internet,[4] then the user experience is the vehicle through which it circulates and delivers value. It affects all of the soft metrics that reflect customer loyalty, and it offers an accountable environment for delivering the brand promise and building customer relationships. Nearly every financial metric can be tied to a similar user-experience metric.

Like trust, the user experience produces both active results (customer confidence in the relationship) and passive ones (the reduction or elimination of worry or suspicion). With the impetus to deliver on the same metrics for success in real-world relationships, the user experience must deliver value, be respectful of the relationship, acknowledge mistakes, and be proactive to make amendments. In short, the user experience has to satisfy many of the requirements of being trustworthy.

At the same time, the user experience must walk a fine line between building trustworthy customer relationships—which ultimately lead to shareholder value—and delivering a trusted experience to the customer. Because the user experience now collects a detailed record of a customer's buying behaviors, privacy can easily be invaded through the creation of a complete, 360-degree view of the individual customer—and his or her buying habits and history. Marry this profile data with other, more detailed records—such as the U. S. Census—and there's an opportunity for serious privacy invasion. Arguably, public fear in the Toysmart.com case was most likely overblown. Would customers really have been at risk for privacy invasion if their buying records of toys were acquired by another firm?[5] It's unlikely. However, had the site attracted customers engaging in nonmainstream behaviors, the invasion of privacy and damages that resulted might have become an issue. Companies that understand trust building in the user experience practice the art of proactively addressing the user's concerns about privacy. They make their privacy policies explicit and clearly accessible.

If the user experience fails to deliver a trusted experience, the results can immediately be seen in the measurement of loyalty. Users will cut short the relationship—in effect, saying goodbye—or else redraw the boundary of the relationship so that the firm no longer plays a major role in that customer's life. For example, a financial site might hinder a customer from easily completing critical tasks such as executing a trade, aggregating accounts, or getting live customer support when needed. It would eventually lose "wallet share" to a competitor who delivered a better, more trustworthy service.

Customer relationships are increasingly being developed in online environments. Therefore, those who own the customer experience—typically, senior marketing professionals—need to understand how to drive and evolve the user experience in the service of driving profitability. These owners have to "get" user experience and make it part of the lifeblood of the organization. They must understand the impact of technologies that enable relationship-building tactics, such as personalization. For this reason, those who ultimately control the customer experience need to have strong understanding of technology and how it will impact the user experience from both qualitative and quantitative perspectives. Ultimately, business schools will need to prepare marketing managers to better own, manage, and measure electronically mediated customer relationships. Customer-experience owners must both understand the analytics that are part of measuring the success of the user experience and learn how to continually work to make the experience better.

Executed well, technology tactics such as personalization can have a huge impact on building trust online. Some successful sites that enjoy high customer loyalty reach critical mass by offering personalization, which increases the value of the experience for the user over time. More so, personalization increases the barrier to switching to competitors and satisfies the business metrics of retention, allowing the experience to deliver highly targeted information, which advertisers value. Portals such as Yahoo!, which has over 200 million users worldwide, represent one of the most successful user experiences ever developed on the Web. For this reason, portal architecture has influenced other areas of knowledge management such as corporate intranets, because it's an effective user experience that builds loyalty and trust.

Trust in User Experience: Emode.com

One user experience that has successfully employed a form of personalization to build trust and retention is Emode.com. The site creates an online experience in which visitors explore their personal issues and interests through personality surveys such as "The Ultimate Personality Test" to find the answers to such questions as "What breed of dog are you?" Through the ongoing dialog, the site builds a relationship with visitors who want to return because the payback—in the form of personal results or personal email with suggested products and services—delivers increasingly more value with each visit. Every personality test that the user completes adds to the amount of personal information—or personalization—that the user has invested in the experience. This is reflected in the quality of the personalized recommendations about products and services—served up with an attitude. A big part of the trust-building aspect of the experience is the privacy policy, which is validated by TrustE, an independent nonprofit privacy organization that awards its "trustmark" to Web sites that adhere to its privacy standards and comply with TrustE oversight. Emode.com's privacy policy included an exhaustive FAQ (Frequently Asked Questions) list with answers to many questions about the site's use of personal information, in very clear and customer-friendly language. Another aspect of trust building is the open communication to the firm, in this case the Privacy Officer, available via email.

Employing a strong brand personality of cutting-edge "hipness," the Emode.com experience strives to be "a fun, unique experience on the Internet," says CEO James Currier, "where members can compare and rank themselves with their friends across the country, all the while learning more about themselves." Becoming a member allows a site visitor to have access to complete tests and results. He or she can also receive personalized email with product suggestions based on the interests and preferences of the user. The experience has value, as evidenced by the degree of loyalty at the site. As of this writing, Emode.com has over nine million registered site members. As a pure Internet company, the Emode user experience *is* the brand experience.

Enhancing Trust Online: Pioneer Investments

Another good example of a firm that is focusing on trust building in the user experience is Pioneer Investments, a mutual fund company in Boston. Pioneer Investments is the first mutual fund firm to employ humanlike software robots—"bots"—to help prospective investors and clients understand such things as the basics on mutual funds to specific benefits of working with brokers. Pioneer Investments' goal is to surpass traditional goals such as cost savings and operational efficiencies by concentrating on creating a Web platform that can be leveraged to focus on customer relationships—which is the Pioneer way of doing business. By using natural language and a three-dimensional graphical display of the bots (see Figure 3-2), the experience engages the user in a dialog that is like the conversation with a real financial planner.

The benefits to Pioneer's business of having this type of user experience are twofold. First, through the interactive dialog between site visitor and bot, the business enjoys better qualification of leads for Pioneer's funds, which are sold through brokers or financial advisors. Second, the firm sees an increase in cost efficiency by allowing better self-service through the user experience. Intelligent agents can

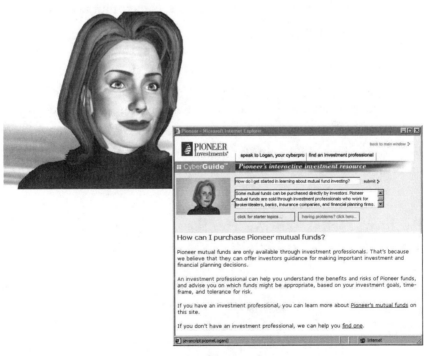

Figure 3-2. Pioneer Investments' software robots.

handle the kinds of basic questions online that would typically be answered by a human representative on the telephone. Pioneer is also seeing evidence in the log files that site visitors trust the bots and feel more comfortable with them when asking "dumb" questions. Pioneer ecommerce team members review the log files on an ongoing basis and have seen statements such as "Thanks, I was afraid to waste the time of a real person on the phone." In a subtle way, the bots are building trust with users who would otherwise feel uncomfortable about asking the same questions with a human representative.

Pioneer Investments understands that this effort is not just an ecommerce effort based on transactions but a relationship-building one—and it will take time to see results. They continue to develop their analytical model for tracking customer activity, but early feedback is extremely positive. Iang Jeon, Pioneer's senior managing director for ecommerce—and a veteran of successful ecommerce projects who has a career that has spanned firms such as Fidelity, Scudder, and Forrester Research—admits that building trust online is "an ongoing process" demanding a close collaboration among team members with distinct skill sets and goals. Says Jeon, "As a first step, you have to get everyone on the team to understand that you're talking not just about a Web site, you are actually touching a human being at the other end of the keyboard or the line." Success ultimately comes from aligning the team toward building the best customer experiences. The next step is analyzing the data and feedback from users and determining the relevant and appropriate data to watch closely—and the right metrics to use in measuring business results.

Building Trust Online Is Like Building Trust in the Real World

Building trust through the user experience is an ongoing holistic process—not unlike building trust in the real world. It requires quantitative and qualitative analysis and testing, and continual refinement. It is often easy to fix small aspects of the user experience that have a big impact in overall trust. Like the tipping point that Malcom Gladwell describes in his book *The Tipping Point*,[6] trust can be lost if enough of the prerequisite conditions are present and one or two minor occurrences serve to "tip" the customer's mindset to lose trust in the site experience. Perhaps all that is needed for a customer to lose trust is a bad individual experience. Trust is incredibly difficult to earn, yet it's very easy to lose, so the user experience must consistently strive to build and enhance the trust relationship with customers.

At MIT Sloan School of Management, Glen Urban[7] and his colleagues have studied trust online and found that Web trust is built like trust in the real world. As in the real world, first impressions can have an overwhelming impact on a relationship, and the quality of the ongoing experience goes beyond the presentation or visual style: The quality also involves the connection, the judicious use of bandwidth, and the simple demonstration of respect for the user's time. Case in point: Users bail out of sites that take too long to download the home page, before they see the site.

To analyze how the user experience impacts trust, the researchers designed a site called "Truck Town" to demonstrate how agents—humanlike software "advisors"—can influence trust on the Web. One of the strongest indicators of trust in Urban's experiment was the perception of bias in the user experience.

Urban and his colleagues suggest that trust is built in a three-stage cumulative process that establishes three things:

1. Trust in the Internet and the specific Web site
2. Trust in the information displayed
3. Trust in delivery fulfillment and service

In the Truck Town research, users visited a site where they interacted with a conversational advisor—an actor dressed like a car mechanic. This choice of persona was based on earlier surveys that indicated that customers are more likely to trust car mechanics than car dealers, salespeople, or others who are involved with advising on the purchase of automobiles. Through conversation designed to probe for underlying preferences of users—price, power, style, and performance—the advisor would recommend how well specific types of trucks matched the user's preferences and what similar customers had purchased. The user could then view complete specifications on the truck (including horsepower and towing capacity), side-by-side comparisons with other truck specifications, and evaluations of other users. Also available were magazine articles and advertisements about all of the trucks presented. Users could also choose to converse with others in a live chat session with other customers with similar needs. In all, 82 percent of respondents said that they trusted the software advisor, and 76 percent agreed that the information was trustworthy. That users were presented with unbiased advice and potentially competing products in the user experience was shown to have influenced their perception of trust.

Truck Town's design also illustrates how subtle elements of the user experience, such as navigational structure, can affect trust. Truck Town's information architecture and design allowed users to exert considerable influence over information acquisition—they were free to use the advisors or to navigate the site directly. Not asserting control over the user's navigation style is one way the user experience helped to build trust in a subtle way.

Trust building in user experiences can't be described as a single best practice or user-interface mechanism. In the same way that marketers use more qualitative means to measure "the relationship," building trust is a cumulative, relationship-driven *process*. Measuring trust becomes a matter of correctly choosing the parameters that affect the trust relationship—and then tracking them over time. As it becomes apparent which different elements of the experience are adding value and enhancing customer relationships, these can be enhanced or pushed to the fore of the experience. Mechanisms that decrease trust can be minimized or removed. The Web offers a platform for testing experiences, quickly doing real-time concept tests, and then killing the ones that aren't working. It's a form of Darwinism, with the evolutionary process producing successively better and more effective user experiences that build trust and deliver business value.

Successful Experiences Deliver
on the Trust Promise

Amazon.com is a good example of a user experience that builds trust quickly. At any point in the relationship—starting from the first visit—the user experience engages the customer in a respectful dialog. The site experience answers the major criteria for building trust by giving the user easy access to just enough useful information and then delivering on the promise of fulfillment. Though the initial purchase transaction process involves more steps than other ecommerce sites, the extra screens add value by helping users understand the choices and what the results of their actions will be. After completing the "buy" transaction, users are kept up to date with emails that allow them to know what to expect, and when. Subsequent visits to the site deliver value in the form of "proactive personalization"—without users having to actively do anything other than visit the site, the experience has begun to evolve toward something that they might find useful. Opinions of other readers—not necessarily endorsements from the publisher—help to provide multiple perspectives so that the site experience avoids bias, which affects trust online as the Truck Town example demonstrated.

Important transitions in the relationship can signal the evolution of trust and be used as a basis for success measurement. For example, when a site visitor to Amazon.com decides to register for the "1-Click" buy, that indicates a desire on the part of the user to further the relationship. That simple act then delivers a huge payback for the user in subsequent site visits.

Like other successful user experiences such as at Yahoo! Finance, the Emode.com user experience delivers concrete value to the user—in the form of entertaining results of a personality test—without him or her necessarily having to provide personal information. This helps build trust because it allows the user to control the evolution of the relationship. It also exposes prospective members to the benefits of membership in a respectful way—one that does not demand that they enter personal information.

Privacy is addressed in a straightforward way throughout the Emode.com user experience, and this helps build trust at critical points in the experience relationship. At any point where the user is asked to enter personal information, a highly detailed and clear privacy statement and listing of privacy principles[8] is a click away. This privacy statement clearly articulates Emode.com's privacy principles (see Table 3-1), displays the TrustE membership seal, and gives a detailed FAQ (Frequently Asked Questions) list, which explains exactly how site usage data is collected and how it is used. The privacy statement goes further than ones in most other sites in explaining the distinction between data that identifies an individual, such as name and email address, and information that is used to personalize a site visitor's Emode.com experience, such as demographics, interests, and responses to test and poll questions. Details are given about how Emode.com does not share information in a personally identifiable format with any third party. But the company does collect and store certain technical and other information about the online activities of users—whether or not they are registered—on an aggregated (or collective) basis, and that, too, is explained.

The Emode.com user experience builds trust by respectfully engaging the user in a conversation that delivers value at every stage of the dialog. Part of the value in the experience is the strong attitude and personality, spanning the experience at the actual site, as well as in subse-

---

- Your privacy is protected at Emode.
- You control your personal information.
- You can end your membership at any time.
- We will never disclose your personal information to any third party unless you expressly tell us to.
- We will not sell your personal information to any third party.

Table 3-1. Emode.com's privacy principles.

quent emails that are sent to users, with suggestions for products that have personal value for the user. The user experience is very proactive, helping the user know how to proceed or to understand what's coming. For example, a "progress meter" is available to help the user understand how long until the survey is completed, and how much more effort is needed to see payback—in the form of survey results.

Every subsequent survey completion is an indication of the amount of loyalty that a user has to the site. Therefore, a metric that measures the number of a user's survey completions over time, as well as the completion of surveys that are considered more "personal," might be a sample metric for trust.

Measuring Trust Online

Trust is difficult to measure. To accurately reflect the perception of trust in the user experience requires the use of a holistic set of measurements, using a hybrid approach that blends financial and relationship metrics. To establish relationship metrics that accurately reflect trust in the user experience, the user-experience mechanisms or processes that affect the level of trust must be understood. Then ways must be found to continually measure and improve on those mechanisms. For example, an ecommerce firm might measure trust through relationship metrics such as wallet share, frequency of purchase, or number of users who initiate a purchase and then abandon it in midtransaction. As part of an ongoing process for enhancing trust, firms should continually work to enhance the usability features of the user experience—such as purchase initiation, transaction completion, or customer service access—that impact trust for their particular type of business.

Trust affects retention, a major metric of online loyalty. Trust can prevent a site visitor from engaging in an ongoing online relationship that deepens over time; one bad experience might cause you to think twice about revisiting the site. Or a bad experience in the middle of a transaction might cause you to dump the shopping cart and click over to another site or, worse for the ecommerce site, reach for the phone to call customer support. It's important to distinguish between evolving a good online relationship and just building site "stickiness," a term used to describe engagement-enhancing tactics. For trust to be successfully developed in an online experience, mutual benefits have to be present. Some sites undermine trust by trying to be too sticky, too aggressive. Using brute force is the wrong approach: sites that disable the Back button and hence force visitors to remain at the site, unable to escape, are the online equivalent of having tree sap on your fingers. Continuing to click just makes the experience more frustrating, and it increases the likelihood you won't return. In this case, stickiness does not necessarily mean more trust is being built in the relationship; it's a risky form of retention.

Like any relationship, trust building in the user experience is an ongoing, strategic-level process, not a static tactic that can be executed once and forgotten. Trust is difficult to earn and easy to lose; success is measured by both results and process metrics. Results metrics include retention, loyalty, and increased wallet share over time. Process metrics include continual analysis and enhancement of aspects of the user experience that impact trust. For example, the success rate of critical features like account registration, or the effectiveness of navigation, might be monitored.

One of the most simple and important processes that can positively impact the customer experience, is monitoring search logs and refining the user experience based on analysis of user behaviors. Search logs show what visitors are looking for, and if the record of entered search terms show that customers are looking for items that should be easily apparent in the navigation, such as "Open an Account," that presents a good case for changing the navigation to be more useful. The result of updating the navigation to reflect users' needs can easily be measured. For example, the number of successfully completed account registrations should increase.

In the next section a model for trust is proposed that can expand to include experiences that are delivered to mobile wireless devices as well as to personal computers.

A Trust Model for the User Experience

The following paragraphs present components that make up a trust model for the user experience. The model is based on surveys of the current research and practices in building trust online coupled with input about what users expect online. Results were generalized into specific practices for the user experience. This model can form the basis of a process to ensure that a firm is doing everything possible to satisfy the requirements for building trust online—and to measure its effectiveness.

Presentational

The physical presentation of the user experience has an immediate effect on trust, particularly the first time a site is visited. Like a well-lit retail store, the physical appearance has a huge impact. Companies should ensure that the user experience satisfies the appropriate aspects of presentation, which include the following:

- *Fulfillment of expectations.* Upon first use, does the experience deliver on the brand promise?
- *Ease of use.* Is it clear to the user how to proceed to make progress?
- *Stylistic treatment, including the use of branding and identity.* Is the experience accurately translating the firm's identity and brand equity to the experience? Does the experience look like it has been professionally designed?
- *Clear disclosure of information that will impact the relationship.* Is the privacy statement readily accessible, and does it address the needs of customers in a language they understand? Are the ecommerce components such as the return policy readily accessible? Are prices, taxes, and shipping totals readily apparent?
- *Architectural and navigational model for the site.* Does the experience encourage progress for all target-customer segments? Does it help them initiate their tasks to complete their goals effectively?

- *Clear and efficient value proposition.* Is the initial presentation of the experience one that demonstrates efficiency so as to not waste the user's time?
- *Perception of timeliness.* Is the content up-to-date?

Experiential

Beyond physical presentation, the engagement and interaction experience influences perception of trust. Companies should measure experience aspects of the site that will impact business goals, including the following:

- *Navigation.* Does clicking on a selection take users to where they expect to go? Are they prevented from progressing through a path to complete a task?
- *Tone and manner.* Is the tone of the experience appropriate to the relationship, and appropriate for the customer segment?
- *Bias of information.* Is the information biased toward selling only the site's products, offering only that perspective? Is there an opportunity to see other competitive products and services?
- *Efficiency of message.* Is the experience respectful of the user's time, and does it deliver enough valued information? One of the most common mistakes is to employ aggressive upselling on every page, or to devote too much room to advertising or marketing without enough of the information that users are seeking. Users want the valued information without any additional noise.
- *Accuracy and completeness.* Can the user easily find valued information such as pricing and shipping totals? Is it accurate and complete?
- *Quality of connection.* Is the experience bandwidth-efficient? Does it deliver a high-quality connection consistently?
- *Consistency.* Is the experience delivering on expectations and being consistent in the delivery of value to the user each and every time? Do channel-integration issues prevent the user from having a good experience that spans channels, such as picking up the phone to complete a transaction that was initiated online?

Furthering of the Relationship

Experiences that build trust encourage a furthering of relationship by assuring that each interaction adds a positive check in the "experience ledger" for the overall relationship. Best practices for furthering relationships online include the following:

- Be consistently respectful of the user's actions at every step of the dialog, employing no undermining tactics such as data mining and selling without consent.
- Clearly display a timely and relevant privacy policy in customer-friendly language. Include appropriate contact information for inquiries regarding privacy and a guarantee that personal information is secure.
- Handle errors in a respectful and graceful way.
- Build in high degree of proactivity, such as during the transaction process or during error conditions. As more consumers become empowered to engage in online transactions, they will require more proactivity to be able to successfully complete transactions.
- Deepen the relationship over time, at an appropriate rate. For example, ask questions that are appropriate for the stage of the relationship. Don't ask personal questions such as birth date that aren't relevant in the registration form of a retail portal site.
- Allow easy access to help and customer support—and access to helpful humans, if the user gets into trouble.
- Make it easy to initiate a relationship with the firm. If registration or opening an account are complex or difficult to complete, they can compromise trust among early users.
- Personalize. Many major portals have successfully employed both active and proactive personalization tactics in the user experience to drive loyalty. Users are more likely to trust a site if they have spent time and effort to personalize the information that is presented. Adaptivity of the experience based on repeated usage also helps build trust, if each visit delivers an increasing amount of value over time, and demands less effort on the part of the user with each visit. More value with less effort builds trust in the user experience.

Encouraging furthering of the relationship, especially in the initial phase, can be as simple as making the initiating action simple and easy to complete, with the benefits clearly shown beforehand. Registration should require a minimum of input of personal data about the user: some retail financial portal sites ask for personal information such as birth date at the time of registration for personalization. Questions like this undermine trust because they are inappropriate and irrelevant at this stage of the relationship.

For best practices, MyYahoo! offers the most streamlined, frictionless registration process. By allowing users to view others' customized portals—organized around themes such as finance, entertainment, or sports—the benefits of personalization are made clear early in the experience and are available without requiring the user to actively personalize the site. Like looking over the shoulder of a friend who has already personalized the portal, this practice allows the user to see benefits of customization immediately in a no-pressure manner, with an obvious offer of "membership" always only a click away.

Environmental or Contextual Cues

Trust on the Web can also be influenced by the perception of the Web by the general population. Public confidence in privacy policies—like the Platform for Privacy Preferences Project (P3P), an emerging industry standard—can also be an environmental influencer of trust. Trust can also be affected in terms of its perceived quality of information. For example, it's widely believed that citing sources of information found only on the Web is risky, because it's so easy to publish but not always easy to verify facts.

Other cues that affect trust include the following:

- The perceived quality of the connection can influence perception of trust of the site. Affecting perceptions are such factors as whether or not the transaction will take place over a secure connection, or whether the experience will degrade because of a slow modem or faulty connection.

- Popularity of specific sites as the originating source—a sort of Social Citation Index for online information—can influence trust. Sites that show up early in the results list of relevance-ranking search engines like Direct Hit, for example, are perceived as quality ones by Web users. Users are more likely to perceive a site as being authoritative if it's the one that most people go to for information about the topic.
- Using links from objective third-party sources can help build trust. For example, an excellent write-up from *Consumer Reports* or a respected research firm would be beneficial.

Accuracy and Appropriateness

Beyond the presentational aspects of information on the site, the accuracy of the information can impact trust. Accurate pricing that is easy to access builds trust. In some industries, this factor is more critical than others: A wrong date or price on a retail ecommerce site isn't necessarily going to damage the customer relationship for good. However, for financial services firms such as asset managers—under the SEC-regulated pressure of compliance—accuracy can have an all-or-nothing impact on the trust relationship: One wrong price quote, and trust is broken.

Reputation and Adherence to Guidelines

Using third-party sources to establish reputation or creating customer communities that present customer feedback are other means to reduce risk, and they encourage trust building in a site experience. The following are some examples:

- Some of the most successful experiences have built a form of trust among communities of users. Employing such means as reputation helps to employ third-party objectivity into the community.
- Another source of trust can come from an appropriate spokesperson for the site experience. Fidelity.com makes excellent use of a

human spokesperson Peter Lynch to build and maintain investor trust and confidence—*a human interface* into Fidelity.com

- Third-party seals of approval can help develop trust in the user experience by delivering cues to customers that the site complies with standards for audits and privacy. These means, however, should not be relied on to be the only ones for establishing trust in the user experience. Companies that serve a global market online should not rely on U.S.-centric seals of approval for user experiences that are targeting an overseas user population.

Transactional Fulfillment

The fulfillment of expectations is one of the more tangible aspects of building trust. With regard to transactions, this means delivering on promise, in a manner that respects the relationship.

Aspects of transactions that can impact trust include several phases:

- *Preparatory.* Indicate clearly how to initiate a transaction.
- *During the engagement.* Use clear directions during the active engagement phase of transacting. Users can become lost or disoriented on the path to completing a purchase because of unclear directions on how to proceed or how to deal with errors. Failure in this dimension can compromise trust. Having cryptic error messages during the transaction is one of the fastest ways to push a user to pick up the phone to call customer service.
- *Fulfillment.* After successful completion of the transaction, confirm that the product or service has been successfully received by the customer.
- *Postfullfillment.* Have means in place for the user to contact the firm if something is wrong with the product or service.

The opportunity to build trust is greatly increased if the experience delivers exceptional value during an error condition or dire situation. Imagine how impressed you'd be with a Web site if, in the middle of the purchase process of an item you really want, the machine crashed. And suppose that upon rebooting you found a friendly message in your email with a URL that returns you to exactly where in the transaction you left off, with the data you already entered saved and ready for you to continue. You'd be more likely to return to the site, because you trust it to deliver value based on your experience in a problem situation.

The transactional aspect of the user experience will demand better practices for building trust as more and more consumers—not necessarily technically savvy early adopters—conduct more transactions online. They'll need more help to be assured that they can successfully initiate and complete transactions, with more proactivity available in the process. Trust-building practices will eventually become transparent in the user experience. So, for example, you may one day naturally expect your cell phone to alert you to the fact that your flight has been canceled and that your automatic travel insurance policy has been initiated.

Trusted User Experiences Promote Customer Loyalty

Companies such as Amazon.com consider the holistic user experience, from the first time the prospect visits the site through all of the purchasing experiences to when the product arrives in the box at the customer's door. Each touch of the customer, on the site or via email, is designed to add value to the cumulative relationship. Each purchasing experience proactively gathers information about the customer's interests so that subsequent visits enhance the value proposition established earlier. Every click works in the service of enhancing the customer relationship.

Presentation is also highly regarded at Amazon.com, and the care that they put into rendering the personalization concept is evident: Users' favorites are highlighted in the navigation with a small, subtle heart. These user-experience mechanisms are truly subtle, and truly useful, and they do not place a burden on the customer to manage or remember the categories. Such proactivity in the user experience can add increasing value over time while also demanding less active participation on the part of the user.

To develop successful user experiences, trust-building strategies must inform the user-experience strategy. For companies with a brick-and-mortar brand, the attributes must successfully be delivered in a user experience that exhibits the relevant aspects of trust from the model proposed in the previous paragraphs. For companies that don't have a physical presence, the user experience is the major vehicle for building the trust relationship. Those firms that have sussessfully built online brands—such as eBay and Yahoo!—built trust by paying careful attention to delivering user experiences that continually build confidence with customers.

Trust Relationship Driving User-Experience Process: State Street Global Advisors

For State Street Global Advisors (SSgA), the customer relationship in the brick-and-mortar world is centered on a high degree of trust. As the sixth largest money manager in the world, SSgA provides investment strategies and integrated solutions to clients from thirty offices around the globe. The customers they have—institutional asset managers, pension managers, high-net-worth individuals, and financial advisors—all have extremely high expectations for the customer experience.

Ever since SSgA set out to define an initial Web strategy in early 1999, the trust relationship has been core to every step of the strategic process and continues to be at the basis of all user-experience enhancements. "Quality, speed, reliability, accuracy, and privacy were all important in building trust," notes SSgA principal Peter K. Bennett, who initiated SSgA's Web strategy. Initial strategy meetings revolved around the central question, "What is an experience that delivers the most value to the customer?" The approach was based on what SSgA could deliver to customers and prospects that was truly useful. They didn't want to just stampede along with the crowd onto the Web and provide the latest technological bells and whistles, many of them useless. The goal was to deliver a user experience that would not compromise customer relationships in any way.

The business case was in the planning stages, with the goal of leveraging the Web to expand the mindshare of SSgA to be more than just an asset manager to prospects, such as financial consultants and pension consultants. Due to the supply of money managers and the demands on these consulting firms, they tended to put all money managers in a box—without much differentiation. By developing a more compelling Web experience—providing thought leadership in research and commentary—SSgA intended to expand its opportunity to enhance the perception of asset managers and consultants.

The first step was to define a model for the business case—the metrics for measuring success. SSgA began by listing the areas of value that they felt would deliver the most to customers and to the firm. The next step was benchmarking according to business metrics set to measure success for each value area.

For example, taking into account the business drivers and the appropriate business metrics, they had the following considerations in mind:

- Expand mindshare to target prospects, and promote interest in contacting SSgA (Metric: the number of requests for proposals (RFPs) from new prospects)
- Deepen existing relationships with clients (Metric: new contributions to accounts)
- Validate that SSgA is a world-class asset manager (Metric: awards and notices from analysts and the press)
- Expand interest in SSgA overseas (Metric: qualified leads from geographic locations overseas for the global offices)
- Attract top-quality talent to the organization (Metric: the number of career inquiries and hires attracted through the site)

As part of a longer-term strategy to build trust online by delivering highly relevant and personalized experience to its valued customers, SSgA also chose to deliver enterprise-level private extranets accessible only via login and password. These extranets enable a client firm to have private access to investment-program relationship information such as communication and alerts from relationship managers. Whereas the public site serves as a marketing channel for SSgA, providing site visitors with access to investment strategies, investment research, and corporate information, the private (password-protected) sites enable SSgA to evolve and deepen its relationship with its existing clients: A Client's Corner is available for institutional asset-management clients, and a Consultant's Corner is for asset-management consultants. Each site provides a unique user experience that features access to investment programs, research and commentary, and direct communication from SSgA relationship officers.

To reduce risk and decrease the likelihood of any compromises in the user experience, SSgA chose to put off facilitating transactions until a later phase, when the legal, security, and technology issues would be better understood. Another aspect that was central to the trust-building effort was the single login, deployed to make it easier for customers to access their accounts. Using only one login and password, customers with multiple accounts could access all of them at any time after the initial entry. They had just one relationship with SSgA, a single user ID, and one password that they needed to remember.

SSgA chose to employ a rapid prototyping methodology, which produced an information architecture (IA) that detailed the site experience along the most critical paths of value (see Figure 3-3). The strategy team first validated the architecture among all owners, including members from marketing, relationship management, content management, technology, and compliance. Then they set out to define the overall look of each user experience by envisioning the critical transactions and screens that the end user would see (see Figure 3-4). Each site became a real estate–versus–revenue question, as the team worked to balance the user's needs for information with the need for marketing materials to be delivered through the site. Ultimately, SSgA developed an experience that blended the value propositions for both the firm and for the end user, and this was validated with target customers.

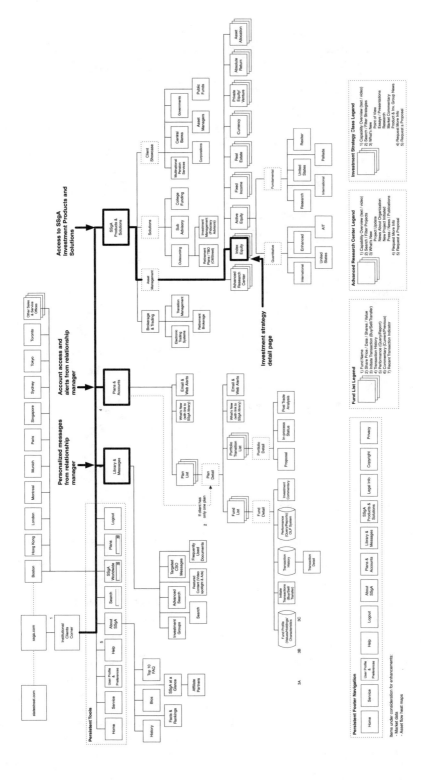

Figure 3-3. Information architecture for State Street Global Advisors' Clients Corner site, with critical paths highlighted.

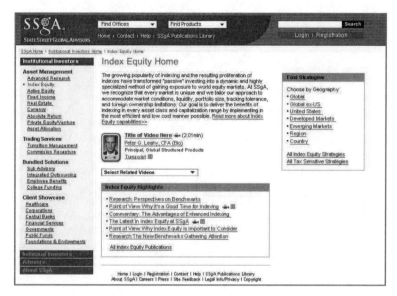

Figure 3-4. Example of envisioning prototype of critical screen for SSgA's Client's Corner site. This example of an Investment Strategy detail screen shows the Index Equity investment product—one of SSgA's key products—with key highlights and a streaming-media presentation by the portfolio manager. To make finding other specific investment strategies easier and faster, searching using categorization criteria that is designed around institutional investors' needs is featured (at right).

"Going Global" with the User Experience

In setting out to expand the user experience to accommodate a global audience, SSgA chose to employ innovative streaming-media technology in building enhancements to the user experience that would build upon the trust-building components already in place. These streaming presentations—fully navigable by clicking with the mouse—allowed SSgA to effectively deliver an initial presence for the local offices in countries such as Germany, Canada, and Japan. They did so without having to resort to complete language translations for the site content, and these presentations helped put a "human face" on the investment professionals and thought leaders in the global organization (see Figure 3-5). Along with compliance and

Figure 3-5. Global office streaming-media example from SSgA's Web site, featuring a navigable index (at right) in German.

regulatory risks, a complete site translation would have meant substantial resource and time commitments. Internally, SSgA hoped that very careful and evolutionary investments would produce exponential learning in the organization. They also hoped it would help build a global network of collaborators to formulate a strategy that would ultimately result in a single database—one representing all of global product content for all represented languages and cultures.

As no global office had any representation on the SSgA site, each global office was initially given a one-page template with samples to show the use of streaming media for presentations to be made in multiple languages. Local offices quickly learned to become streaming-presentation authors. They taped their own videos and sent them to the Boston office for post-production and posting on the local site along with products in the local language. In France and Canada, SSgA executives delivered an introduction to their office in both languages, along with an active outline so that site visitors could move around and choose parts of the presentation that were most interesting.

This approach to using streaming presentations was a great boon to SSgA. It helped enhance the user experience while avoiding some of the risk in translating complex investment-product presentations—the streaming presentations were translated by the subject-matter authors and then represented in the appropriate local language. Within those streaming presentations, SSgA integrated real-time links to related products as they were being discussed—in multiple languages such as in German or Japanese. This approach to enhancing the user experience by using streaming media resulted in a very low-cost, high-impact learning process. This effort expanded around the global offices, and SSgA now produces over 500 videos per year that are delivered over the Internet to audiences in more than fourteen countries.

Trusted User Experiences Deliver on the Business Case

Ultimately, the SSgA site has enjoyed a steady stream of traffic. This has generated leads in the public site and produced increased engagements by clients who have originated through the extranets. This success has been measured by the number of relationships that have been initiated and deepened through the user experience. To deliver such an experience, the site experience needed to employ best practices to enhance and maintain trust in the online user experience.

Employing a trust-based strategy throughout the development process can set the framework for establishing customer loyalty and developing long-term, trusted relationships online. Achieving this goal requires fastidious attention to the aspects of the user experience that impact trust building and delivering an experience that articulates the brand proposition while continuing to enhance the trust-building aspects of the site as the site evolves. Based on the work of the SSgA team over the last eighteen months in building multiple, large-scale online advisory extranets, the following best practices have been found to help deliver trust in the online experience.

Although they were developed specifically for the asset-management experience, they can be generalized to any online experience:

- *Develop a physical presentation designed to deliver brand experience in an efficient and easily understood manner.* Make it easy for the user to proceed through the experience. Employ minimal graphics to allow the site to download quickly. Design each screen to articulate the message in the clearest and most jargon-free language possible. Use concise, explicit directions on how to proceed to make navigation of the site as easy as possible.
- *As much as possible, deliver experiences that are appropriate and relevant for the audience, and make judicious use of the user's time.* For example, in the private clients' extranet, SSgA kept nonessential marketing information to a minimum in key areas of the site.
- *Minimize clicks to important transactions.* Mission-critical information such as investment strategies should be made available early in the experience using a minimum of clicks and an indexing scheme that allows efficient searching. By delivering an experience that shows that the company understands the needs of customers, trust can be built.
- *Maintain adherence to accuracy standards.* All institutions that publish financial information must maintain a standard of compliance with a wide range of regulators, which govern appropriateness and accuracy of published information. SSgA took the novel step of including a compliance officer into the earliest stages of the design process, so that the intended experience would be in compliance with regulations at all times.
- *Use technology that reflects the appropriate level of "intelligence" in the experience.* Users have higher expectations of systems that exhibit intelligence. SSgA has chosen to employ appropriate technology in the service of both enhancing the strengths of the human relationship managers and gaining efficiencies in the processes that don't require human management. All contact with relationship managers is routed through a redundant system so that no customer's request goes unanswered.

- *Display and maintain an up-to-date privacy statement.* Establish a privacy task force to develop an industry-appropriate privacy statement, and put in place processes to track and update it.
- *Incorporate rapid iteration of user-experience feedback into the site.* SSgA uses a quantitative and qualitative approach to measuring the site's effectiveness, by reviewing usage logs and conducting interviews with target customers and asking them about their workflow, their use of the site, their expectations, and their reactions to new mockups that have been created on a testbed site.

Trust in Next-Generation and Ubiquitous User Experiences

Ubiquitous computing will require a new model of negotiated trust among devices and appliances attached to the network that are live and aware at all times. When a mobile worker with a handheld mobile device arrives in the zone of a wireless local area network (LAN), the worker's device will need to establish a form of "real-time" trust to be able to participate in the transfer of information. The notion of ownership will take on new meaning in ubiquitous computing: Devices will have clear owners, but they will participate in a shared ownership of knowledge. Though these ubiquitous experiences will help users escape the limitations of the desktop computer and offer richer, multimodal experiences, they will make the job of experience designers more challenging. End users' expectations will increase, because there will be many more consumers using many more types of devices. Many of the cues for building trust—especially the visual ones—will be removed, elevating the importance of the mechanics of delivery. How information is delivered and received will become more important than ever. The message will be even more intimately tied to, and dependent on, the medium.

Ubiquity will be known to be succeeding if the number of bashed devices that are delivered to electronics repair shops begins to decrease. Indeed, National Public Radio (NPR) recently reported that the number of smashed mice, keyboard, and monitors has been on the rise. Sheepish owners admit to repair-shop personnel that they were upset with their machines and took it out on their computers and peripherals. If a decrease in this kind of behavior—and fewer smashed devices—is evident, something is obviously being done right.

Increasing the humanistic aspects of the ubiquitous experience might help increase the odds of being able to develop trust in the user experience. Indeed, a new field called *Affective Computing*[9] has emerged that addresses the emotional needs of users and determines ways to enable the machine to respond appropriately. Innovations in such areas as natural language, autonomous software agents and bots, and intelligent streaming media offer opportunities to create a more humanistic experience online, increasing the high-touch factor in user experiences. Using innovations in technology to enhance trust by increasing the humanistic aspects of the user experience is a two-edged sword. Designing experiences that can scale to deliver value across many browser profiles and the many plug-ins can be a challenge (or a disaster, depending on whom you ask). The expectations of users can be set too high so they expect the machine to be more intelligent than it really is. That approach can backfire badly when the experience consistently fails to match users' expectations. And the experience has to be "respectfully anthropomorphic." A virtual pain in the neck is still a pain in the neck. Just ask the winking desktop paperclip who won't leave you alone.

More consumers are becoming networked purchasers—and placing increased proactivity demands on the user experience. So user experiences will have to understand the expectations of users before they have been expressed—and do so for a much wider audience. Technology that enables a customer-service representative to take control of the user's browser remotely—just before the user asks for it—helps add a human touch to dialog in situations that call for it.

One aspect of the user experience that will greatly impact trust will be appropriateness. If the experience proceeds appropriately, I'll continue to trust it. If it doesn't, then I won't. The work required to make this happen is huge—intelligence, integration, sensing technology. All are in the works, but ubiquity won't truly work without all of these pieces of the puzzle in place.

Trust across channels is the next step in ubiquity. We see trust models employed now in cross-channel relationship-building tactics for creating loyalty. A good example of an experience that transcends platforms can be found at Emode.com: The engaging experience on the Web site is maintained by targeted email sent to the user for special events or containing personalized updates. When an Emode.com user receives an entertaining email, the engagement factor of the brand is extended to another channel. As more user experiences link desktop and networked appliances and wireless devices, building trust across environments will continue to be a challenge. Best practices exhibited by firms like Emode.com hint at the kinds of practices that will become necessary as mobility enters the equation.

Trusted experiences in the ubiquitous world will be more like real-world relationships because they will not be conducted through the current abstractions we use to communicate with machines today: the desktop, folders and files, the mouse, the modem. They will be experiences that deliver appropriate value in the way that users choose. Going beyond the browser, new business models will emerge to offer value-added services that add layers to these transactions. Each layer will enrich the user experience with more contextual awareness and intelligence that won't necessary be visual—but will still play an important role in building trust with users. Many of the basic aspects that have a huge impact on trust—which Glen Urban at MIT refers to as "trust busters"—will still be applicable in ubiquitous and pervasive computing environments. But, as with Federal Express, the value will be in the delivery of the appropriate information in the appropriate packaging.

The mechanics of delivery of experiences will still be a critical aspect of trust, but the visual cues will go away, navigation will be done using other modes such as voice recognition—often in concert with other forms of input. Executed well, transactional experiences of the future will be like using FedEx—transparent and trustworthy, demanding increasingly less effort of the customer over time for increasing returns. As a customer you know that FedEx will work, every time, to get a package delivered to the right location, in the appropriate package, in the most efficient way. Over time, you don't even need to fill out any forms—they are all prefilled—and you don't have to travel to the drop box—FedEx sends a truck to your house.

New businesses will emerge that exploit this rich, new transactional landscape—managing the infrastructure for dealing with transactions will be a big business. Trust between machines will be more complex but will enable them to "do the deal" together, without us.

Best Practices for Building Trust in the User Experience

Only recently have best practices and specific online trust guidelines begun to emerge in the ecommerce industry.[10] Companies are under pressure to build trust in their specific online experiences, but at the same time the loss of collective trust (again, think of the Toysmart.com example) means that site-specific trust building is subject to the greater environment of the Web. Firms that undermine trust erode the community of trust for businesses and customers alike, especially when they use tactics like recording clicks on non-advertiser-sponsored pages or selling personal information. When a firm gets caught with a *"hand in the cookie jar"* everybody participating in commerce online suffers.

Developing a user experience that builds trust depends on a clearly defined business strategy and an appropriate trust model, and it requires a platform for testing and refining the experience against this model. As in the real world, trust models help to establish the guidelines in which a market works, and they allow a firm to better serve the market. Companies will benefit by explicitly defining a trust model for the business case and applying process metrics to ensure that trust is optimized in the user experience.

Defining best practices for trust building in the user experience requires, first, a holistic model for describing trust and, then, approaches to satisfy each aspect of the model. Firms should follow these steps to ensure that the model is being employed:

1. Establish the driving business strategy. For example, "Increase customer loyalty among the high-value-customer segment."
2. Clearly define the tactical approaches. For example, "Offer personalization in the experience as a means to build trust."
3. Choose the trust-building components of the trust model that impact the business, and determine a method to measure their efficiency over time. "Transactional Fulfillment," for example, might be an important component whose efficiency metric might be the percentage of incomplete transactions (or "repels") out of the total sum of successfully completed ones.
4. After launching the initiative, track the trust-building components according to the method for measurement. For example, the percentage of incomplete transactions should decrease over time.
5. Make enhancements based on the measurements gathered in step 4.

strategic
experience
envisioning

4

capture what customers want in the user experience

One Click Can Matter

Incorrectly targeted user experiences compromise business success. Imagine if Amazon.com's "1-Click" buy had instead been "Three Clicks and a Pulldown Menu Buy," and the importance of translating business goals and experience requirements into useful, valued user interfaces becomes clear. When the experience fails to satisfy the target audience, the results can have a huge impact on the business. If customers can't engage with the site because they don't like it, or if they can't quickly understand the value proposition or how to initiate tasks, they won't continue the relationship.

Successful user experiences deliver the value proposition—essentially the brand promise—to customers in the most effective and appropriate way. If users can't engage in the full brand experience because of usability issues, the value proposition is diminished, so usability should be intrinsic to the DNA of the planning and development processes. Companies should develop a model of usability that reflects the business metrics—such as transaction initiation, successful transaction completion, or "pickup" of new features as they are added. These usability criteria should be matched to corresponding financial metrics—such as measuring cost per lead, conversion rates, and cost per new customer. Track the model and metrics on an ongoing basis to enhance the user experience, and flag any issues that will impact profit. All key team members involved in the design—the marketing, technology, design, and content teams—should understand the connection and impact of usability to profitability and the metrics for success. Regardless of the type of user experience—broadband, wireless, desktop Web—management and the development team need to better understand the connection between usability and profitability.

Case in point: A vice president of Marketing for a Fortune 500 financial-services firm called in a panic: "Why can't our customers use our site?" The Web site enabled customers to use interactive calculators to estimate the amounts they would need to save for future events like retirement or buying a house or to learn about concepts such as risk and return. After the site was examined, the problem became immediately clear: The calculators were too complex and demanded domain knowledge about investing. The target users were average consumers, many of whom were also novice investors. The problem was the mismatch between the user population, with their aptitudes and attitudes, and the user experience. Most likely, it resulted from an inexperienced product manager working with even more inexperienced designers. Unable to grasp the handle that opened the door to the experience, customers had no idea how to start. Had customers been technically savvy early adopters, this user experience would more likely have been successful. Early adopters will put up with a huge amount of pain because they value the experience in terms of *what* it's delivering, not necessarily *how*.

Another aspect to targeting the user experience frequently gets overlooked: What the business team needs to be able to measure success from the user experience. If the business model is based on advertising or partnerships that require frequent usage reporting, then the user experience must be architected, from both the user and the technical perspectives, to deliver useful and relevant data back to the marketing team. Trellix Corporation initially sold its Web-authoring software as a desktop product that was loaded on the user's machine, and the measure of success was the number of new sites the user published to the Web. All of the activity that occurred prior to publishing—the user's actions and attempts—was invisible to the marketing team. Yet when Trellix migrated its authoring tool to work as a server-based product on the Web, the infrastructure of the user experience changed, along with the business reporting structure. Now, marketing had a detailed record of every click for each authoring session, and the reporting back to strategic partners needed to be based on usage and page views, not just publishing a complete site to the Web. Trellix was able to alter the experience architecture to evolve along with the business needs and deliver the relevant data that the marketing team needed to satisfy business-partner relationships.

As we saw at the outset of Chapter 1, a mismatch can occur when the user experience fails to deliver the value proposition in a way that satisfies customer's needs and goals. Though there's a long history of human-computer interaction which has evolved through the last twenty years, much of it was ignored during the Internet heyday as flimsy business models drove the design of even flimsier user experiences. A return to more rigorous practices needs to happen, and fast. There's less capital available now, and firms want to minimize risk. At the same time, developing successful user experiences has become more difficult because of the following:

- Marketers speak a different language than designers and technologists. These groups have different goals and metrics for success for the user experience. Yet all of these parts of the organization influence the user experience, so the need for shared metrics is important.
- The online user experience can represent many kinds of customer relationships that demand unique "experience propositions": a software application, an ecommerce site, or a marketing communication site.
- Customers want one relationship with a firm, which can now span multiple channels, and they want business to be conducted where

and when they choose (e.g., at a brick-and-mortar store, on the phone, online, on a wireless device; at 3:00 p.m. or 3:00 a.m.)

- The link between the business drivers and the product experience can easily get lost as more people—including outsourced talent—participate in the design and development of user experiences, often in physically different locations.
- Online experiences are evolving toward more transactional capabilities as pervasive computing becomes a reality, enabling customers to accomplish tasks using a new class of intelligent and portable network devices. Their development processes resemble that of software-product development, and this demands new skills from marketers—who now are responsible for the user experience.

This chapter continues the strategic process from Chapter 1, focusing on the capture and translation of customer goals and requirements into useful experiences (see Figure 4-1) that deliver a consistent customer relationship regardless of channel. The chapter examines why it is important to translate the business strategy into the experience strategy at the outset—in effect creating a single roadmap that the entire team understands and can follow, maintaining the linkages between the business goals and the needs of customers. Also covered is what is required to drive and manage the process and a framework for capturing customer requirements and translating them into experience requirements—helping make the process more effective and ultimately deliver a better product.

Why User Experiences Fail

User experiences fail because they don't effectively blend business goals with true usefulness, which is often a result of poorly executed project management or incorrect goal-setting. The business goals can get diluted as development proceeds through conceptual prototype to ultimate execution—and the final design cannot support the original business goals. An ecommerce site whose revenue depends on ease of initiating and completing a purchase can fail if the

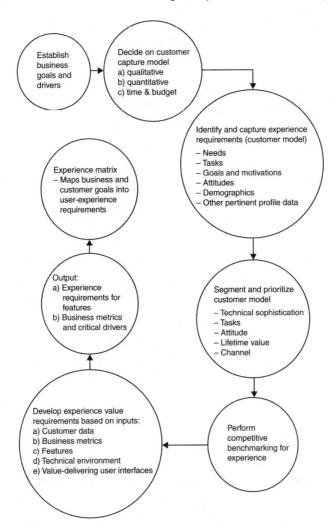

Figure 4-1. Capturing customer expectations depends on understanding the business drivers and the needs and tasks of customers, against the background of technology platform and competitive landscape with an eye toward evolution and scalability.

call to action—the purchase button—is cryptically hidden in the design or the purchase transaction difficult to complete. It's not built for use. Perhaps the marketing manager falls in love with beautiful graphical mockups and successfully sells the concept to the organization—and ultimately the technology team can't execute because

HTML does not enable a page layout that matches what Photoshop can produce. The result fails to deliver the appropriate experience to satisfy the tasks users need to complete. The issue might be organizational: Team members responsible for the execution may not understand or be aware of the underlying business strategy—and may not care—and therefore the business strategy is weakened by poor execution. The sales team may promise deliverables for which they don't entirely understand the complexity—or the impact on the schedule. The development team may be located in different time zones. For example, many eservices firms are now outsourcing work to development teams in India and Eastern Europe. So there's a potential risk in execution if the team is geographically or culturally distinct. The change management may fail: End users may not want to change their behaviors to use the system. Another reason may be the use of disparate teams: Outsourced development or design with team members who may not have strong enough skills, which makes the customer experience difficult to own and manage. Or perhaps its difficult to maintain the criteria for brand, utility, and usability throughout.

The challenges of managing multidisciplinary teams can impact the quality of the user experience. Issues such as a lack of understanding or awareness among the teams can lead to communications breakdowns and affect the quality of the user experience. For example, design process is not clearly understood by many outside the discipline. Marketing or sales team members often have little or no understanding of how design or experience architecture works. So, in cases where ample time has not been left in the schedule, design can unfairly be seen as a bottleneck. As a result, the design process can be accelerated beyond the breaking point, resulting in a compromise to the user-experience deliverables. Technology teams too can be seen as bottlenecks when product management brings an incomplete set of requirements or asks for too many features that cannot be coded in the available time—and then refuses to budge on the end dates. Companies that work to organize teams around "customer relationships" and break down communications barriers among groups—sharing knowledge about process and creating cross-functional teams—overcome these issues by creating a mutually respectful culture.

User experiences also fail because firms don't know enough about their customers—their behaviors, their interests and skills, and what they need in order to be successful in a relationship with the firm. This lack of knowledge impacts the design of the experience. Who mistakenly thought that users would want a mobile Web experience displayed through a cell phone that required using number keys to enter complex character strings like "http://"? Performing that task is an excruciatingly painful experience. Didn't someone think about the economics of the business, and what kinds of behaviors customers needed to engage in to ultimately drive profitability? Examples like this show how a good idea can suffer from bad usability—and compromise any hope for a business return in the process.

User experiences can be difficult to fix, and the all-important first experience can end a customer relationship forever. So doing the customer capture work beforehand—before launch—will pay huge dividends later on, even though it might lengthen the development process. 3G is a communications infrastructure for delivering high-speed wireless connectivity to handheld devices that needs the appropriate user experiences to help deliver the value proposition—and a return on the $125 billion that has been invested so far in its development. Companies should be skeptical on wireless technology and carefully consider the benefits to the end user and the impact on the user experience: Emode.com is a dot-com that has over 9 million registered users who return consistently to take personality tests and receive personalized email and product recommendations—with an attitude. CEO James Currier remarks: "We're less bullish on wireless, [even though] our experience is a narrowband one—we assume everyone is 28.8 [Kbps] and below. Our user experience ports well to the wireless environment, but we think there won't be as much trust building going on there." He notes the impact of trust on the user experience for Emode: "We have to press flesh—it's not going away."

As brand experiences continue to cross and integrate customer channels, firms will need to manage their portfolio of commerce experiences to maximize customer relationships. Says marketing strategist Kathryn Blair: "One of the fundamental issues facing electronic commerce is understanding what part of the commerce should be made electronic and would better service a consumer or business market—and what part of the buying or selling experience should be done in person. When buying a car, for example, we need to know what part most buyers must experience in person in order to buy." Blair thinks this information could be gathered by testing potential and actual customers in at reasonable cost, and that this information would prove valuable as an input to the design of the user experience.

Less Like Paper, More Like Product: Good User-Experience Design Now Resembles Best Practices for Product Design

As the Internet economy developed, many firms created processes and methods to enhance the product development life cycle. "Products" in the context of the Web meant many things: traditional desktop software applications ("fat client"), an ecommerce site, a hybrid of desktop and browser components, or purely marketing communication. Producing a product *on Internet time* typically meant that the process was accelerated at every point of the development cycle. As shown by Microsoft in the development of Internet Explorer,[1] sometimes this produced good results. Sometimes the results were disastrous. (Think of how many bygone dot-coms had a flimsy ecommerce experience).

On the positive side, the result of so much Web design and development activity in the last few years has meant that companies now have a better framework than ever before for designing experiences for new contexts. Designing for the Web meant that new frameworks were learned—especially designing for a constrained environment. Says Philippe Stessel, user experience practice lead at Plural, Inc.: "We've come to the point where the limits of the medium have led to innovative solutions. Complex navigation, for example, when properly handled and designed, can cross-promote a firm's different business lines without confusing the user. And, of course, we've gained tremendously from the connectivity. We're still developing a common language for design, and the new designer will understand many contexts."

The body of knowledge about design amassed during the dot-com era will help inform design for the wireless Web, because more is known now about how to create user experiences for constrained environments than when the Internet first became a customer-relationship channel. Proving the importance and impact of good usability has also become easier. Good examples of these frameworks include the design of navigation systems to afford the most efficient experience for the end user, which have standardized into a left-hand vertical or a top horizontal layout, using minimal graphics and HTML text instead of graphical buttons—practices that ecommerce firms had to learn by trial and error. The collective learning and thought leadership of many eservices and ecommerce firms meant that new methodologies and practices—those that blended best practices for business strategy with those from design and software development— were shared among the development and design communities. This knowledge-sharing influenced practices, and has now begun to work its way into the vernacular for user-experience practice.

The bottom line has become important again in the founding of new companies. So some of the more rigorous processes available before the Internet economy have to be applied to the accelerated practices acquired during the dot-com era. The result can be the creation of good experiences that more closely match business requirements. Best practices for user experiences now resemble good market research and the highly iterative processes of architects and designers. New forms of usability testing—far more informal and "on the fly"—are being incorporated into development cycles. Most importantly, the customer's needs and goals are being incorporated earlier in the development process, because that has been shown to lead to more successful products.

Capture Customers' Experience Expectations at the Outset

The Internet economy put the power of the commerce relationship into the hands of the customer: With competitors only a click away, the inconvenience of switching was low, so customer retention became paramount. The user experience began to substantially impact the business goals of building loyalty and trust, as measured by metrics like retention. Companies knew that adopting processes that placed high value on customer-centrism was important to maintaining their own value and to their survival. Successful software methodologies such as Extreme Programming—which tightly integrates software design and testing—have emerged. Feedback from customers is being integrated earlier and earlier in the process and "usability and user experience are the mantras now" says Plural's Philippe Stessel.

Having knowledge about the customer's needs, goals, behaviors, and expectations is critical to success. Doing the research on what customers want is not a phase that companies can accelerate or try to skip: Aspects of the experience that will deliver value to users must be understood, and work needs to be done to capture the expectations for the experience before development begins. Helping to lower the risk of designing products and services that customers don't want and can't use makes good business sense. It also increases the likelihood of a return on development investment.

Common mistakes that result in failure to meet customers' expectations include rushing new concepts into development without adequately testing them among target users to guarantee that they are meaningful and easy to use. Many reasons may apply: Most often the culture does not value "process," so management may not "get" user experience; instead they use tactics like drop-dead dates to drive the development of products. Another mistake is blindly adding features just because competitive products offer them, without any thought about how useful or valuable they are to customers. Although the product might get produced on time, if it's not the right one or if it is not valued by customers, nobody will use it and the development investment will have been wasted.

Firms will have less room for error in the design of ubiquitous experiences: Big mistakes will mean big money wasted. A tighter link must tie user-experience requirements to profitability in the future. The user experience will be considered a major asset to be protected. Perhaps firms will develop risk-assessment groups dedicated to minimizing risk or creating pro-forma models for the development of the user experience—much like the insurance or financial services industries do.

Early Customer Input Is Key to Success: Fidelity Investments' PowerStreet Pro™

When customer feedback is incorporated early in the design of the user experience, the likelihood of success increases. Case in point is Fidelity Powerstreet Pro™, one of the most successful ecommerce applications, whose development cycle incorporated critical customer feedback at the very outset. Designed in stages from a product concept to final launch in just under six months, it was developed by a cross-disciplinary team with clear business objectives, a rich and detailed customer model, and immediate access to target customers, whose voice was incorporated early in the design process.

The site features online tools and resources exclusively for qualified active traders who want a single online environment through which to control their finances. Users have access to real-time and Nasdaq Level II quotes, the ability to place trade orders (including complex options orders such as straddles and spreads) through an integrated user experience that displays centralized real-time quotes, account holdings, watch lists, third-party stock charts, and news. The user experience allows the trader to customize the layout and use advanced tools within watch lists such as drag-and-drop sorting for columns and right-click mouse functionality to insert and delete rows.

The overall user-experience challenge was to satisfy Fidelity's business goals and customer goals and create a branded, easy-to-use customer experience that abstracted the complexities of trading in a rapid-pace environment. Fidelity's customer goal was to increase satisfaction among active traders with a user experience that was easy to master and easy to incorporate into a trader's everyday work flow.

Using a small team made up of executive management, product team members from design, technology, brokerage, project management, and target customers (a critical component), the team participated in an ultrarapid brainstorming process to capture customer requirements against the backdrop of the business drivers. This was done offsite, away from corporate headquarters, to assure that the team was left alone to work intensely and without interruption.

The team developed a conceptual demo of the product's user experience for use as a "talking piece" with potential customers. Using hand-drawn sketches that were shown to target users who participated in the session meant that the immediate feedback could be incorporated into the design. The first design employed an aggregated interface with access to market news and education: Users rejected this design by telling designers that they wanted to navigate using a "security-centric" model and to have access to trading on every screen, especially where securities were displayed. These concepts felt foreign to the design team. The notion of placing a trade button on every screen wherever a security name appeared seemed to fly in the face of good design principles. The team redesigned the interface using the feedback from customers. After this redesign, it became clear that the target users understood the value in the experience.

The entire process—from initial brainstorming sessions, to hand-sketched iterations of user experiences, to working mockups for user testing—took one week. Mockups were handed off to a prototype development team overnight, usability tested in the morning, and enhancements and adjustments added into the prototype by midday. This prototype was presented in a formal presentation to executive management.

The initial design that the team developed was the basis of the user experience that ultimately became the product's interface (see Figure 4-2). It was also designed with flexible modules and screen components such as watch lists and portfolio elements, so that as Fidelity later added new functionality, these features were easily incorporated as new components within the flexible user interface architecture.

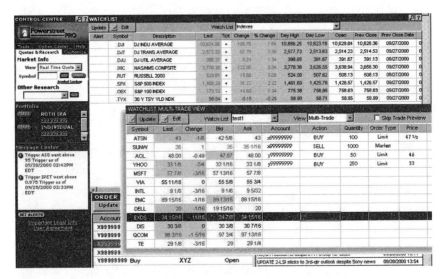

Figure 4-2. Fidelity Powerstreet Pro.™ *(All copyrights and trademarks of the PowerStreet Pro™ product are owned by Fidelity Investments.)*

Understand the Brand Experience

It's a good practice to validate—as early as possible—that the brand proposition is deliverable through the user experience and in the proposed technical environment. Users must be able to fully experience the brand proposition online: Imagine trying to enjoy a steaming mocha latte at Starbucks yet being forced to sip it through a coffee stirrer. The full experience is degraded, and the value in the experience is lost.

Boo.com had a strong and unique brand personality of cutting-edge cool fashion. Their fully animated personal agent, "Ms. Boo," was an innovative concept that defined an edgy brand personality. Yet the brand experience could not be adequately delivered to the customer because of bandwidth limitations: At the other end of the pipeline, users were left frustrated, peering at the screen, waiting for the experience.

Ubiquitous, Transactional Experiences Will Demand Even More Customer-Centric Design

Ubiquity will elevate the importance of design—and of style—in the user experience. Like Swatch watches, the form factor will impact how we feel about the experience of using these networked appliances more than ever. And as user experiences evolve to become more transactional and less tethered to a single location, understanding the expectations of customers becomes increasingly important to ensure a consistent relationship—especially one that spans multiple channels.

"Wireless experiences are really about little information tasks and transactions," says eRoom lead user-experience designer Glenn McDonald. He should know. Nothing makes him happier than receiving the scores of the European soccer leagues on an ongoing basis, especially during the championships. He does not want to waste time in his busy day navigating a Web site to look for the obscure teams he follows. He created his own custom wireless application—his private killer app—by creating a program to go to the soccer Web site several times per day and gather the latest scores for only the teams he is interested in. Once this information is gathered, it is sent to his cell phone in a discreet and simple message that he can pick up while in meetings or anytime during the day.

Glenn, being the gifted technologist that he is, values the transaction and the information that is relevant to him—and nothing more. The user experience balances constraints with simplicity and delivers a truly satisfying experience—one that I'll bet he would probably pay for, if he were unable to program the code himself.

User-centrism will become more important as ubiquity becomes a reality, because users will be mobile, so the user experience will have to span different contexts. Users will judge the quality of the experience based on the appropriateness and relevance of the information they receive. Ronna Tanenbaum, chief creative officer at software company Alexa Internet, thinks that for ubiquitous computing the user experience must blur the line between technology and information. Says she: "Do what makes sense to people in their lives by making the information flow like a story—making the line between the content and the tool disappear, because the focus is on the information and the anticipation of how it reveals itself. Stories provide a context which make it more comfortable to make decisions—and in user-experience design this translates to action."

Capturing Customer Demand for a Wireless and Mobile Experience: FitSense Technology

For a good example of how a complex concept can be successfully executed when customer feedback on mission-critical features is included early in the design cycle, consider the user experience for FitSense. FitSense Technology was founded by fitness enthusiasts who saw an opportunity to answer the age-old questions, "How far have I gone? How much energy have I burned?" This information cannot be measured while walking and running on trails and roads. Never before has it been possible to accurately track the human stride, because stride length is highly variable as the result of changing speeds and conditions while running or walking. But FitSense has developed a patented foot sensor called the FS-1, a sensor that clips to a runner's shoelace and monitors data such as speed and calories burned. The sensor automatically adjusts to each stride to give a highly accurate measure of pace, distance, speed, and caloric expenditure. A wireless digital link sends the data from the foot sensor to the watch on the runner's wrist. Later, this information can be downloaded to a personal fitness Web site to track progress over time. The watch has been designed with a display that faces up and slightly inwards, enabling the runner to glance at the reading without having to lift and twist his or her wrist to read the watch's face—a truly useful wearable wireless appliance.

The founders of FitSense knew there was a need in the market, but validating the concept with no demonstrable prototype meant that capturing initial customer-demand data would be challenging. In order to validate what customers wanted in the user experience, FitSense team members used concept sketches on paper showing the watch and sensor. They discussed the rendering with focus groups, using qualitative verbal descriptions to describe features such as the shoe clamp and the ability to easily see the speed and distance on the watch. They asked participants if the concept was clear and if the experience was one they would benefit from. From these sessions, FitSense executives were able to gather qualitative data and feedback based on reactions of focus-group participants. One of the most critical features was that runners did not want to have to bend and lift the wrist to view the face of the watch; it had to be easily viewable while in motion. Capturing this kind of qualitative data was key—and would ultimately lead to one of the design features that made the FS-1 unique and useful.

AN "INTIMATE" USER EXPERIENCE

The next step of answering the question "What is the user experience?" was a "constant challenge" says FitSense president Sam Joffe. "All of the specification for the physical form as well as features was difficult to gather into a specification. There were many differences in perspective among the team members, each distinct group having its own language and goals." The executives worked to align the organization around customer needs, and they used that as a basis for decision making. From the data they collected in the focus groups, they created a portrait of customer value in order to be able to answer questions about how much customers would value the FS-1 experience. They used this information to understand the need for the product, gauge interest in it, and influence the design of the user experience and the underlying technology architecture. They were helped by the fact that the founders themselves were target customers and had a strong vision for the user experience. "We also had the benefit of a small organization," says Joffe, "so the designers understood the major goals and drivers." Indeed, making sure the design and engineering teams were aware of the business goals was key, although sometimes business imperatives, such as speed to market, were not always shared by the engineering team.

To deliver the user experience, FitSense had to develop a unique wireless system to allow the runner's foot sensor to communicate with the wristwatch. The experience design had to include the physical hardware, the underlying wireless infrastructure, and the graphical display of the watch. FitSense chose to outsource the industrial design of the foot sensor and the watch to a firm that worked closely with the internal teams. "This was the right choice for us," says Joffe, because FitSense understood that "user experience for industrial design is a refined art and demands a unique skill set."

The design of the watch became a critical part of the FitSense user experience, because it's an extreme motion for a runner to bend his or her elbow and lift the wrist to read the watch display. Runners demanded that they not have to push buttons or scroll to get the critical data while in motion. By placing the watch display in a slightly twisted position so that it sits on the inside of the runner's wrist pointing upwards, the watch delivers instant feedback at a glance without forcing the runner to break stride (see Figure 4-3). The

Figure 4-3. The FitSense watch delivers instant feedback at a glance without forcing the runner to break stride. The watch display is placed in a slightly twisted position so that it sits on the inside of the runner's wrist pointing upward. A single glance at the watch face answers runners' critical questions, such as "How far have I gone?"

design of the watch face features four fields that answer runners' critical questions in a single glance, all relevant information on a single view. Ultimately, this "intimate user experience" delivers the key value for the runner while minimizing movement of the wrist—something that is important to runners and makes a difference in the quality of the experience. This innovative design smoothly marries the action of reading the watch into the gesture of the runner's arm while in motion: the ultimate "frictionless transaction," offering a model for the way that experiences will be designed in the future for mobile and wireless devices and appliances.

Ultimately, the design of the FitSense user experience has been a success: FitSense has sold several thousand units to very enthusiastic and loyal customers. And the product has begun to gain traction in the world of organized sports: Olympic track-and-field gold medalist Michael Johnson used the FS-1 at the U.S. Olympic trials in 2000.

Planning the User-Experience Strategy

How will you develop and evolve your user-experience strategy over time? What must the user experience satisfy to deliver short-term results right away? And how, at the same time, can it scale and evolve to enable broader experiences—ones that reflect the growth of the business and deliver long-term value in the form of loyal customer relationships? What kinds of team members are necessary, and what should their skill sets be? And how can the output of the process—which becomes the input to the next stage of architecture and envisioning a prototype—never lose touch with the underlying business drivers? These are the questions that best practices for user-experience strategy can answer, in effect forming the first piece of a blueprint that will ultimately express the experience requirements.

Many firms try to accelerate the process of user-experience design and try to skip the customer-capture stage. Why? Because it takes time, and it can be expensive. In a sense, this stage is akin to marketing research—the early stage of proving that there is a market need for the product or service. There are measures you can take to guarantee that the user experience you plan is the one that users want to use, but it's important to do this at the outset, not at the end. Usability testing just before launch is not the time to find fundamental mistakes in the targeting strategy. Firms need to put in place the framework for the right user experience the first time, because it's difficult to scale and build one that has been incorrectly targeted and based on a shaky framework from the outset. It may look like a great experience, but it's not the one your customers want. And it won't scale to new platforms and environments.

Translating Marketing Strategy into Actionable Designs: State Street Global Advisors

Successful user experiences translate customer goals into great experiences: The interfaces enhance the customer relationship by delighting the user, adding value at every opportunity, leveraging the technical environment's strengths and minimizing its weaknesses. For example, Amazon.com's translation of the customers' goal of easy online purchasing into a 1-Click buy is a great example. The one click is simple and doesn't require any special code or knowledge; it's the *atomic unit of value creation* in the experience. At any stage in the Amazon.com customer experience, the most relevant and appropriate information is presented. Even on the first visit, the user is never more than three clicks away from buying a book. Yahoo! Finance's financial portal gives the most efficient experience for the target user (technically savvy investors) with a portal interface, aggregating a large amount of disparate content into a single, unified interface. These users are loyal. Have you ever tried to get a Yahoo! Finance portfolio user to give it up and migrate to another financial services portal? You can't get them to budge; the experience is that great.

At State Street Global Advisors, it became apparent that institutional investors such as pension managers—a high-value customer segment—needed an online product. These customers were asking for Web access to their investment programs, and SSgA had no product for them. Apparently there was a demand for a new kind of online customer experience: What institutional clients needed was a secure and private extranet, one that enabled them to have an online relationship with SSgA that complemented their existing one with their relationship managers.

Marketing executives at SSgA defined the business strategy, which included creating loyalty and expanding the relationship through the Internet channel. From there the team defined a capture model to gather input from the specific owner groups who would be responsible for the development—the relationship managers, the sales and business development team, marketing, technology and compliance officers.

The effort began by brainstorming through the business goals and defining metrics for each of these goals. An example of a goal might be to grow revenue. The corresponding metric would be the number of new accounts opened within a time period.

Features were developed that the team members felt would be valued by customers, including:

- Account access
- Communication with relationship manager
- Access to products and services
- Library of investment knowledge

These key features were then analyzed for their business opportunities and the specific product features that were required for each part of the experience.

Team members then took the customer's perspective. Each of the key product features was considered, as well as what the experience needed to deliver for it to be successful. Customer demographics showed two things: that customers were experts in their industry-specific knowledge of information (i.e., they were "domain experts") and that they were split evenly between technically savvy early adopters and novice Internet users. Using that knowledge, the team developed a model that described in words what each of the segments would need to experience in order to use and value the product.

The next step was to prioritize features according to management goals and gain better understanding of users' work flow. SSgA created scenarios to explain the behaviors and tasks that specific user segments would exhibit in the course of their everyday use of the extranet. These scenarios gave the team insight into the work processes of users. They also drove the definition of the information architectures—part of the next stage of planning the user experience—used to envision the extranets through rapid prototyping techniques.

Planning, Staffing, and Resources: The Team

The customer-capture process requires input from several teams, including business development, marketing, technology, and design. This process is typically managed by the product manager or the product marketing manager, and the strategy for initiating the design process is driven by the business goals. Typically, the marketing executives will be involved in this step to set the tone for how the process should evolve and to set expectations.

The customer-capture step can be done by outsourcing the entire process, or it can be done in-house by a dedicated team. The trade-off is time versus resources: The internal team may have the interest and the skills, but not enough time. If the time frame is critical, or if the user experience is particularly complex or requires a refined skill set, use of an outside expert is a better approach. Either way, the process requires input from all team members who will be responsible for shaping the user experience. It's a matter of deciding at the outset who has the most relevant knowledge for stating the customers' requirements and making sure that the experience satisfies the business goals and is deliverable through the technical platform and environment.

There are now a host of new job titles that reflect the changing landscape of skill sets required to develop user experiences, a list of which is shown in Table 4-1. User-experience strategists work on the

Business Team	Experience Design and Creative	Technology
Business strategist	User-experience strategist	Technology architect
Marketing manager	Information architect	Technical manager
Product manager	Creative director	Software engineer
Product marketing manager	Designer	Webmaster
Program manager	Content manager	Quality assurance
Project manager	Documentation writer	
Analyst	Copywriter	
Business-specific Competencies	**Usability**	
Compliance officer	Usability professional	
Legal	Moderator	
Customer advocate	Usability analyst	
Relationship manager	Research assistant	

Table 4-1. Contributors to user experience have many functions and job titles, some of them new.

strategic planning and development of the overall requirements for the user experience, often in concert with the business owners and senior technology and design team members. Information architects have skills that span business strategy, technology, and user-interface design. They translate business, technical, and user requirements into a blueprint that incorporates flow and narrative into the user experience. One of the key team members is the program manager, a position that is common in software-development companies, whose goal is to deliver the right product at the right time. Program managers work as simultaneous translators among business owners, development teams, and end users. They translate business requirements into specifications for designers, engineers, and the documentation team. The experience matrix—a capture framework we suggest at the end of this chapter—can serve to help the program manager track the design over its life cycle to make sure it is answering the original business and end-user goals.

The team members responsible for the design and development of the user experience should have exposure to developing similar—not necessarily the same—types of products. Designers who primarily do consumer work may not have the skill sets for doing business-to-business experience design. Or the design of a complex transactional user experience may require a designer with domain knowledge of the area and strong technical skills. User-interface designers typically have more software-development experience and technical skill. A more thorough examination of the work of these team members is discussed in Chapter 5.

Managing an Interdisciplinary Team

Managing an interdisciplinary team in the design of user experiences relies on a complex collaboration among marketing, technology, design, and product management. Each team has different goals, processes, and metrics for success, often with no idea about the work processes and challenges faced by the other. Ultimately, these competing agendas must combine to deliver an experience that delivers value to the customer—and drives profitability.

Despite the disparity among these cultures, a good approach is to focus and align the teams along customer relationships instead of on functional areas such as technology or design. Communicating the importance of the customer relationship to each team member in his or her unique language and skill level is valuable. This approach only works if it's driven—and practiced—by senior management.

One way to encourage this is to make customer-centrism part of the fabric of the culture and to tie compensation into this goal. "Take a look at your existing compensation system," says Hollie Schmidt, president of Lifting Mind, a Boston-based management consulting firm. "If it already includes elements like pay for performance or goal-based incentives, and if customer focus is a new strategic imperative for the company, then consider introducing user-experience metrics as one of the factors that determine compensation." She also recommends that firms only link compensation to user-experience metrics for people who are directly responsible for the user experience.

Collaborative multidisciplinary teams need to better understand the business goals and use shared metrics—which could be thought of as "experience metrics"—to effectively drive and develop good user experiences. In these post-dot-com-boom days, when profitability matters, everyone involved in the process of developing the user experience must understand the underlying business drivers that will create success. Designers and technologists, who typically don't carry profit-and-loss responsibility for the user experience, will benefit by understanding how their contribution impacts the bottom line. Marketers will benefit by understanding some of the pressures and challenges faced by designers and how they do their work; the complex processes involved can often be misunderstood by members of the team. All will benefit from better understanding the challenges and complexities faced by software developers to design and build experiences in an increasingly complex and dynamic technical environment. The most successful collaborative efforts happen when there's open communication between team members and mutual respect for the different disciplines.

Managing the team effectively means allowing each team member to grow and develop her or his talents while contributing to the goal of developing a superior user experience. Encouraging team members to be owners of a specific aspect of the user experience is an approach that has worked successfully for usability consultant Chauncey Wilson of Bentley College's Design and Usability Testing Center. While employed as a product manager at a large software-development company, Wilson assigned individuals on the development team to be responsible for and own a specific part for the experience, such as "Error Messages," "User Interface Consistency," or "Purchasing Transactions." The team members became known among their peers as being "experts" and recognized as having special and unique skills that contribute to the overall success of the group—and to the user experience.

The most successful designers and technologists in the dot-com-blowout culture will understand how the business will impact their work, and vice versa, and be able to make sure that the business is defensible. The creative producers, the designers and technologists, need to be committed to developing and designing things that are good for the end user, not for their portfolios. Designers also need to understand when to sublimate their own creative aspirations for the good of the end-user experience: If extra screens or design "bells and whistles" don't add value yet cost a lot to develop, they should not be done. This holding back has been a challenge. The most usable experiences are often not the sexiest. Says James Currier, CEO and founder of Emode.com: "Many user-experience people turned it into a moral crusade for five years, took a holier-than-thou attitude, and refused to understand the business needs. We ended up with development projects that produced art but did not achieve the business concept." Now, the demise of the booming dot-com culture has left some designers whining about being victims of bad business strategy. Better to be an active participant in the business strategy and cognizant of the *why*, not just the *how*.

The Process

The process discussed in the following paragraphs and shown in Figure 4-1 is a general guideline for best practices in planning the user-experience strategy. Driven by the business case, this approach uses an experience-level approach as opposed to one based on feature definition. Often, companies already have in place a process for developing products that is specific to an industry. For example, the process might be more formal at a software-development company than at an ecommerce firm that is less dependent on documentation.

Most companies use some sort of guiding product-features document, such as a marketing-requirements document, which states the business drivers and defends why the strategy makes sense for the company and for customers. A good practice is to define a one-page document with the strategic goals and benefits clearly listed, such as the following:

- What is the goal of the user experience?
- Why is it business-relevant?
- What is the value to customers?
- What is the underlying metric (or metrics) for business success?

This strategic document can be used to inform the design and technical briefs that will follow for the specific teams. These documents can serve as agreements among team members and are used to define delivery dates and development milestones. Some companies have a formal process for signing off on delivery dates that each development group agrees to; others are more informal.

The process for capturing the user-experience requirements follows these steps:

- Establish business goals that drive the customer experience.
- Establish metrics for business success in the customer experience, including the short-term and long-term return on investment (e.g., the "Just Good Enough" model suggested in Chapter 1).
- Develop a customer model: Establish the customer segment(s), their goals, tasks, attitudes, and needs along with the technical environment in which the user experience will be delivered.
- Perform competitive analysis for the user experience.
- Establish experience benefits and expectations for all product features.
- Define an experience matrix, including tasks and product features, experience requirements and metrics, best practices and user interfaces. (See Table 4-4 for an example.)
- Deliver the experience matrix to drive architecture and envisioning.

The first two steps, covered already (see Chapter 1), must be clearly understood before the customer-capture process can occur. Companies that try to skip over these crucial steps risk executing on a plan that is driven by tactics, not strategy.

Establish Metrics for Business Success in the User Experience

At the outset, gathering answers to the questions that follow helps to initiate the experience-design capture process. Drive the user-experience strategy by asking these questions of the business owners at the outset, then collecting and prioritizing the results.

Start by clearly articulating the major aspects of the value proposition of the user experience:

- Who are the customers? Are they also the end users?
- What are their goals?
- What would they value in the experience of this product or service? Why would they use it?
- What do they lack, and how does the product or service address this need?
- What are their relative expectations of such an experience, as compared to other experiences?
- What is a customer's relationship with this product or service over time?
- What are the drivers of relationship and retention in the experience?
- What does the current competitive landscape look like? Who are the other players, and what do they do well?

For each of the business and customer goals, the appropriate success metric should be defined. Distinguishing between the goals of customers is important if the end user is different from the direct customer, which is a common situation for a B2B user experience. For example, for an institutional brokerage site, BrokerX, the business might be the processing of transactions for executing the buying and selling of stocks. The direct customer is the brokerage house, but the end users are the traders who work for the broker. The brokerage house wants to enable as many transactions to be completed with as few errors as possible, and it seeks to gain efficiencies from traders. The direct customer's (i.e., the brokerage house's) business goals and success metrics are shown in Table 4-2.

The end-user goals, shown in Table 4-3, are very different from the direct-customer goals, as comparison between Table 4-2 and Table 4-3 reveals.

With BrokerX, the user experience must facilitate the goals of the firm (increasing the number of error-free trade executions) and be easy and fast to learn. As Tables 4-2 and 4-3 show, the goals of the direct customer and the end user align along the dimensions of desired efficiency and throughput. In situations in which there is a misalignment between the goals of the firm and the goals of the end user, a decision must be made as to whether the cost to the customer relationship will have negative impact on the business proposition.

Customer Goals	Success Metrics
Increase revenue	Increase in transaction flow and resulting revenue
Gain efficiencies in productivity	More trades successfully completed without having to scale physical infrastructure or add personnel
Decrease risk from trade execution	Decrease in trade-execution errors

Table 4-2. Direct-customer goals for the BrokerX user experience, with success metrics.

End-User Goals	Success Metrics
Be able to trade more efficiently without having to read a manual or sit through a class	Rapid adoption of system into trading work flow
Be able to execute more trades with fewer execution errors	Number of successfully completed trades, and number of execution errors
Look good in front of my boss and in front of coworkers	Increase in stature of organization: seen as a "player," promoted to head trader

Table 4-3. End-user goals for the BrokerX user experience, with success metrics.

For each of the metrics of success, be sure that the data required to measure and report progress is made a priority in the technology architecture. With BrokerX, the back-end system must be capable of tracking each user's transaction flow as well as execution errors. It also must report this information in a format that marketing can use to perform analysis and produce ROI reports that measure against the success criteria.

At the outset of the process of establishing metrics for business success in the user experience, define the specific business mission for the product or service and be specific with relation to the brand position. For example, "to create the premier online money management experience for affluent customers" covers the brand position ("premier") as well as the target customer segment ("affluent customers"). Be aware of any aspects of this mission statement that will be affected by your brand. For example, if your firm is a blue-chip financial services firm, the concept of "premier" will have to include high levels of security, privacy, and high-touch service consistent throughout the user experience over time.

Know the Customer Well: Develop a Customer Model and Establish the Demand

Developing a customer model means capturing the appropriate and relevant information about customers to be able to design—and evolve—an effective user experience that builds loyalty for all customer segments.

Know as much as you can about your customers: their goals, attitudes toward and comfort level with technology, their needs and behaviors. That knowledge enhances the relationship you can build online. Like a seasoned salesperson who puts a customer at ease, the user experience must satisfy the needs of different types of customers and be able to gracefully adapt to continue to deliver value as the Web attracts more and different users each day. Early adopters are more technology-savvy, and they don't need much hand-holding.

Therefore, they might want rapid access to information they value: their accounts and records, for example, and the ability to search using specific terms. Novices might feel more comfortable with a more structured experience, with step-by-step processes they can follow, and with navigation mechanisms that facilitate more general searching, much like browsing. As they become more expert, they might require "training wheels" in the user experience, ones that can be removed and replaced if need be.

Develop a general customer profile model to quickly capture and update customer information. This is a good practice regardless of the type of development methodology a firm employs. Segmenting customers by business-relevant dimensions such as lifetime value, attitude,[2] or channel and qualitative inputs such as goals and expectations (see Figure 4-4) helps to develop a detailed model of the customer life cycle, a valuable input to the user-experience strategy. Establishing the demand of each segment helps determine the best way to allot resources to development. It also helps define the best order in which products and services are to be rolled out and what channels are to be used, based on what makes economic sense. Knowing that the user population is split evenly between novices who are technology laggards[3] and affluent early adopters with lots of

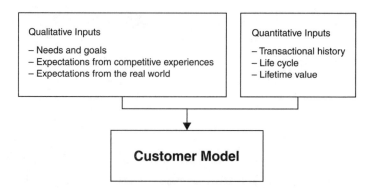

Figure 4-4. Segmenting customers by business-relevant dimensions, including qualitative and quantitative inputs, helps to develop a detailed model of the customer life cycle—an important input to the user-experience strategy.

devices such as wireless PDAs is important. That knowledge helps you to correlate aspects of the user experience with what these specific users need while at the same time minimizing risk by designing for demand. Figure 4-5 shows an approach to use to segment users along the normal distribution curve, ranging from novices on the left to early adopters on the right.

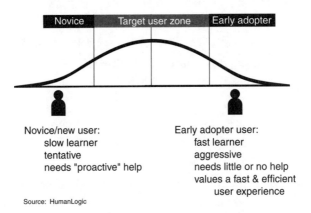

Figure 4-5. An approach to segment users along the normal distribution curve, ranging from novices on the left to early adopters on the right.

Typical customer models can include qualitative information—good for capturing "soft" aspects such as attitudes and opinions—such as:

- Demographic data
- Work-flow and task-flow information
- Surrounding technical environment, where and how the user experience is going to occur
- Expectations based on comparable or competitive experiences
- Critical features that the user considers useful
- Attitudes toward technology and product features

Other quantitative information can also be included in the customer model, if available, including a historical record of transactions or marketing segmentation models.

Many methods can be employed to gather this customer data, including traditional qualitative market-research methods such as focus groups, surveys, and ethnographic research (where users are observed in their natural settings performing their behaviors and activities). Other methods of capturing customer data include creating user profiles, from real (or fictitious) customers who represent the spectrum of target users. These profiles can then be used to develop user scenarios that use techniques such as storyboarding to illustrate work flow and the tasks that users perform over a period of time: an hour, a day, or a week. Another method is task-flow analysis, which uses flowcharts that illustrate the natural progressions of all tasks that users proceed through, usually in concert with the user scenarios.

The capture process for user experience is beginning to resemble more traditional market-research methods.[4] The inputs to the process include the business goals and strategy and the knowledge about customer segments, for example, the skills they bring to the experience and background knowledge about their behaviors and tasks. The output of the process is to map these inputs into the framework and expectations for the experience and to set direction for the next phases of architecture and envisioning.

This information is only useful if the research the marketing team has done is rigorous enough for the design and development team to use. Often the marketing team is really marketing-communications-focused; as such they are more interested in the outward-facing message, not necessarily the inward-facing one that is required to bring useful market research to the product manager and development team. Today, product managers are stretched thin, being responsible for the product concept, development, delivery, and experience enhancement, so they don't have time to conduct in-depth customer research. Instead, they must rely on market research for the input. And if it's not good input, it's not good for the customer.

Another thing to consider during this phase is the risk of not doing each of the steps in capturing good customer data. Measuring the cost of doing each against the risks of not doing each should be part of the ROI model employed at the outset of the process. For example, for a new product whose development cost is $1 million, spending $10,000 to validate customer requirements for the user experience is well spent if it flags critical issues before the prototype is transformed into real software ready to be shipped to customers.

Questions to Ask When Developing a Customer Model

As a guideline, the most important questions that must be answered in the phase of developing a customer model are the following:

- Who are the customers, and what are their skills?
- What technical environment do they use?
- What are the limitations of delivery through a channel or on a platform?
- What tasks do users need to be able to complete to have a valuable experience?
- What user-experience features will they value, and how critical are they to business success?
- What is a typical day in the life of an end user, as it relates to the business?
- What are the typical customer life cycles for each segment? Are there any specific events that catalyze customers to use a product or service? For example, for an asset-management site that caters to affluent individuals, is there an event such as the selling of a company or an initial public offering (IPO) that might instigate customers to use this product or service?
- What exactly are the aspects of the online experience each customer segment values? Efficiency in transactions? Access to a wide selection of choices? Promptness in response from customer service?
- What does each customer segment consider to be an ideal online experience through which to deliver your value proposition?
- How will the user experience impact the business success?

Keep in mind that the administration of the user experience might also represent a target-user segment. Administrators are responsible for updating and maintaining content, much like a Webmaster. The user-experience strategy should include provisions for making the interface for administrative work flow as effective as possible.

The data gathered in the customer-capture step provides the necessary input for the team to begin to brainstorm concepts about the user experience and to define its features. Writing scenarios for each of the customer segments, describing the actions and tasks of each user through the course of an hour, a day, a week, or during any events that cause them to engage with the product is a good way to capture the requirements. If possible, bring these scenarios to customers—as FitSense brought concept sketches to focus-group participants—and ask them if they would value these kinds of solutions or if they would agree with the scenarios.

Perform Competitive Analysis for User Experience

At this stage, analyzing the competition is important in order to understand where they fall short or deliver big value in the user experience. Think "out of the box" for experiences that might be able to be leveraged from totally unrelated areas, such as brick-and-mortar retail experiences. If the goal is to build loyalty and retention, look for other, totally unrelated user experiences that satisfy these goals.

Analyze the business model and how it is being expressed in the competitive experience. Ask the questions: For a portal, is the site engaging? For an application service provider (ASP) model for an online tool, does the environment encourage engagement and facilitate task completion, which lead to real productivity gains? Performing a usability test, even an informal one, on competitive user experiences is a good way to gather data on what works well or what fails.

Analyzing competitive user experiences should focus on gathering best practices for satisfying the strategic goals of the user experience, and it should not be limited to the vertical industry for the firm. For example, a bank that is planning a portal for its retail customers should review other banking sites, but think out of the box and leverage best practices from areas that have evolved more quickly in developing in successful online experiences. Successful retail ecommerce and consumer-portal sites that deliver outstanding experiences should be studied, because they satisfy the bank's site goals of driving transactions and building loyalty quickly, even though they aren't related to retail banking.

Questions to Ask When Analyzing User Experience

Answer these questions when analyzing the competitive landscape of user experiences:

- What are the strengths of the competitor's user experience? The weaknesses?
- What compromises have your competitors made in their online customer experiences? For example, is access to key transactions difficult to find or navigate?

Develop the Experience Requirements for User Experience

After the business goals and customer requirements are captured and analyzed, they should be translated into experience requirements and, ultimately, features. A set of guidelines for defining a feature set and the corresponding experience requirements would include the following:

- *Context.* What will be the platform for delivering the experience? A browser on a desktop machine? A wireless device such as a Palm VII, a PocketPC, a cell phone?
- *Environment.* In what environment will the experience occur? In an office? On the road? At home? In dimly lit or potentially dangerous environments? Is the experience on a single platform? A desktop machine? A handheld device? On a cell phone?

- *Scalability and extensibility.* What likely evolutions will occur that will demand that the experience evolve? For example, the Handspring Visor device, a portable electronic organizer, can be extended to include a cell phone adapter.
- *Expectations.* What other experiences will the user likely have had that will impact the expectations and intentions?
- *Flow.* What is the typical task or scenario flow in which the experience is utilized?
- *Navigation.* What are the critical tasks that the user must be able to complete, and what are the pathways that will make this most effective?
- *Transactions.* What are the key transactions? How will they be initiated and completed?
- *Qualitative.* How will it feel to use it?
- *Quantitative:*

  - How long should it take to complete tasks?
  - If there are tools such as Search, how many clicks are necessary?
  - How long should it take to complete the first-use case?

Define an Experience Matrix

Understanding the kinds of experiences that best express the product features is a combination of good design and understanding the technology platform and the surrounding constraints. Ultimately, using an experience matrix such as the one in Table 4-4 allows the team to map the business goal through to product features and the corresponding experience requirements. This also gives the team a clear roadmap for validating that all business goals are accounted for in the design.

For each business goal, identify the features that contribute to this goal and one or more user-experience mechanisms that can satisfy this goal. For example, for the business goal of increasing trading transactions for a brokerage firm, a contributing factor to satisfaction would be encouraging trading activity. This might be achieved

Business Driver and Success Metric	Tasks	Product Features that Support Business	Experience Requirement	Best Practices	User Interface	Metrics	Testing Plan and Acceptance Criteria
Increase trading activity among high-value customer segment Metric: 1. Increase in trading for segment	Create Portfolio 1. Create New 2. Search for a security 3. Add the security 4. Repeat step 2	1. Portfolio 2. Search 3. Add	• Rapid ability to add a security • Easy, fast, and applicable search • Ease in looking up forgotten ticker symbols	• Yahoo! Finance • Midnight Trader	• Trade button prominent and pervasive in user experience • Simple, clean design that is fast-loading	• Two clicks to add security • Successful completion at first-use case • Feature used at each user session • Leads to a trade on the security • Number of securities added per session is increasing	• Quality Assurance (QA) will test each feature, and usability team will validate • Will also check usage logs every three days for behavior patterns
Increase loyalty Metric: 1. Increase frequency of trades, size of trades 2. Increase retention rate 3. Increase mindshare, replace all other trading tools	Personalize portal	1. Customization wizard 2. Clear benefits statement on screen to drive push to personalize	• Ease in initiating and learning • Fast to complete, no lengthy initialization	• My Yahoo!	• Addition of a "Personalization" tab to navigation scheme	• One click to initiate personalization	• QA will test each feature, and usability team will validate interfaces • Will also check usage logs every week to calculate number of users who have customized

Table 4-4. An example experience matrix, which allows the team to map business goals (in the first column) through to product features and the corresponding experience requirements.

in the user experience by having an easily accessible trade button and a clear, easy-to-complete trading transaction process.

A key piece of knowledge in completing the experience matrix is to understand what constitutes the "atomic unit of revenue" in the user experience: What are the actions of the user that directly add business value to the firm? For example, for the brokerage firm, the value-adding action is the trade transaction. This key transaction is critical to revenue, so anything that degrades the experience for the user puts its success at risk.

Develop a set of features for the user experience, based on the data gathered up to this point. To ensure that the experience delivers what the user expects it to and that the customer is using the features, let's trace an example from the business goal (and shown in Table 4-4).

Company A is a brokerage firm that wants to leverage the Internet as a channel to increase revenues and productivity. The measure of success for this initiative is the level of successful trading activity. The tasks that contribute to this goal include trading and using the portfolio to track and analyze stocks. The product features that contribute to the goal are the portfolio and the trading transaction. The experience requirements include efficiency, security, and help for when the trader forgets the symbol for the stock. Competitive analyses of other firms show that both eTrade's and Fidelity's sites have great trading interfaces, very fast and efficient. Based on interviews with traders, it's clear that they will only tolerate up to a few clicks to be able to securely complete a trade, and they won't sit through a training session, so the system has to be easy to use from the first time onward. The number of clicks becomes a metric for the success of the experience, because it's only by answering this requirement that users will engage in the activity that drives the business case—trading.

The important elements to capture in this exercise are the possibilities for satisfying the business goals in user-experience mechanisms that also satisfy end-user goals. Look for opportunities to deliver a big win for the customer, which will, in turn, deliver a win for the firm. Look for areas where your competitors have compromised in the delivery of their customer experiences: Can you deliver a better experience more effectively, more consistently, or in a more engaging way?

For example, the Palm Pilot's hardware button that instantly turns on the machine is a simple interface mechanism that has huge perceived value.

Choose features wisely. Think about what features of the user experience will cause users to exclaim: "I don't know how I ever lived without it!"

The knowledge captured in the experience matrix (Table 4-4) provides a supporting framework that will drive and inform the user-experience strategy throughout development and launch. The entire team—marketing, technology, and design and content—can clearly trace the underlying business goals and see the resulting experience requirements, and they should have ready access to these requirements at all times. This document can be posted to a shared intranet or printed on a wall-sized poster to keep the information accessible to the team at all times during development. Assigning someone on the team to be responsible for validating the features against the experience requirements is a good practice, and it guarantees that the business goals are being maintained through the design.

The User Experience Blends Art and Science

The successful user experience artfully blends features that satisfy the business success metrics with those that the customer deems to be adding value. For example, for the brokerage site, the business goal is to maximize the trading activity, so the user experience must offer the trade opportunity at every point where users might value it, and in a way they will value it. And in terms of the business, in the user experience *all paths should lead to a trade*.

A good design solution might include an experience that enables traders to use either a step-by-step wizard to execute a trade or a single trade-entry area for expert users. It might also include a single screen with a minimum footprint of displays: a window for watchlist, a window for alerts, and a window for actively trading stocks. Most critically, the navigation is security-centric, as it reflects the way that traders think as they are working through the trade. The ubiquitous trade button is available on every screen: It's the central action that delivers the value to the user. Coincidentally, it also drives the revenue: It is the *atomic unit of revenue generation* in the user experience.

This framework can carry through updates in business models or technology: Simply apply the same approach for updating or enhancing the customer-experience strategy, and validate the new experience against the new business goals.

Deliver the Experience Requirements, Not Just the Product Specifications

Ultimately, the result of the customer-capture process is a document or collection of documents that delivers the experience requirements against the framework of the business drivers, not just the functional requirements for the features. It's a basic blueprint for collaboration driven by the business drivers that provides a roadmap for the next phase of architecture and envisioning—and for ultimately delivering the best experience to customers.

BEST PRACTICES

1. Segment customers by business-relevant dimensions such as lifetime value, channel, or attitude.
2. Determine the life cycle for each segment in relation to the business goals—and the demand for the experience for each segment. Answer the question: "Do users want this experience, and will they incorporate it into their everyday work flow?"
3. Make sure that the entire team understands that designing the right experience has implications for the business and the end user. Make business and experience goals easily available so all team members can access them.

4. Assign a compliance officer for the user experience who is responsible for tracking each of the components of the experience matrix throughout the development process.

5. Get the right team and infrastructure in place before setting out to develop the user experience. Make sure team members' interests are aligned along the needs of the customer, not along their own needs such as designing cool stuff for their portfolios.

6. Don't skip competitive analysis. It's important to have a finger on the pulse of the experience landscape and know what customers will be expecting. Study real-world situations that can influence the design of the experience such as retail merchandising in brick-and-mortar shops. Study online competitors, both direct and indirect, as well.

7. Capture the experience benefits for all proposed features, and assign relevant success metrics.

8. Brainstorm to develop the experience matrix as fully as possible, mapping the experience requirements to the best user interfaces.

9. Create a "Report Card for User Experience," with the aspects of the user experience that impact success from both the customer's point of view as well as the business's. Use this report card to perform ongoing analysis to ensure that the user experience is delivering value.

architect and envision:
marry the business model
to the interface

In 1990, the architectural sketches of A. G. Rizzoli were discovered in a garage in San Francisco. In the late 1930s and early 1940s, this lay draftsperson had created a breathtakingly meticulous collection of architectural drawings, with lovingly crafted narratives of the daily activities of the inhabitants of utopian skyscrapers and cathedrals. Yet there was one crucial caveat. None of Rizzoli's structures—skyscrapers and cathedrals soaring hundreds of floors—could be built using materials known in that era. These structures could never be useful to anyone. Like a real-world Howard Roark, the brilliant but unyielding young architect in Ayn Rand's book *The Fountainhead*, A. G. Rizzoli had created his vision of paradise, yet it was unbuildable using the materials known to architects in the early twentieth century.

Now imagine back to the early 1900s, just prior to when George Fuller invented the first steel skyscraper, the twenty-one-story Flatiron Building in New York City. Until that time, the best-known materials for building tall structures included iron, wood, and masonry. Architects could only employ a codified approach using a frame with thick supporting walls usurping a disproportionate amount of floor space. Imagine the architects' excitement upon learning that steel would allow them to design taller buildings that could touch the sky, with thinner walls that could support the floors as well. Yet armed only with their understanding of "iron, wood, and masonry" design models, they were no doubt frustrated at not immediately knowing the possibilities, and the constraints, for such a novel material as steel. To be successful, architects needed to break out of their old "wooden" thinking to exploit new strengths of steel, such as its malleability and tensile strength, that would allow for spires reaching thousands of feet in the air. It meant a lot of concept testing, failure, and redesign—and a steep learning curve.

Many of the user experiences that are designed to be delivered over the Net today suffer from this type of "wooden thinking": stunning visualizations and cutting-edge technology are now part of many Web user experiences, yet the overall customer experiences are often unsuccessful because their architects have not understood the strengths and limitations of the medium. By failing to consider the needs of their audience, and the relationship between the experience and the business, they have failed to understand the constraints of the context.

But this failure need not happen again as we move toward ubiquity and pervasive computing—new forms of experience design. As we evolve to a new context, experience architects have a framework on which to base their work in developing experiences. What we learned from designing for the Web was that the process was about designing experiences against constraints. We now know how to do that: We know that navigation has settled comfortably on the left-hand side of the display or that scalable layouts that expand and contract with resized browser windows are now standard. We now have methods to help inform design that we can carry over to the wireless medium—a further constrained environment. Despite the constraints, however, combining multiple channels offers potentially new and exciting ways to develop digital experiences—ones that delight and engage customers and enrich the customer relationship.

This chapter discusses the role of information architecture (IA) in the customer experience and explains why this phase is arguably the most mission-critical in terms of its impact on the bottom line. While the following paragraphs won't delve deeply into the processes of creating information architectures,[1] they will discuss what managers need to understand to drive the process and why it's important to execute well now and increasingly so in the networked environment. The envisioning process will also be explored as will reasons why it's important to arrive, quickly, at a prototype experience that can be validated with customers. These two steps translate the business strategy and customer-profile research captured in the experience matrix in the last chapter into an experience framework that can be validated with customers, and they set the stage for the technology evaluation and execution phase, covered in Chapter 6.

The Goals of Information Architecture and Envisioning

The goals of the information-architecture and envisioning stage include the following:

- Synthesize the business goals and the customer model from Chapter 5 into a structured experience framework to be used as a working document among members of the development team.
- Enable the technology teams to initiate their process of evaluation to establish the technical platform, architecture, and integration needs.
- Allow the design team to develop working prototypes that validate the user experience with target users, in areas such as navigation, interfaces for all product features, and transactions.
- Allow the design team to have a framework upon which to establish the stylistic guidelines and branding issues for the user experience.
- Enable the usability team to plan their testing procedure to uncover any issues of usability.
- Enable the QA team to plan their testing procedure.
- Allow the content and documentation team to plan their development needs and process.

- Enable any other business owners who need to be kept in the loop or have input about the development to have exposure to the blueprints for the user experience. For example, in financial services, Securities and Exchange Commission (SEC) regulations apply to the appropriateness and accuracy of all financial information that a firm publishes. The Web has become a new medium for distribution, so compliance teams now need to be exposed to the information architecture and user-experience strategy early in the process so they can have input as to what content will be included and how to address any legal issues that may arise.

Information Architecture Is Business Critical

Information architecture is a highly refined skill, a creative process that blurs the line on the boundary between art and technology.

Architecture is a critical part of planning a user-experience strategy, providing a strategic blueprint that articulates the needs and goals of end users in a rigorous, scalable framework that at the same time also satisfies some goal—in the case of this book[2]—driving business profitability (see Figure 5-1). In metaphorical terms, the information architecture is the roadmap that translates business strategy into actionable experiences to satisfy distinct audience segments. Incorrectly planned and executed, it can collapse, resulting in a bad customer experience. The results? Customers can't find products and services, can't initiate and complete transactions, and can't build trusted relationships, all resulting in the loss of the "Three Rs": reputation, relationship, and retention.

Although it's possible to accelerate other stages such as "Look and Feel" (a product with bad graphical treatment can often get by with a decent architecture), a flawed architecture strongly impacts a product's usability in critical areas such as navigation and transaction completion. Attempting to skip the IA phase and move directly to envisioning screens is attempting to substitute tactics for strategy. Like teenagers who don't want to hear that drinking milk is good for healthy bones—but who think that *skin* is everything—firms need to

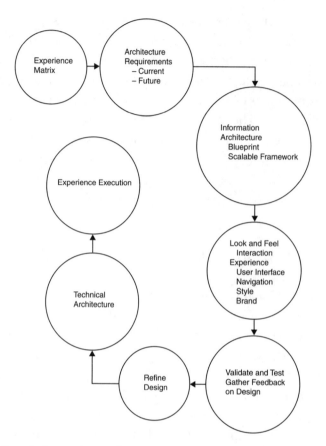

Figure 5-1. Information architecture is a critical part of the life cycle of user-experience strategy.

focus on the supporting experience structure—and concentrate less on the "look." To the business—and to profitability—the "bones" of the user experience matter more than the "skin."

Envisioning the user experience—the next step in the development process (see Figure 5-2)—depends on rigorous information architecture. Companies make a big mistake when they attempt to skip or accelerate the architecture process and proceed straight to screen design. It's impossible to design the "look" of a screen, or the navigation or the user interface, without understanding the flow of the experience, the structural requirements, the patterns of usage, or

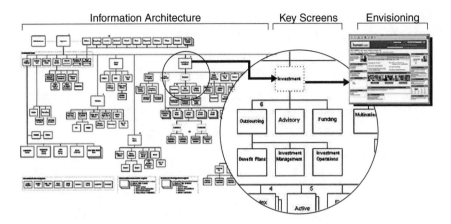

Figure 5-2. Information architecture should drive the envisioning stage of the user experience.

the types of scenarios that would typically drive customers to engage in the experience. Ultimately, it's the customer who suffers. This stage can be beset by challenges: inappropriate or lacking skill in information architecture and envisioning; lack of understanding about the technical environment; insufficient input about customer needs, goals, and tasks; or a timetable accelerated beyond the breaking point.

Mistakes in the information architecture impact many business-critical aspects of the user experience, such as navigation and transaction completion. A site with navigation that reflects the firm's corporate structure and not information the user desires, is an example of an information architecture that offers a mismatch between the user's needs and the needs of the firm. A customer who wants an inkjet printer does not care that Hewlett Packard has multiple corporate divisions.[3]

The business strategy and customer requirements, captured in the experience matrix in the last chapter, are required inputs to an IA. The output of the IA results from a creative process that blends the inputs into a map that satisfies the business goals for all audience segments, detailing the interaction paths to complete tasks and transactions. The architecture blueprint forms the basis of the next stage of prototyping: Envisioning the experience using screens or a testable mockup. If the information architecture is thorough, the resources can be assessed in terms of time and budget based on a review. This assessment is possible because the IA both reflects the scope of the front-end user experience and defines the requirements of the back-end development that will be needed to deliver the intended user experience.

As a blueprint that contains the strategic plan for the entire team to use to collaborate, the IA enables project management, marketing team, content developers, and the design and technology team members to share a common roadmap and to organize their collaborative process.

Besides providing a strategic-planning tool for the development team, the construction of the IA itself has a huge impact on usability because navigation and transaction completion are closely tied to the information architecture. Customers can't establish a relationship with a company if its user experience is unusable, so the impact on profitability is clear. For this reason, information architecture will continue to play an important part in developing frameworks for ubiquitous experiences—even though the output of the process won't necessarily look like a blueprint on paper.

The most critical aspects of IA that experience owners must understand are the following:

- Structure the IA around users' tasks and goals (not, for example, around the organization of the firm).
- Encourage a deepening of the customer relationship over the course of the customer life cycle.
- Architect for experience extensibility (e.g., to accommodate later stages of development such as personalization or expanding to include global offices or audiences).
- Provide the best experience within the constraints of the given medium, whether it be the Web, a wireless device, or any other means of communication.
- Architect for evolution of the business model.

- Plan for the life cycle of the customer relationship for all customer segments.
- Design a single, seamless customer experience across channels.

The basis of good information architecture is structuring it in a way to facilitate the tasks and goals of users—in effect, expressing "empathy" for them. A company that sells investment strategies might use "asset class" as an organizational structure—instead of the common organizational schemes like alphabetical, chronological, or geographical order—because asset class is the means by which the target users, investment managers, organize and think about investment strategies. Critical to utilities such as searching, the IA needs a taxonomy—the language index that will define the way that users can ask for and retrieve information in the user experience. Another important part of IA is analyzing and understanding the drivers of the experience: The tasks and underlying transactions that drive profitability should readily be reflected in the IA. An experience that has goals to drive loyalty and retain customers should be based on an information architecture that is constructed to support these goals in all possible ways. For a retail ecommerce site, the information architecture might deliver the best possible buying experience. For an equities trading system the information architecture might afford the most effortless and easy-to-access trading experience. The IA should be designed to help each customer segment evolve along the path of increased lifetime value—by delivering an appropriate and useful experience that is appropriate for the stage of the relationship.

Many methods exist for designing information architectures, such as those based on task-centric approaches as the means for organization. Metaphors—commonly used in the personal-computer desktop environment as a means for helping users understand new or unfamiliar concepts—can also help define the organization of the IA. Often, the IA will accommodate multiple audiences by using audience-segmentation schemes. These break a user experience into separate paths that in effect create audience-specific mini-sites, sometimes called *microsites*. Depending on the desired effect, these mini-sites can be architected to serve as, metaphorically speaking, "luge runs" in the user experience, paths that do not allow the user to navigate to other areas of the site. Or they can be more flexible to allow navigation between audience-specific sections. The luge-run technique is appropriate when the audience segments are so distinct that it would be confusing for them to be blended into a single experience or one that allows for cross-navigation among the distinct experiences. State Street Global Advisors uses a luge-run technique to prevent institutional investors from being exposed to the user experience that is specifically crafted for individual investors. They are uniquely distinct audiences and require unique experiences.

The Evolving Practice of Information Architecture

The practice of information architecture continues to evolve as technology evolves to afford more personal experiences. In the future, IA will be less about crafting a hard-coded content framework that exists as a visual blueprint and more about defining a task-centric environment where the user's actions and environment shape the experience. The underlying intelligence of the machine will enable dynamic and on-the-fly personalized experiences.

As more devices and appliances become part of the user experience, new hybrid information architectures for the wireless Web will marry and extend the desktop Web experience to parts of the experience that are displayed on other devices. In the near future, some user experiences may employ information architectures that combine visual and invisible components. For example, a wireless device may track the user's location and alert her to deals at local retail shops as she strolls by on the sidewalk. But those experiences will still rely on the experience architecture to provide the framework that enables users to successfully complete tasks and transactions in different contexts and environments. The information architecture for ubiquitous computing will be less like a fixed framework and more like behavioral guidelines for the experience in different locations and scenarios. By maintaining the same task and goal-specific requirements of the IA, these experiences can be extended beyond the desktop.

The next generation of information architectures will adapt dynamically to the end user's context and appropriately to the stage of the customer relationship. The information architect of the future will be more of an experience conceptualist, able to transcend any medium. At the same time, specialists will emerge, just as there are architects who specialize in the design of residential or commercial buildings, or resorts or amusement parks. These experience architects will possess deep understanding of user's behaviors in a specific medium and focus area, such as wireless devices or networked appliances, and they will understand how to build an experience for that medium and platform.

Case Study in Scalable Information Architecture

At State Street Global Advisors, the initial U.S. launch of an institutional extranet preceded the launch of microsites for SSgA's thirty global offices around the world, with offices as far abroad as Japan, South America, and Europe. State Street Global Advisors used a phased approach to information architecture. Phase 1 (shown in Figure 5-3) allowed for the United States–centric site to be launched with content appropriate for that audience. Slots were used on the information architecture to show the team what the next-phase architecture would look like when the thirty global offices were added to the site. When the site was redesigned for the phase 2 launch, the original information architecture now afforded the new global offices to be accessible. Also offered were several new content areas, each of which had been designed to offer new functionality such as communication with relationship managers, and a new searchable library of investment strategies and services. The new architecture was far more complex, but it rested on the original framework of phase 1. This is an example of creating information architectures that can scale to accommodate changes in the business or the user population.

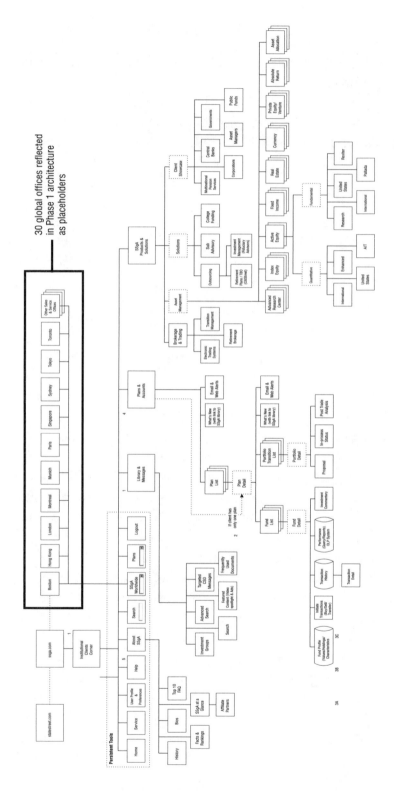

Figure 5-3. Information architecture for State Street Global Advisors' Client Corner extranet site.

As we've seen by examples of successful ecommerce user experiences at Yahoo! and Amazon.com, the information architecture can affect relationship building because it helps in making users feel comfortable about engaging—and returning. Comfort while browsing and purchasing is a big part of making a successful ecommerce experience. The IA supports and enhances the evolution of the customer relationship. The rewards can be huge: fiercely loyal customers who have put energy into personalizing their user experiences can be difficult to dislodge.

The Role of the Information Architect

Allowing a complex user experience—not an online brochure, but a transactional application or ecommerce experience—to be designed by an inexperienced information architect is like handing a trowel containing wet cement to a first-year architecture student and asking for a custom-designed skyscraper. It may look fine on the outside, but would anybody want to step inside?

The role of the information architect is to understand the business mission and goals and translate them into an experience framework that satisfies users' goals. Satisfaction is achieved by defining the interaction process and the narrative flow of the user experience. The information architect also defines the framework for the content, functionality, and navigability. Aspects of the user experience such as searching will be designed by the information architect. He or she must have a knowledge of the underlying taxonomy that will be employed and any technical issues, such as the metadata, that will impact the searching experience.

The information architect is a key member of the team who must be able to understand the business drivers, empathize with the end user's point of view, and drive these toward a solution that delivers the best experience architecture. When the team is assembled, especially if the team is outsourced, those selecting team members should ensure that this key IA position is filled by someone with appropriate experience in different methods for developing experience architectures. That IA person should also be able to test and validate the design to see that they are indeed solving the intended goals of the experience from both the end user's perspective, as well as from that of the firm.

Information Architects: Skill, Intuition, and Empathy

The information architect develops the overall atmosphere and framework of the user experience—as opposed to the individual screens, page layouts, or graphics. The best information architecture is intangible and translucent: It should only be noticed when it's not working well; otherwise it should allows users to glide effortlessly toward satisfying their goals and completing tasks.

Information architects come from different areas of industry and academic backgrounds. Most often they come from graphic design, industrial design, computer or library science, or other disciplines that demand a deep understanding of how to translate a complex landscape of information into one that is useful and simple to understand. They often have training in technology. The best ones have been found to understand the details of the medium and how it works. Information architects can exploit technology's strengths in the service of delivering the best experience to the end user—while avoiding its limitations. Like the best master craftspersons, information architects blur the line on the boundary of art and science. Part draftsperson, part storyteller, the information architect must knead and cajole the experience out of thin air onto paper and into a wireframe model or storyboard. That person, using the model, then has to express the essence of the experience to persuade the rest of the team—and management—of its value.

Experience strategist Deborah Frieze thinks that information architecture requires a "spatially oriented mind, one that is focused on the dynamics of the experience of the end user, with a natural thought towards answering 'how do people move through this?'" She asserts: "Although they may not have the orientation on motivation and behavior, information architects intuitively understand the notion of movement motivation, and the best experience designers understand that 'users are here to be intrigued.' They possess a great orientation for synthesizing complex and interactive motion into a complete and engaging experience." As more channels and devices become part of the customer relationship, the practice of IA will continue to evolve and become more complex than ever, demanding a unique hybrid of skills.

In her book *Longitude*, Dava Sobel writes about John Harrison, who architected a solution for the "longitude problem" that beset scientists in the eighteenth century. Up until that time, sailors were unable to measure their longitude while at sea, resulting in the loss of thousands of lives and causing ships laden with fortunes to go careening off course. In the quest for a solution, England's Parliament offered a reward—a king's ransom—for a solution. Many clock designs were offered—but one of the challenges was that any metal parts would rust in the salt air, rendering the longitude device unusable. Harrison, a master carpenter and clockmaker, designed a longitude clock that used a self-lubricating tropical hardwood called lignum vitae, so that the internal clockworks ran without the need for oil. Understanding the problem, the end goal, the constraints, and—without benefit of a microscope—the molecular structure of the medium of wood enabled him to architect a better, useful solution. Information architects need to possess this kind of deep knowledge about materials and constraints to design the best user experiences that are useful, elegant, and scalable, regardless of location and environment.

User-experience experts will have to have a hybrid of skills that combine neuroscience, technology, design, and business strategy. The demand for these more rigorously trained experts will increase, but demand will exceed supply. The profile of the experience designer will be closer to Jeff Hawkins, the brain scientist/engineer responsible for the design of the Palm Pilot and the Handspring Visor. One of the challenges facing industry right now is that there are few courses of study at the university level for studying information architecture. Lead user-experience practitioners lament the dearth of a talented pool of trained practitioners—and the lack of institutions where students can receive rigorous training. Another challenge is to find time to develop and refine the IA skill set, despite the pace and pressure of the market. Information architects are not unlike real-world architects who practice the craft over a lifetime and, like Phillip Johnson or Frank Geary, only a few will be capable of truly great architecture. Companies that want to develop great user experiences will have to foster a learning culture that seeks to develop experience architects over the long term. They may operate much in the way that "mentoring relationships" do at the white-shoe consultancies, where it takes years to make partner, through practice and refinement of the craft, and careful observation and emulation of more experienced senior partners.

Information architects need a hybrid of skills that span the left and right sides of the brain: technology, human factors, cognitive science, design, and business strategy. Most important, they need to have empathy for the end user: They need to know and feel their desires and frustrations.

Mistakes in Information Architecture

Information architecture is a difficult craft, existing on the boundary between art and science. Like designing a house, a cathedral, or a skyscraper, designing an information architecture involves many different levels of complexity and scale. Designing a house and designing a skyscraper both rely on architecture, but the economics, the scale, the materials, and the usage are very distinct. The most common mistakes that are found in user experiences are the following:

- A mismatch between the goals and tasks of the end users and the IA: Users cannot complete tasks because of flaws in navigation or the points of initiation
- Inconsistency of the IA: a lack of consistency in navigation or use of objects in the information hierachy
- Inability to search for and act on search results

- A mismatch between the IA and the type of content—or its treatment: for example, a navigation scheme that is too complex to be accurately rendered, as in cases where graphics are used to display navigation that would be better represented as text
- Inexperience of the information architect for the type of site experience
- IA that cannot scale to afford a good experience on other platforms

Information architecture also requires the appropriate context: Any user experience will fail if the data architecture of the enterprise makes it impossible to be a good experience for the end user. Bad legacy systems—the pre-existing information systems of a firm—can kill a great information architecture. Without good pipes and plumbing, the best user experience in the world is like surface detailing: The experience can't flow well.

Conditions change: The business needs shift, the audience changes, and technology platforms evolve. So scalability in the information architecture is important to consider at the outset. Tearing down the entire design and launching a completely new one can be disconcerting to users: They don't want to have to relearn everything about how to use the system. Often when a firm engages a new vendor to enhance or update the site, the design will change completely. Sometimes this can be for the better, but it's important to keep what is good and useful—and not throw away everything for the sake of a having a clean slate. To design information architectures with scalability in mind, consider the next generation of technology, such as broadband or wireless, as an active part of the strategy.

MidnightTrader.com: Establish the Demand for Wireless, Extend the User Experience

Companies should validate that the business need for wireless exists and that users will want and use the service. After establishing the need, the firm must make sure that the underlying network architecture can support the delivery of appropriate content to the appropriate device in a timely manner. The underlying transactional infrastructure and technology integration issues need to be solved first, before anything can be designed. Lastly, the information architecture needs to scale to accommodate the delivery to these devices. A good example of a firm that took a conservative and winning approach is MidnightTrader.

MidnightTrader is a retail portal that serves the investment community as a source for aggregated and real-time after-hours electronic equity trading news and data. As Electronic Communications Networks (ECNs) began experiencing exponential growth, Brooks McFeely, the founder of MidnightTrader, himself a seasoned trader, knew that individual and institutional investors lacked the useful data, news, real-time pricing, and analytics to be fully informed participants in this market. In setting out to design a site that would deliver the news and information that these investors wanted, the firm took a conservative approach. Using very little capital—just over $10,000—they designed a bare-bones Web presence that delivered real-time after-hours news, analysis, and data. They also created unique educational content to enhance the offering to customers, who paid a subscription fee of $29.95 per month. They used the site to establish demand for the service and to set up content partnership deals. Partnerships with online brokers such as CyberCorp and MyTrack allowed MidnightTrader to deliver retained customers to these partners for trading. Content partnerships, such as with Screaming Media and Comtex, enabled MidnightTrader to package new forms of after-hours market content and supply them to partners for delivery to business clients' enterprise portals.

After establishing the demand for the service—with no advertising, and only by the byline "Source: MidnightTrader" showing up on content partners' sites—the site had over 1000 new unique visitors each day. The business-strategy team decided that the time was right to architect a robust Web presence that could scale to accommodate a large critical mass of end users and partners. It was also time to facilitate the billing and administration of the site, which up until that time had been handled by hand.

The team—including owners from business, marketing, finance, user experience, technology, and design—all brainstormed for several days to define the business goals. They included the following:

- Create a unique branded site that revolves around after-hours trading.
- Increase conversions of browsers to subscribers.
- Gather better demographic data to help with business partnerships.
- Increase traffic to the site.
- Increase retention and engagement of end users.

To satisfy the goals, the team broke into several groups, each of which focused on a specific area of the business case. The business team wrote the value proposition for each of the customer segments and refined the business case. At the same time, the design team worked to develop an information architecture that would both satisfy the goals and deliver a useful and easy-to-learn experience.

After delivering an information architecture (see Figure 5-4), the team worked to define a series of rapid sketches of the user interface, which were tested with end users (see Figure 5-5). The wireframes were delivered to the technology team to allow them to develop the technology evaluation plan and strategy for handling the data-integration issues. The team then worked to deliver the screens for the new design, incorporating a new branding scheme into the design. The rigor of the process, which took about a month, meant that at every step the design was validated against the guiding business goals. Capital investments were again kept to a minimum by trimming excess functionality, such as a portfolio area, from the first release to only focus on delivering core value, and by keeping the team small and outsourced, using highly experienced team members. The metrics for success included a model that tracked relationship metrics such as conversions and amount of activity over time on a weekly basis. The new technical architecture includes provisions to deliver this tracked information to management.

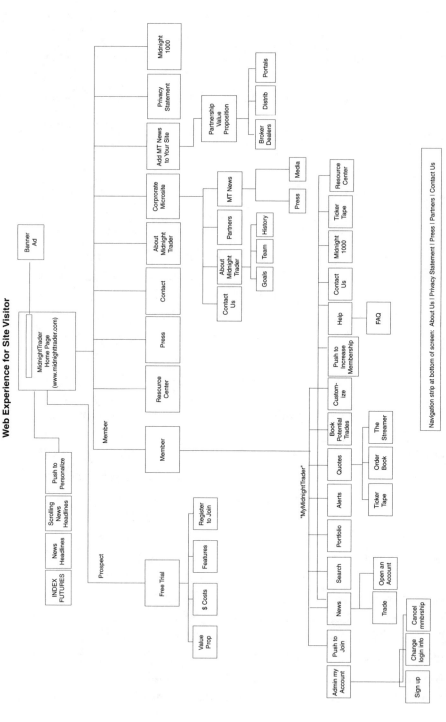

Figure 5-4. An information architecture for the MidnightTrader Web site.

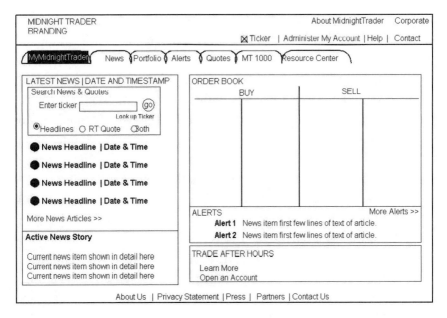

Figure 5-5. A wireframe sketch of a key screen in the MidnightTrader user experience.

The process has worked well for MidnightTrader. Target users are responding very favorably to the design in usability testing. For an investment of under $100,000 MidnightTrader now has an engine for revenue that can scale up to millions of users.

Because users were demanding that after-hours market updates be sent to wireless devices such as cell phones and beepers, MidnightTrader decided to look at developing wireless functionality. They carefully considered the information architecture and how it could be extended to include the delivery of after-hours information to other devices. They also examined the value proposition to customers who use these devices. After considering the amount of capital necessary to build such functionality and looking at the costs versus benefits, they decided to proceed: software would be developed that would extend the information architecture to accommodate delivery to other devices. Fortunately, the information architecture had been designed from the outset to accommodate users' goals and tasks and deliver transactions that would drive profitability. So it could easily be scaled to accommodate the delivery of information to these new devices.

MidnightTrader developed a user experience that satisfies both business and end-user goals and evolves to accommodate the wireless Web. They did so by carefully considering the demand before building and then crafting the user experience around the demand. Says MidnightTrader CEO Brooks McFeeley. "A significant causal factor in the recent demise of many subscription-based Web sites and free portals was the faulty business model focused on getting eyeballs over dedicated users. What really matters are relationships, not eyeballs. An attractive yet intuitively simple user experience is essential and directly supports relationship development. Increasing user-based revenues are more closely tied to customer retention." By staying focused on the needs of end users, MidnightTrader has produced in a better return on the capital invested in the site development and has put in place a scalable framework that can grow as the business expands and the needs of their end users change.

Strategic Envisioning of the User Experience

When the information architecture is defined, the framework is in place to envision the user experience by creating a rapid prototype, as we saw in the MidnightTrader case study. This phase also serves to validate the information architecture with target users—to make sure that the paths that the user will traverse through the experience are indeed clear and useful.

Rapid prototypes can take many forms, depending on the delivery medium for the user experience. For Web-based experiences, this step involves creating sketches of several key screens—typically the home page and one or two key principal screens to illustrate the experience of completing transactions and using major features.

Rapid prototypes can range from hand-drawn sketches on paper to wireframe diagrams created with a graphics or diagramming tool or HTML. The goal of the rapid prototype is to show concepts in a form that can be tested with target customers. Feedback can help the development team flag any issues with usability and stimulate discussion among team members about what the ultimate user experience should be.

Designing Web experiences means defining new experience frameworks that leverage well-established standards—and breaking those that are no longer appropriate. Time-worn user-interface standards, such as placing the OK/Cancel button on the bottom right of the screen for a desktop dialog box, are no longer appropriate in an environment where it's more important to *not* require the user to have to scroll to get at important information. eRoom, a Cambridge, Massachusetts, firm that develops collaboration software, needed to break from the Microsoft Windows standards for their user experience when they migrated the product to the Web. "Pushing experiences through a browser has allowed us to break the standards in the interest of creating a more natural conversation with the user," says lead user-experience designer Glenn McDonald. "Placing the OK/Cancel button on the top left of the screen means that the user does not have to scroll the page to proceed through the transaction." Pushing the boundaries of design in the interest of creating the best customer dialog is exactly the kind of thinking that needs to happen as we move to the highly constrained Wireless Web and the networked world of appliances.

Increasingly, as more ubiquitous and mobile experiences are developed, the envisioning stage will come to include the creation of prototypes of physical materials, or represent environments in which transactions will occur. A new form of prototyping that revolves around scenarios will develop. Think about what it means to envision the experience of paying for drive-through fast food with an E-ZPass: It includes the experience of driving the car into the fast-food restaurant, ordering, driving to the pickup window, and having the purchase completed by a device that is hanging on the windshield.

With no visual interface, these scenarios will play an important role in the design processes for ubiquity, because they will help give clues as to usability issues associated with actually having used the experience. These scenarios will help to validate that the multimodal experiences of ubiquity—combining voice and transactions, for example—are useful and easy to use. These narratives will tie together the interactions that span the physical and visible worlds with the ones that are the virtual and invisible.

Envisioning Case Study: Trellix Corporation

To trace the evolution of the information architecture through the envisioning process, consider the example of Trellix Corporation,[4] a leading Web-authoring software company in Boston, founded by Visicalc co-inventor Dan Bricklin.

Trellix Web started out as a desktop application that allowed intranet users to easily create and view documents online and enabled small-business owners to easily create Web sites. Later, as the business grew and evolved from a B2B model to accommodate consumers who wanted an easy way to create Web sites, the user experience needed to expand to accommodate a wider audience—one that would also include novice consumers who were new to the Web. By analyzing the needs of the new consumer-user segments, Trellix chose to accommodate these new users by creating a bridging device in the interface, to help novice consumers get over the initial challenge of creating a Web site and successfully publish it to the Web through an Internet Service Provider (ISP). The business model at that time depended on revenue from hosting sites built by Trellix users who published their sites to the Web. Trellix developed a new interface for novice consumers, a wizard-like dashboard, that afforded new users an easy way to have a good experience the first time they attempted to create a Web site.

As Trellix's business model evolved again to include ISPs and their member communities as customers, Trellix needed to adapt the product's user experience to allow users to make Web sites while on the Web, not having to download and install client software to their desktop machine. What would need to be developed was a server-based equivalent of TrellixWeb, now called the Trellix Publishing Platform. The major functionality would need to include the ability to create a new site, and insert text, images, and links as well as embedded ecommerce objects called Web Gems. And that functionality would need to be accessible and easy to use through the browser, a much more constrained user interface environment than the Windows desktop.

On a tight development schedule, the business strategy and planning phase began in December of 1999. The development team, led by a product manager with substantial experience in software development, met to work out a viable schedule for launching the product in the late spring. The information architecture was developed in January 2000, after a thorough analysis of competing products and the product-features specification list.

The subsequent envisioning process produced a rapid prototype in the form of several principal screens (see Figure 5-6) which were first developed as hand sketches and refined into black-and-white wireframe drawings that represented the look and feel of the user interface: the navigation, the screen layouts, toolbars, the labels on buttons, and placement of branding elements such as the Trellix logo. Key wireframe screens were handed off to the usability team to test on paper with target users in Trellix's in-house usability laboratory. Feedback from the tests was included into the next iteration of drawings.

Developing visualizations of key screens that illustrate tasks and functionality is a good way to validate the information architecture and make sure that the design enables users to complete tasks easily. Choose the paths that represent the key transactions and critical tasks as the initial screens to envision.

Concurrent to the envisioning stage, the design team began to work on creating stylistic treatments for the screen design—including the color and font choices, the style of the graphical

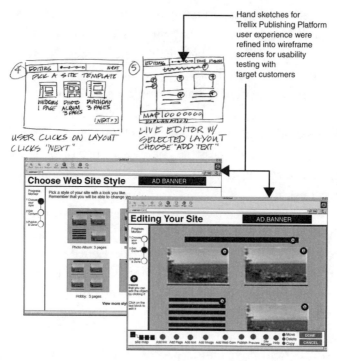

Figure 5-6. Trellix Corporation used hand sketches early in the process of the design of the user experience, which were refined into black-and-white wireframe drawings that represented the look and feel of the user interface. These screens were tested with users in the usability lab, and the feedback was integrated into the next iteration of the design.

items such as icons for the toolbar—that would ultimately become the graphics for the final design. Product management shared the documentation with the entire development team to keep them abreast of the process, and they had access to the information architecture diagram and the storyboards and wireframe screens. The technology team also were given these documents to review, as they began to assemble their team and expose them to the design that was in process. The next step in the envisioning process was the development of a complete storyboard to illustrate the interfaces for all features and tasks and to work through all of the interaction processes.

During the development process, the product manager served as a simultaneous translator among the needs of the end user and the various development teams. The storyboards were used as a basis to finish wireframes of all of the screens. These were all validated by the usability team and the feedback was incorporated into several iterations of the design.

By February, the information architecture and envisioning processes were complete, and the process was ready to proceed to the technology evaluation, architecture, and execution stage. Ultimately, the team delivered the final product (see Figure 5-7) to customers at the outset of the summer. The coherence of the team—members had worked together before—and strong project management helped the product to eventually win several awards for excellence.

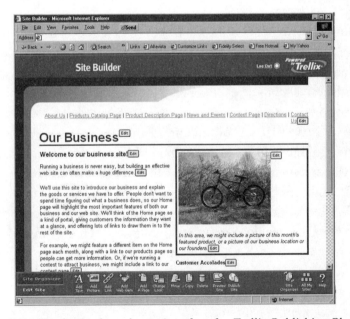

Figure 5-7. The final released user interface for Trellix Publishing Platform, the award-winning Web-authoring software from Trellix Corporation. The released product was the end result of early customer testing with several cycles of rapid prototypes and rigorous usability testing.

Information Architecture Influences Technology Architecture

The information architecture influences the technology architecture in the same way that an architect's blueprint for a building influences the materials to be used or the methods of construction. Business and user requirements are reflected in the information architecture, which in turn impacts the technology strategy. A good example might be the design of a trading system in which real-time market data—stock quotes or news—must be displayed and updated in real time on the user's screen. The value to the user might be in the real time display of the information as it happens. There would be no opportunity if the market were to move in the time it takes to get the information to the user's screen. This user requirement means that the back-end technology must be able to integrate multiple data sources and deliver the information to the user's screen in real time; even a delay of ten seconds can be too long.

Another way that the information architecture can influence the design of technology might be through the use of techniques such as personalization to drive retention and loyalty. If the business case depends on the user experience building loyalty, personalization might allow the user to customize the user experience—through the graphical look, the type or amount of information. The information architecture must adapt to accommodate the choices of the user, and this adaptation influences the way that the back-end technology is constructed. This type of experience design requires technology that is aware of the user's identity (through the use of technologies such as cookies) and can deliver a custom user experience by managing the relationship with each unique user. The back-end server technology and middleware are more complex for these kinds of highly adaptive systems, and they require substantial resources so that they can be built, hosted, and maintained.

The information architecture and envisioning processes are now complete: The validity and usefulness of the design have been validated with users and found to be satisfactory. The next step is to define, evaluate, and execute the technology, which is covered in the next chapter.

6

make it happen:
build for extreme usability
and business evolution

After the experience architecture has been defined and validated with customers, it's time to focus on technology architecture and execution. In the execution phase lies plenty of risk: The best product concept or user-experience strategy can be dealt a fatal blow by a critical but unsolvable bug that nobody anticipates or by a design that cannot be built because of technical limitations. Other risks include misjudgments in planning how long development tasks will take—and not including time for critical steps such as quality assurance (QA) and usability testing. Timing pressures from external sources, such as competitors' launch dates and pressure from venture capitalists, can come into play and apply undue pressure to the design and building phases. Yet another risk is when execution happens in a vacuum—and without an evolutionary process in which users are exposed to the design as it evolves. With the technical complexity of the desktop and browser environments in which software is now built and delivered, issues such as multiple browsers, the ever-evolving platforms, and challenges of integration make flawless execution challenging. Project managers, marketing, and the technology team need to understand that customer-centric thinking—and maintenance of the goals and vision of the previous stages of development—extend through the execution stage.

Because of the risk and complexity of execution, coupled with time-to-market pressures, new software-execution models have evolved during the years of Internet economy. Thirty years ago, sequential development, such as the "waterfall" model, was the norm: Fully formed, specification-driven development meant that nothing was built until it had been fully specified in documents. That model has now given way to a more evolutionary process, one that employs a highly iterative approach: Customers test an actual version of the software, not just a rapid prototype. In effect, the customer is incorporated as a development partner much earlier in the process then previously. This approach has spawned a new name: Extreme Programming. This is a software-development methodology, characterized by rapid development cycles, that releases key features to customers early and often, and tests daily through exhaustive "localized" testing. This evolutionary customer-as-design-partner approach has now elevated usability to strategic importance because the Web has made usability a customer-relationship issue.

The paragraphs that follow discuss why usability should be considered a strategic part of user-experience execution and the software-development process. Highlighted is the execution process after the information architecture (IA) and look and feel are completed (see Figure 6-1). The process is followed through technology development, iteration and refinement, and the all-important launch.

Usability Will Become Increasingly Business-Critical

On the Web, usability has a higher profile than ever before, because usability is now a customer-relationship issue. Customers' expectations are high: On the Web, experiences are expected to be easy to use by a wider audience, the first time. Compromising usability means that customers are underserved. It also has immediate disastrous effects on business-success metrics like retention and browser-to-buyer conversion, all of which is immediately apparent with analysis of the clickstream.

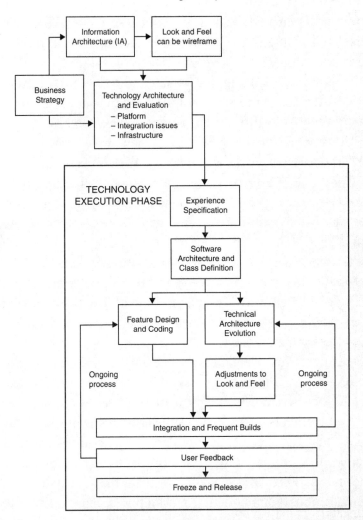

Figure 6-1. The execution process follows business strategy and occurs after the information architecture (IA) and technology evaluation/architecture phases have been completed. Frequent builds are iterated through testing and adjustments before launch.

In the pre-Web era of desktop software development, usability happened at the end of the development cycle. Now, for many firms whose value is heavily dependent on their user experiences, usability impacts both the top line (i.e., revenues) and the bottom line (i.e., profits).

For many companies, usability will be a major source of competitive advantage, and it will be critical in moving toward profitability. Successful companies know this and concentrate on efficiently enhancing the user experience by using the Net as a live testbed. For example, Amazon.com routinely tests distinct user experiences with different product features, say, A versus B; based on analysis of usage data, decision makers know within a few hours whether A or B will "live." This process works well because Amazon.com can collect the data from a large user base in a short amount of time. The search engine Google has proven that making usability central to the user experience—and focusing on delivering core value to customers without overextending the offering—can result in a successful business. Google processes 70 million search queries daily, half of which are through its own Web site and the rest through portal partners that license Google's engine, such as Yahoo! The interface is simple and efficient and satisfies the goals of customer and end users. And the business makes money.

To be successful, usability has to be an intrinsic part of both software products and the culture of development as never before. This won't happen without a commitment by firms to educate management and members of cross-disciplinary teams about how usability impacts business success, and how to practice user-centric design principles that are based on logical thinking from the point of view of the end user: the customer. Leading firms like Fidelity Investments make a serious commitment to usability because they know its impact on the bottom line: Besides having a state-of-the-art usability lab that features testing equipment for tracking pupils and new forms of biometrics, the company offers a yearly course on usability for Fidelity managers, developers, and designers; the course is prepared and taught by Dr. Tom Tullis, vice president of human interface design, who uses 200 slides in the presentation. His vision is to help everyone involved in the development of human computer interaction have access to both sides of the equation—the human and the computer sides—and to understand how to design and develop the best user experience.

Yet we don't really know how to accurately measure usability and apply it to the business metrics, especially with regard to revenue and profits. We need new metrics for measuring usability that are accurate and precise yet not difficult to incorporate into ongoing business practices.

Being able to show that a firm's user experience is becoming 25 percent more usable each year would be a great measure to have, but it would also need to be tied to profitability. Calculating this kind of return on usability requires that a model be defined that correlates it with business metrics. For ecommerce businesses, return on usability would need to be tied to metrics such as buyer conversion, transaction initiation, and completion. For software products, it would need to be tied to the rate of adoption and ongoing usage of new features introduced during the customer life cycle, and the number of phone calls to technical support, the types of calls, and their duration and outcome. For corporate portals, return on usability would need to be tied to employee productivity and measured in productivity or efficiency gains for the particular type of employee—say, saving 5 percent of a marketing executive's valuable time.

To benefit from this kind of analysis, companies will need to commit resources to define a model for usability that consists of the appropriate measures—and a mapping to business success—and perform ongoing measurement. A clearly defined usability-to-profitability model simplifies the data collection and analysis and allows firms to concentrate resources on enhancing the user interface, not just analyzing reams of Web log data. In effect, such a model provides a "dashboard" for analyzing the business's usability-to-profitability activity. These measures will require both qualitative and quantitative components that answer the following questions: Will customers like the experience? Will they incorporate it into their work flow and daily lives? Will the experience ultimately deliver a return on investment? The challenges to usability professionals include understanding what data are needed to calculate the return and getting access to the data; for example, gaining access to the call logs and billing records for technical support.

This evolution is also demanding that marketers—marketing managers and executives—own a new medium for creating customer touchpoints; they need to work directly with usability experts early in the process, not just at the end of the cycle. They must understand the process by which user experiences are developed, the risks involved, and the ways in which the medium will impact the message. In the future they will need to become fluent in the use of tools to measure and analyze the effectiveness of the user experience. They will become like portfolio managers, constantly adjusting the mix of methods for analyzing and measuring the effectiveness of the user experience, ultimately to produce profitability.

There is an opportunity in the years ahead to get marketing managers to really feel the desires and frustrations of customers. Ultimately, perhaps, their compensation will be tied directly to the measures of customer satisfaction in user experiences.

Customer-Centrism Is a Cultural Mindset

"Our users aren't that stupid": Overheard conversation of one software engineer to another while watching through one-way glass at a test subject struggling to complete a task. Unbeknownst to the engineer, the test subject held a doctorate in physics from the Massachusetts Institute of Technology.

Part of the effort to change cultures to be more customer-centric involves encouraging a marketing mindset (meaning one that is "customer-facing") for team members who otherwise would not think that way and creating a culture for shared metrics across the enterprise. Engineering would need to understand the customer-value proposition and adopt usability as a mantra for its process. The design team members would need to understand the business case that is driving the design. They would also need to be dedicated to designing what is being measured by the business metrics, not just to think what would look great in their portfolios. Technologists would need to have customer-centrism at the heart of their planning. Firms such as Amazon.com clearly understand the impact of usability on profitability; they make sure that all of the developers are committed to creating technology that enhances—not hinders—the user experience. Says Maryam Mohit, vice president of site development at Amazon: "We make sure that we hire developers who are excited about creating things that are useful for customers. If you have that fundamental point of view, you have the ability to solve the business."

The practice of usability has changed from an end-of-development process service hidden in the research-and-development department to the forefront of product development. Usability is now strategic, because it impacts customer relationships—and profitability—more than ever before. New methods should be developed to integrate usability practices into a firm's development processes. One model to borrow from is that of the Extreme Programming software development methodology. In use since 1996, Extreme Programming is based on a philosophy of simplicity and streamlining to improve the development process and employs many small and daily testing procedures threaded throughout the development process. Usability practices can borrow from the practice of Extreme Programming, because usability also needs to be applied frequently, daily if possible, to the tasks and features that are critical to the user experience, especially in the execution phase of software development.

Usability can be incorporated into the design-strategy process by doing the following:

- Assure that the technology team is well aware of all the usability requirements and features for the user experience. This applies to a global audience, not just to users in the United States.
- Validate designs against a set of usability criteria, including how execution will impact the design and performance metrics. This applies to a global audience, not just to users in the United States.
- Make sure that the data that needs to be collected to validate performance and business success can indeed be collected by the system.

- Verify the development phase against the original user-experience strategy, including the information architecture and the experience matrix.
- Have the technology team review the user tests—either as they are being conducted or on videotape—to "feel users' pain" as they attempt to complete tasks.
- Create an ongoing learning culture that invites multidisciplinary dialog around areas of usability and brings usability issues into frequent discussion among the development team. Having usability team members present in informal sessions over lunch is a good example of this kind of practice.
- Make the executive decision to compensate and reward development teams based on usability and usefulness of products and services as well as collaboration with team members responsible for usability and design.

Chauncey Wilson, director of the Bentley College Design and Usability Center in Waltham, Massachusetts, creates a culture that fosters a multidisciplinary dialog around areas of usability by speaking to development teams over lunch about the "Top Ten Usability Issues We've Found" to get team members thinking about the issues in an informal setting. Other means Wilson has used include making posters that highlight usability issues, which are rotated among the walls of conference and meeting rooms. Screen shots and callouts are used that illustrate issues in the design, and analysis and recommendations for sites are given, along with justifications. These posters create dialog among team members and keep usability-centric thinking flowing throughout the development environment.

The Team

The experience of the team has been shown to be crucial to successful delivery of software that brings value to users. Yet "experience" these days is not necessarily measured by age. The collective experience of the development team is key, and technology team members should be known to have developed and shipped comparable—not exactly similar—types of software. Just as important, a customer-centric attitude is key.

These new integrated teams—comprising marketing, design, technology, information architecture, user-interface design, and documentation—form a new type of development team that places user advocacy at its core and has to collaborate to execute on the vision. A great user experience emerges from the integration and balance of these distinct disciplines, orchestrated by strong project management.

Marketing managers have evolved to become customer-experience drivers, the keepers of the user experience who own the overall project and budget. In some environments, such as software development or ecommerce companies, the user experience is usually owned by a program manager, an internally facing marketing professional who serves to simultaneously translate the customer and development goals and push the process ahead. That manager also deals with usability issues. Regardless of the way the firm is organized, the owner of the user experience needs to have the knowledge about the business goals and the end users, and he or she must consistently own and drive the project requirements and schedule. This position requires strong project management skills and a clear understanding of business process, market-research and requirements gathering, and multidisciplinary team building. This key team member must understand what it means to guide the user-experience strategy through the execution phase and to guarantee that the blueprint and vision is maintained.

Just as important, marketing managers will be responsible for measuring the success of the user experience when it's actually in use. As in product development, the user-experience owner needs to drive the process and define a set of evaluation criteria that makes sense for the product. For example, a model for usability needs to be developed that includes both quantitative measures, such as the rate of completion of key tasks or the rate of adoption and use of key features, and quantitative measures, such as how enjoyable the user experience is for the customer.

Usability professionals have eclectic profiles and backgrounds. Most have training in human factors or engineering psychology. And most have backgrounds that include technology (usually computer science or electrical engineering) or social psychology, anthropology, and many design disciplines such as graphic or industrial design. Recently, there has been an influx of usability professionals from quality assurance. They are often driven by strong professional and personal interest in increasing the effectiveness of user experiences that span software applications, Web sites, and any other electronically mediated systems. Most usability professionals design and conduct a variety of usability tests and produce analysis and reports with recommendations for improvement in the user experience. They can also run focus groups and remote (online) studies, heuristic evaluations, and targeted surveys in addition to more traditional usability tests.

Usability Metrics Will Be Tied to Business Metrics

The most successful usability test I ever participated in was one where the major flaws in the design were cited and tied back directly to the business-success metrics, showing where failure in the user experience was immediately impacting profitability. It caused the chief technology officer and founder to sit up straight and take notice—and call in the CEO to listen to the rest of the presentation.

Product managers will need to develop a model for user-experience evaluation that includes checking that the design complies with the original information architecture and design prototype and answers the requirements in the experience matrix. In addition, product managers will need to measure the viability of the design by analyzing feedback and data from usage—both qualitative and quantitative—to continually deliver incremental enhancements to the user experience.

The best practices for correlating user experiences to business metrics include the following:

1. Check compliance of the design, features, and user experience against the experience matrix requirements.

2. Develop a model for measuring usability, such as the adoption rate of feature usage or the time to complete tasks. Continually measure this process to look for trends that indicate problems. Use logfile analysis tools such as WebTrends or usability-testing services such as Vividence to do the measurement.

3. Develop a financial metric for every feature in the user experience that impacts business revenue and profits. For example, to measure loyalty for an ecommerce site, measure the usability of both the conversion process (buying the first time) and the purchasing transaction by the number of transactions that fail to be completed; then compare that number to the number that are successful.

Usability Criteria

Usability criteria for browser-based applications include both qualitative and quantitative aspects that answer the following questions:

Qualitative Criteria:

- Is the first-use case, the one in which the user attempts to use the experience for the first time, successful?
- Can the user explain how to initiate critical tasks (e.g., search, other transactions) from the first-use situation?
- Does the user feel comfortable engaging in and completing tasks?
- Do the user interfaces consistently present themselves in ways that naturally lead the user to action?
- Does the site help the user be more effective?
- Does the site behave rationally when there is an error? Are the error messages clear and appropriate for the context?
- Is the information clear and legible?
- Does the experience make best use of screen real estate, especially for the user's display?

It's important to incorporate good design, such as error messages, into aspects of the user experience. As in the real world, where trust can be enhanced by performance under duress, the system can deliver help by way of meaningful error messages, ones that can help the user get out of a situation without having to resort to picking up the phone to call customer support.

Quantitative Criteria:

- Is the first-use case successful? Did the user do anything other than sit on the page? (Base your determination on log-file data.)
- Does the user experience require that users employ plug-ins (such as QuickTime) that they may not have available?
- Is the navigation not allowing the user to find information that should be obvious? Is the searching tool made obvious in the navigation? A look at the log files will provide the answer.
- Did it take too long for the page to load?
- Does the navigation help users use the site and find what they need? That is, after users state their goals, can they satisfy them? How long does it take, or how many clicks?
- Does the experience help the user complete the tasks effectively? That is, how long does it take for users to learn and complete transactions successfully, or how many clicks does it take?
- What is the degree of relationship engagement as measured by the rate at which the user begins to utilize features?

Evolutionary Software-Development Process Is Key

The advent of the Web changed the process by which software products are developed.

The original waterfall model from thirty years ago was designed to enable the management of large-scale software-development projects (typically, for the military). It featured a highly structured approach that required the development team to write an exhaustive specification before any coding was done. From there emerged a rapid prototyping model, which put prototypes into customers' hands before any development to establish customer preferences. Now, evolutionary and highly iterative processes' put actual working (but highly limited in functionality) software into the customers' hands as early as possible. This highly iterative process works well, given the speed with which software products in the Internet economy are being built. It has been successfully employed by companies such as Microsoft in the rapid development of products such as the Internet Explorer browser. This process now resembles the highly iterative way that architects and other creative professionals have been working for many years.

Alan MacCormack's research at Harvard Business School on Internet-software development has found that successful software development is evolutionary in nature[2] and has pinpointed these successful practices for Internet-software development:

- Release a low-functioning version of the software into customers' hands at the earliest opportunity.
- See that rapid feedback on design changes is incorporated into daily software builds.
- Build a team that has experience shipping a broad spectrum of products.
- Make major investment in the design of the product architecture and infrastructure.

MacCormack's team found a correlation between these best practices and the quality of the resulting software products. This approach allows the product to evolve in response to customer feedback, and it does so early enough in the design cycle to influence the outcome.

In an evolutionary-development process, the team first develops software based on the functionality that constitutes the major value for customers—the three most critical functional areas, for example. It then uses this framework to further evolve features over subsequent development cycles. A working version of the software with these three initial features would be built, allowing the development team to test how the code components work together, and it would be given to customers to enable them to provide feedback.

This process allows for flexibility and adaptivity in the development cycle. As in any development process, however, major structural changes can have an impact on the development and execution time frame. Examples of changes that can be made in this phase include tweaks to the information architecture, such as trimming or adding a navigation choice to a pre-existing set of choices. Major structural changes, such as adding an entire branch of navigational flow or designing in a new feature, will impact the schedule because of its impact on design, content, and technology. These alterations to the user-experience strategy and information architecture must be weighed against their ultimate benefits to the user and the return in value that they will produce. Adding in a last-minute feature to enable customization will have a large impact on the development cycle because it may be technically challenging to execute. But the return on the amount of loyalty that enabling customization might produce could mean the difference between a successful business case and one that fails to build retention with users.

In general, during the execution phase, the types of changes that can be made include the following:

- *Small tweaks to the information architecture.* Choices might be added to or subtracted from a navigational path, for example. Note that this type of change does not mean adding new functionality, which could mean substantial schedule and resource changes.
- *Moderate alterations to the layouts of the screens.* The navigation scheme might be shifted slightly up or down.
- *Alterations to the stylistic treatment of the screen layouts.* The color, font style, or image usage might be changed.

The types of changes that begin to impact the schedule and development process include the following:

- Addition of a major feature area of functionality
- Inclusion of a major navigational pathway to the information architecture, such as accommodating a new user segment
- Addition or subtraction of large amounts of content to be published on the site

Features can be designed into the site architecture that represent what is to come in the next phase of evolution. For example, slots can be allowed in the information architecture to serve as placeholders for new items that will reside there in the next phase. The information architecture can cover a range of evolutions, from visual design tweaks to be done in six months, to process-flow tweaks, to addition of a new business offering from the current information architecture. At State Street Global Advisors, the information architecture for the U.S. site was designed to accommodate a rollout to thirty global offices over the following year. Grayed-out placeholder slots were added for each of the offices. Inclusion of these slots allowed the development team to be aware of what was coming in the next release in terms of technology and design requirements. It also allowed the content team to plan accordingly.

The Changing Role of Usability

Usability used to be hidden in the R&D lab. Software was developed in one department and, when there was a demonstrable system, it would be shipped over to the usability lab, and a series of users would be brought in and tested. During testing, it was often difficult to keep the engineers calm; some of them often had to be physically peeled off the glass behind a one-way mirror and stifled from screaming, "It's the scroll bar, stupid—scroll down!"

The following all had effects in elevating the strategic importance of usability:

- Usability used to be an R&D role; with the Web, it's connected to marketing.
- Usability used to be tactical; now it's strategic and part of the planning process.
- Specialists in usability now work with marketing and R&D, in an interstitial environment, and they often work directly with the design group.

- Professionals in usability are now asked to analyze and test user experiences that serve global markets, often at launch, which demands new cultural fluency and competency.
- The usability process has accelerated to reflect the changes in software-development models.

What has changed is the concept of usability as part of the process, not something that happens at the end, after the process is done. Each and every update must weigh the usability factors that will enhance the customer experience. Think of this concept as "extreme usability": usability that is part of an ongoing, rapid test-and-refine cycle inspired by the ultrafast development and testing cycles of Extreme Programming Methodology. Extreme Programming (XP) is a methodology that has been in use since 1996, and it is based on a notion of simplicity and streamlining to improve the efficiency of writing software. It is a practice based on delivering top business value early and consistently, driven by customer requirements of features and functionality. After input from business management and customers on the features that are most important, the development team breaks the features into stand-alone tasks and estimates the work needed to complete each task. Developers choose tasks and work in pairs to write software that satisfies features and, at the same time, develop the testing procedures to validate that the code is correct. As more features pass the tests for validation, the code is integrated into a release version, which is tested by the internal quality assurance (QA) team, and released to customers as test "builds." This process moves quickly through many iterations, until all the features have been added and all pass the validation tests. This evolutionary approach reduces the cost of inevitable changes to the business rules, programming environment, and software design.

Usability process is rapidly changing, but it rests on time-honored principles of observation of users in their attempts to complete tasks, and subsequent analysis and recommendations to improve the user experience. The testing procedures can take a long time to prepare, run, and analyze: developing the right test plan and acquiring the good data without asking leading questions is still a refined craft. Typically, the business owner—or product management—will buy or contract the usability professional's time for the testing process. The final results will be presented to management, often in the form of a formal report and accompanying documentation such as video. Some usability tests produce reams of results, often inch-thick reports with details. The most important analysis is that which cites problems and issues that need to be addressed in the short term, and recommendations on prioritization of issues for the longer term. This can be a one- or two-page top-line findings summary, which presents the more detailed analysis in an easy-to-digest format. Usability professionals have to be prepared to defend their recommendations for enhancements and changes, because their analysis can have a large impact on the development schedule and budget.

Identifying the usability professional or the team early in the development process is important and having them actively participate in the business strategy and planning process is good practice, because usability testing requires preparation that can take several weeks, even months. After the goals and test procedures are identified, the testing plan is developed. This should be validated with project management to assure that the output will be useful and business-relevant. Test subjects have to be identified and matched to the criteria for target-user segments. Testing the wrong types of users produces wrong results; it's better to spend the time seeking out fewer but better target users than testing lots of irrelevant ones. Identifying the most appropriate testing methodology is dependent on the type of data needed and resource constraints. If the product is already in the market and the user experience is failing, a usability inspection, done by a usability professional, may suffice to uncover the issues and provide feedback to the development team quickly. For new products that are being released to an untested market, a full-blown usability test is more appropriate. Testing a wireframe prototype with target users should validate that the product features are accessible and that tasks can be completed without undue confusion. Though there has been a trend toward using fewer test sub-jects with observational techniques—often only four to six users—it can often require a larger sample size to uncover underlying usabili-ty issues. A good rule of thumb is to test as many users as the time and resources allow, focusing on getting good feedback on the most critical product features first, and then getting feedback on the less-er features as time allows. Rapidly disseminating the results of the testing to the development team is key, and the resulting changes should be discussed among the development team and prioritized to accommodate the launch schedule. Any "showstoppers"—for exam-ple, users not being able to complete key transactions,—should be given a "Red Alert" status to be dealt with immediately. Even when their testing and analysis work is completed usability team members should remain accessible throughout the ongoing development process to serve as ongoing consultants. They would be able to advise on any usability issues that arise as the execution phase pro-ceeds toward launch.

In the near future, usability professionals will act more like port-folio managers, with specific areas of expertise yet responsiblity for managing a "portfolio" of usability techniques and methods for ensuring ongoing usability. The new usability expert might have an area of focus such as ethnographic analysis, but he or she will deftly manage a portfolio of testing and analysis techniques that range from analysis from technology services firms such as Vividence to heuris-tic evaluations to real-time data models. New partnerships will con-tinue to emerge among services firms and usability firms, as evi-denced by the trend for integrators (eCIs) partnering with firms like Vividence to offer ongoing usability and usage analysis. In addition to outsourcing, companies might wish to build an internal compe-tency center focused on user experience and usability. They would have to hire team members who have strong backgrounds in tradi-tional usability-testing analysis and who can quickly learn new tech-nologies and the new testing techniques that these technologies will require. Ongoing education and learning, and attending profession-al seminars and conferences, such as those offered by the Association of Computing Machinery's Special Interest Group on Computer Human Interaction (ACM SIGCHI), will continue to be a major part of the usability team's job description.

Ubiquity and pervasive computing will make the usability professional's job more interesting, because ubiquity will allow usability to break free from the constraints of the laboratory. Instead, users can be observed in their natural habitats: in the real world, mobile, on the go. Usability professionals of the future will be like mobile anthropologists, which will make usability one of the most exciting and ever-changing careers in the next ten years.

The Process of Execution

Let's review the user-experience strategy process so far starting with what was covered in Chapter 4. We'll use the example of a retail B2B exchange. The following steps have been completed, though not necessarily in this order:

- Business strategy and planning have been completed and captured in a strategy document, the result of one or more strategic sessions and user-centric brainstorming.
- Representative users from all segments have been identified through qualitative interviews—in this case, suppliers, vendors, and end users for a retail B2B exchange. Scenarios that describe their work flow, goals, and attitude/comfort level with technology and any other preferences have been captured into a document
- A customer model has been defined, and includes answers from target users about attitude, expectations, and behaviors using questions such as: How often would you use this kind of service? Where would you use it? What kind of machine and connection do you have? What display?
- The experience matrix has been defined that correlates the business goal to the experience design requirements, validated against comparable or competitive experiences.

- The information architecture has been defined and shared with the design, technology, and content teams.
- A protoype has been delivered—in this case, a sample home page and several key screens showing major transactions have been defined and mocked up in HTML wireframe format (plain HTML without any graphics). Keep in mind that many different types of "prototypes" can be the basis of tests, including hand sketches, wireframes, rendered screenshots (for example, in Photoshop), HTML files, and semifunctional (that is, prelaunch release) working site pages.
- The screen designs have been validated with target users to make sure they understand the experience, how it will work, and what the value proposition will be.

The information architecture and user-experience specification—as denoted by the prototype and any supporting specifications documentation such as a product features requirements, design and content requirements, and any branding requirements—are given to the technical team to determine a technology framework. Using these documents, the technical team will perform a technology evaulation and begin their design phase, as well as begin to prepare for their execution phase.

The team profile should include a member of product management, a technical lead who will serve as technology architect and who understands the integration requirements, as well as one or more usability professionals. Members of the technology team should have areas of specialization in areas that will become part of the final design, such as database design, integration, or content management. Documentation specialists who will write the supporting help system or create any instructional text should also be included in the team profile.

During this stage, the team that will perform quality assurance (QA) should also be given this documentation to begin to formulate a testing plan. QA will create a test plan describing which things the team intends to test: which platforms, which browsers, and so on. Depending on how refined the development environment is, QA may write up test cases for distribution to the team, or they may plan to automate the tests by creating custom-testing software.

Keep in mind that the process described here represents an archetype of best practices and is general for product development or Web development. The process may differ among firms, or it may include only certain steps or a combination of steps, depending on culture and practices of the firm involved. These process steps are given as a guideline for best practices only.

Technical Evaluation

The process enters a technical evaluation stage, during which the technical team assesses aspects of the user experience and the experience or product features that will define the technology architecture, such as the following:

- Delivery infrastructure requirements.
- Content management system (CMS) and publication systems needed.
- Issues of security and privacy that are impacted by the technical platform and architecture. Security and privacy are both impacted by the technology platform and in turn impact trust, an important component of the user experience. Users expect that ecommerce transactions will be done using a secure server.
- Identification of integration issues with back-end systems. For example, if the system will need to integrate with another firm whose systems will be sending data such as live content or news feeds, what issues with synchronizing these systems need to be addressed?
- The technologies to deliver the front-end experience to the end user through the target browser or platform. Technical team members must be well aware of the technical environments of the end user—for example, what browser, connection speed, and platform will be used. This analysis will include end users that are customers, as well as end users who are administrative employees of the firm who will administer the site.

This last point is important to keep in mind if the system will require the design of administrative screens to enable employees of the firm to make updates and enhancements to the user experience. These administrative screens must be built and tested for usability as well as to ensure efficiency in the work flow of site administrators.

For systems that will involve the management of large amounts of dynamic content, a content management system (CMS) will be necessary—a common component of most big Web sites. Depending on the site architecture and the content creation and publication demands, a work flow system might be needed to ensure that the creation, editing, and approval processes occur smoothly. Many content-management systems have work flow embedded into their design. A CMS is a major investment and might not make sense if staff is available—such as a Webmaster—to work on the continual updating and upkeep of the site experience.

Integration is and will continue to be a big issue in the development of user experiences and is the Achilles' heel for delivering a seamless experience to the user that spans multiple and disparate systems and platforms. A good metaphor for understanding the complexity of integration for developing large-scale ecommerce or enterprise applications is to imagine orchestrating a United Nations assembly: Each of the delegates represents an application, speaking his or her native language and attempting to negotiate in real time with other members of the assembly. Think about all of the necessary equipment, people, and processes that have to be availabe to make communication happen: The microphones, earphones, multi-lingual human translators, and communications protocols have to be in place so that an extra or incorrect word does not start an argument—or worse yet, a war. This picture begins to paint the complexity of integration now and in the future.

Integration is the messiest part of the development puzzle. Making sure that all of the systems and applications can talk to one another is a huge job. Each of them might run on a distinct platform, with a unique interface and format. Integration impacts the front-end and back-end systems necessary to execute the user experience. For example, an experience might allow a user to fill out a form that is sent directly to a database, which in turn is connected to a billing system. The user perceives a seamless experience, but the integration necessary to enable this experience on the back end can be substantial. And if it is weak, it can have negative effects on the experience.

The technology team must do a thorough analysis of the integration issues and come up with a defensible plan and set of recommendations to tie all of the necessary systems together. And they must do so in a way that will enable extensibility for future releases. Technologies that are becoming common facilitators of information exchange between applications and systems, such as Extensible Markup Language (XML), will help streamline the technology infrastructure and make it easier to develop more seamless experiences for the end user. For example, in the design of a B2B portal, XML can be used to integrate into the portal many disparate systems such as legacy systems and external content feeds.[3]

Determination of what technologies will deliver the front-end experience involves making decisions on how to best render the user-interface mechanisms (e.g., pull-down boxes and radio buttons) as well as the navigational elements (e.g., HTML, DHTML, and Flash). Decisions about which technologies to use must be weighed against the profiles of target users. How "harmless" the experience is to the user's browser or technical platform depends on what plug-ins (such as QuickTime) are introduced, which may or may not be standard for the entire range of target users. The best user experience is rendered useless if the target user doesn't have the appropriate plug-in and does not know how—or does not want to—download it.

The outcome of the technology-evaluation stage, which often is a document that details findings and recommendations, should be reviewed by the management team, so that any issues that impact scheduling or budget can be flagged. For example, a user-experience mechanism that requires custom code might be too difficult to deliver within the time frame or budget; adjustment of the feature set might be required to enable the design to be done in a timely manner. Documents that describe the requirements and deliverables in effect serve as agreements between the development and owner groups, so that timelines and milestones can be agreed upon.

Technology Architecture and Features Design/Coding

The next stage involves the concurrent processes of technology architecture and feature design, in which the design of the product features is initiated in a coding language (e.g., C++, or Java). The choice of technology platform will be driven by issues such as scalability, functional requirements, or the internal platform of choice of the firm. The type of product or service being designed, the demands of hosting and hardware requirements, and the type of database needed (typically either a UNIX system or a Microsoft NT platform) all affect decisions made during this phase. The team must be aware of the trade-offs that the platform choice will have on the user experience. A secure layer for credit card transactions demands a secure layer in the technology architecture that will have to be integrated with the system. If the choice of the platform will impact a part of the user experience such as download time, then that needs to be flagged at this stage and incorporated into the technology architecture. These are all examples of the types of issues that the technology team will flesh out at this stage of the process.

The technology architecture phase allows the team to perform the critical step of defining the business rules that will influence the design of the underlying and back-end technology to enable the delivery of user experience. The inputs from the experience matrix—the knowledge about the customer, the tasks flow, the use cases or scenarios, and so on—all influence the architecture of the business layer that will ultimately talk to the back end. The team also begins to design the code architecture and the classes of objects, such as those that will populate the database or handle transactions, that will translate the business rules into code.

In this phase, the features can begin to be coded in order to test the features on the underlying platform and validate them against the architecture. It is during this phase that the embryonic prototypes of the user experience will begin to function: minimally functioning screens and simple transactions with wireframe navigation. These prototypes will be placed into the hands of users as early as possible to garner feedback. Rapid iteration of the design is key to enhancing the user experience as it goes through the iterative process. Often the "builds" that a team will do will be done daily, and tested with users at the same time. In this phase developers should be allowed to test their individual "units" of code, but ultimately the aggregated system should be put into the hands of the QA team for the real testing, to assure that all of the components work together.

At this stage the detailed production schedule will become solidified, as the full feature set will be known and the technology architecture will be in place.

Architectural Evolution

As frequent builds of code are released to QA, usability members, and beta customers, the technology architecture will evolve to take the shape of its final form. As more features are coded and developed, the user experience begins to emerge: At first, wireframe screens might use dummy text or placeholders as features are put in place, and dummy graphics might appear as members of the design team finish the final graphical treatments for elements like navigation buttons, icons, or branding.

Throughout the development process, the design team will be delivering the final graphical elements in tandem as the technology team continues to develop and code features. The content team will begin to add more final text and documentation. Frequently, design teams will establish best practices and standards for the elements that comprise the graphical design, content, and documentation. At Fidelity Investments, for example, the usability lab under the direction of Dr. Tom Tullis, has helped define a framework for usability best practices that serves as an educational and professional resource for the development teams. The guidelines include provisions for the design of graphical elements, standard navigation layouts, and page layouts and recommendations for other aspects of the user experience, such as the maximum acceptable size of graphical elements for specific bandwidth profiles of users.

The Daily Build: User Feedback and Integration

The working system, whether a prototype or real code, is validated in a phased approach with customers. At firms like Trellix Corporation, an internal dedicated usability team takes builds from the development team and runs ongoing usability tests on the premises, writes up the analysis, and delivers it to product management, design, and technology development teams. The communication of issues can be done electronically with bug-tracking systems, or it can be done more informally with daily development documents that track all outstanding user-experience issues.

During this process, one team member—from product management, QA, or the usability team—should be responsible for continually monitoring the user experience for compliance with the original IA (information architecture) and experience matrix. In this phase, slight modification might have to be made to the information architecture to accommodate changes in the business structure, but any modification to the IA at this stage should be considered for its risk and impact on the schedule. The closer to the end of the development cycle, the more risk exists when any modifications are made to the IA.

Freeze, Test, and Release

After the entire product feature list is completed in code, the back-end technology architecture tested, and the elements of the user interface completed, the system will go through a phase of testing to determine that all components work as required. The build will go through a period known as *code freeze,* where no more features or functionality can be added. Actually doing a complete code freeze is important; testing against a still-evolving software build is a bad idea. This phase, known as QA (or quality assurance), is critical. So allow ample time for the team to test the software on as many possible platforms that represent target environments. Firms often try to cut down on the QA cycle, which is probably one of the biggest and costliest mistakes they can make.

The final deliverable includes the working system and any supporting templates that are needed to add functional screens as the experience design evolves.

What Can, and Cannot, Slide

In the execution phase, some things can slide without hugely compromising the quality of the user experience. Others cannot. The architectural aspects of the user experience—the navigation structure, the information architecture as related to key tasks and transactions—must be rigorously defined and really work in the service of helping the user to be effective.

The graphical or stylistic treatment does not have to be optimal, at this point; it can be enhanced over time. For example, a colleague who is managing the user experience for an online B2B commodities exchange called me to get a second opinion about the interface design a few days before launch: He felt that treatment was not "good enough" and wanted a second opinion. After taking a look, I realized that the underlying architecture was sound but the graphics were less than stellar. My bottom-line recommendation was this: Go with it, because users in that market (commodities traders) aren't particularly concerned with the style, as long as the experience satisfies their transactional needs and users can navigate to and complete tasks. Delaying the launch to enhance the graphics would have set back the team another month, during which they might have lost their market opportunity.

Another area that can "get by" is the degree of usability. The user experience does not have to be 100 percent usable at launch, because it will get better over time with refinement. The goal is to launch with something that users like and will want to use; the detailing or refinement can happen as a process in an ongoing fashion. After launch, analysis of the patterns of site usage begins: Reporting software such as WebTrends can be used to analyze traffic and show what users are doing and where, for how long, and their browsing and buying habits. After a few weeks of analyzing live data, patterns may begin to emerge: At the MIT Enterprise Forum of Cambridge site, a nonprofit group devoted to educating entrepreneurs through events, WebTrends analysis showed that users were stampeding from the home page to the calendar section—and then leaving. The user experience was working, but it wasn't optimal: The calendar received a disproportionate amount of traffic, and other areas of the site were beginning to "atrophy" from underuse and lack of activity. To combat this, the site was tweaked to place dynamic links on the calendar section to make users aware of other areas of the site that were relevant to upcoming or recent events. This small tweak, the result of analysis of patterns of usage, ended up driving traffic to the other areas of the site by leveraging the traffic to the calendar.

On the technology side, infrastructure and integration are critical. If the system cannot support the demands of the user experience, such as allowing searching that accesses multiple databases from distinct legacy systems, then the entire phase for executing the user experience is at risk.

What are the risks of not incorporating usability into the technology-building phase? Consider that most Web sites or Web-based applications can be tested for major tasks and functionality for less than it costs to deliver the average corporate-identity system. Fifteen to twenty thousand dollars spent to validate the usability of the user experience is money well spent if it saves a $500,000 investment in development from failing if users can't see the value or can't figure out how to use the site. Done early enough in the development cycle, validation of usability can allow the user experience to be corrected and put on the right track.

The reasons below often drive the decisions to deliver user experiences to customers untested; they substantially add to the risks of compromising the user experience:

- The culture of the firm does not value it. This kind of thinking is common in engineering-driven firms.
- The vice president thinks he or she represents the target customer and so does not understand the need for the feedback. After the prototype, which might "look" like a finished product, is seen, the software might be assumed to be done and just needing a bit of "back-end integration" to work completely.
- Marketing decides on the final delivery date, and engineering needs to deliver software by that date. This decision is often made without a clear understanding of what needs to happen.
- The development schedule is behind, and the team runs out of time.

Even when the firm does incorporate usability testing into the process, there are still risks that surround the process, such as the following:

- The wrong users could be tested. The users might not be able to be objective because they have already been exposed to the user experience or they might not represent appropriate target users.
- The wrong features or tasks could be tested.
- Testing could be conducted in the wrong technical environment.
- A flawed testing methodology that influences the outcome of the test could be used. Flaws might include using leading questions or allowing users to have too much influence in defining tasks.
- Results could be misinterpreted. For example, feedback that is illogical or does not make sense might be overvalued, and changes might be made without understanding why.
- Test results could be blatantly disregarded. Sometime the business

owner does not want to hear that the design is unusable, or the designer might be on a moral crusade and refuses to change his or her "work of art."

Ultimately the firm—and the customer—pays for bad usability.

Launching and Ongoing Refinement of the User Experience

Launching the product or service means releasing it to customers and continually measuring results and adjusting to make the experience perform better. As a vice president of marketing at an ecommerce company said: "Once you launch the site, in a matter of hours you know if it's successful. If you have done it right, users start hitting the site, exploring, and buying things—and it reaches a steady state of activity."

Becoming expert in the "clickstream analysis" of the site is an important part of ongoing refinement: Understanding the kinds of queries that users are entering at the referring search engines can provide valuable insight into what users are expecting from the user experience. This is an important task and should be done by a team member who delivers regular update to the entire team. Analysis such as checking when users use the search capability—as well as what they enter for search queries—can provide insight into navigation issues and problems they are having with the site, even though they have not expressed their frustrations. If users are entering terms that should be readily apparent in the navigational structure, there's a problem with the design—they can't find what they are looking for. These needs should be documented and discussed among the development team to determine the priority for enhancing and updating the site based on user behaviors—and the resulting return from such enhancements.

Design changes that directly impact the user's task flow should be articulated to the end user in an update or alert, so that the user is kept abreast of new features. Small changes, such as minor enhancements to graphical elements or navigational elements, don't need to be announced. Only changes that will impact how the user will initiate and complete tasks do. If users don't like the updates, they should be listened to. Large ecommerce sites have had to revert back to older versions of their user experience because enough users balked at the new design—which they were given without warning. Some firms, such as Yahoo! continually update the design so that it becomes translucent: The user is never really conscious that the update has happened.

Key Issues in Execution and Launch

1. A highly iterative approach is important.
2. Define a model for a return on usability at the outset, and take a quantitative measure to have a baseline to compare to later.
3. Work directly with usability experts early in the process, not just at the end of the cycle.
4. User advocacy should be part of the culture of the firm.

Post-Launch Considerations

Launching is one of the most truly exciting parts of the design process. On the Web, you begin to get instant feedback: real-time data about how the design is solving, or failing to solve, needs of users. If the development team has delivered a truly valuable experience, the user numbers will begin to reflect this: Within hours, the site usage can reach a "steady state"—a buzzing hive of activity. Indeed, I've thought it would be great music to a marketing managers ears to hear the activity of a site rendered as an orchestra. The more intricate and loud the music, the more activity and engagement occurring.

Let's consider what's important to consider post-launch, before the team begins to worry about the next design. The metric model established in Chapter 4—the measurements of success—should be what is immediately gathered and analyzed. It's important to wait long enough to have useful data, but as soon as enough is gathered, all of the analysis and reporting can begin. For the MIT Enterprise Forum site relaunch, for example, we waited a week to review the numbers to see if they were beginning to climb in the right direction—which they did.

The marketing team can begin to analyze usage and look for what is working as well as be on the lookout for problem areas. The analysis should not be limited to just the click analysis or Web Trends reports: Look at the error logs, the referral logs from search engines. Conducting qualitative tests with target users, or hiring a firm like Vividence or Greenfield to conduct usability or marketing research, can provide valuable qualitative feedback about what is or is not working in the user experience.

The Future of Usability

Looking forward, usability will continue to play an important role in the development of user experiences, but getting usability right in the design of the experiences will become more difficult. There may be no physical component, just the experience. Context will play a greater role: How do you test a wireless experience that automatically delivers an alert to a user's cell phone that his flight has been canceled without the user actually having to do anything? While these experiences will get more difficult to test, firms will have to be as cost-effective in validating user experiences. With the trend toward testing usability with a smaller set of users, testing the appropriate ones will become more important, lest valuable testing time and resources to go waste.

Usability professionals will be pressured to master many different types of testing processes, especially as user experiences become more mobile and wireless and pervasive technology becomes a reality. No longer will usability professionals stay in the laboratory to get their data; the labs will be portable, mobile, and often remote—so that users can be tracked at home or on the road, in scenarios that span days and possibly time zones. And eventually these labs may get small enough to fit on a chip, giving the usability professional real-time access to live data as the user is having the experience.

Though the evolution from print to multimedia and CD-ROM was painful, the leap from multimedia to the Web was less so—and the jump to ubiquity will be even less so. Why? Because for the first time we have well-constructed methodologies and frameworks that have been defined by the many practitioners who developed Web experiences: the "plan, design, build, execute" methods, all with their own subtleties and unique techniques. All of the integrators, all of the teams that developed Web sites—that knowledge has not gone to waste. It will be used again as we move toward wireless and pervasive experiences. The availability of this knowledge will help usability professionals to deal with the myriad challenges that will come with being responsible for validating these new ubiquitous experiences.

In the near future, usability professionals will become like portfolio managers, with specific areas of expertise and responsibility for managing a portfolio of usability techniques and methods to ensure ongoing usability. Being an expert in index-equity strategy will be a model for the new usability experts. Their area of focus might be biometrics, but they can deftly manage a portfolio of techniques that range from Vividence to heuristic evaluations to real-time data models. New models for mapping usability to profitability will emerge. In real time it will become apparent how the user experience is going to impact profitability for the next quarter. These experiences will demand new skills for developing testing procedures and using new testing techniques and methods. Usability will continue to become a focus of the marketing group and probably will end as a function that lives inside the marketing group. Usability in a mobile setting means transparency and that tasks become the unit of transaction. With an impoverished graphical environment, pure tasks are critical.

New techniques and technologies will continue to provide tactical approaches to testing and evaluating the usability of user experiences. Testing services such as Vividence will also be coupled with home-grown analysis solutions that firms will develop. These solutions will produce ongoing reporting for management and development to continually monitor the impact of usability on the success of the product. Although testing technologies such as pupil tracking have been available in the past, better forms of biometric measurements will help usability professionals understand how successful, or stressful, the experiences really are, in all kinds of situations and locations. Prototypes are already being developed that forecast a new form of usability testing. At the MIT Media Lab in 2000, Professor Rosalind W. Picard's Affective Computing Group demonstrated a Galvactivator™, a glovelike device that uses galvanic skin-response technology, similar to that of a lie detector, which detects a person's skin conductivity by measuring changes such as an increase in palm sweatiness.[4] In effect, these kinds of "biometric usability tests" will measure the real-time physiological effect of the user experience, not just observe the user's behaviors but accurately assess the effect that the experience is having on the user. User experiences will become more invisible and ubiquitous, without an obvious interface for users to interact with. So usability professionals will have to rely on data from biometrics and other means of measuring the body's responses to learn whether the experience is really successful—or whether it is causing undue stress and frustration. Biology will meet usability soon.

If customer relationship management (CRM) ultimately is embodied in systems that track every click and create predictive models of user experiences, perhaps the experience will become so intelligent, so translucent, that it will be self-correcting on the fly, attenuating to every user just in time, in the perfect way. When user experiences are adaptive enough to evolve themselves appropriately on the fly, will usability even need to exist as a separate job function? Will there be any need to test these experiences?

If firms get the design of the experience right, with the underlying intelligence and infrastructure to deliver the appropriate experience, to the appropriate channel or device, in the appropriate way, user experiences will perfectly adapt themselves to the needs of the user, any place, every time. In designing user experiences in the near future, usability will be so intrinsic to the process that, like DNA, you can't see it and you never think about it; it just happens as a natural part of the process.

Perhaps, if we're lucky, we can even make "usability" an arcane term.

7

evolving, encouraging, and protecting user experience

This chapter reviews the model proposed in previous chapters, for defining, developing, and measuring ongoing user-experience success, and it makes recommendations for maintaining the model as a central part of a firm's business strategy and culture. Also covered are intellectual-property (IP) issues in relation to the user experience.

Quality of User Experience Should Be the Centerpiece of Online Strategy

The last few chapters outlined a process for developing user experiences that tethers user-experience design to business profitability. This approach reduces risk, and it produces customer-centric user experiences that satisfy an established, customer-driven demand. Regardless of how closely a firm chooses to follow the suggested processes, there is value in being as rigorous at each stage as time and resources allow and of incorporating the notion of "customer as design partner" philosophy in a way that works best for the firm's culture.

The dot-com crash has forced a return to rigorous design process. Now that less capital is available for development and innovation, the industry is focusing on the strategic importance of understanding and incorporating users' needs. Consequently, user experiences will be developed according to schedules that look more like good product-design schedules. These compressed timetables will demand best practices and seasoned talent on the development team. Lead user-interface designer Glenn McDonald of eRoom in Cambridge, Massachusetts, who has designed five separate releases of eRoom's collaborative-workspace software in the last several years, definitely feels this pressure: "I have to be right most of the time now—because there's just not a lot of time to make mistakes," he notes.

Limited time is not the only challenge. The best user-experience strategy in the world can miss the mark if the site is launched into a hostile technical environment or if there is insufficient change management necessary to carry it through. A great user experience is a failure if there are few or no users. Beyond these high-level aspects of the user experience, the design itself—the navigation, the user interface—must be usable and easy to learn. A lot of integration has to happen so that a seamless experience is delivered to end users. Badly integrated legacy systems—ones that don't enable the customer history and current pricing databases to talk to each other—inconvenience end users and waste their time. Think of sitting in a beautiful chair made with ill-fitting wood and bent nails: Your ultimate discomfort will override your appreciation of the elegant design. Likewise, Web-site end users will feel discomfort unless site-design processes are adequately funded and allowed sufficient time to produce truly integrated, customer-centric experiences.

It's going to take time and capital commitments for firms to have customer-centric design processes, and one of the biggest areas that will have to be solved is integration. Only then will end users not feel pinched and poked by bad user experiences.

Another, even bigger challenge is that of change management in the enterprise that will be incorporating the user experience into its work flow. As in any other issue of organizational behavior, the introduction of new technology only works if the end users—not just the people who pay for the technology's development—accept that it will enhance their life and work.

Successful User Experiences
Change Users' Behaviors

Consider a B2B exchange: a trading portal that a firm builds to raise its efficiency in trading with business partners. The portal will only deliver a return on investment if the end users, the employees of the firm responsible for trading and administration, will use it. The world's greatest user-experience strategy will fail if it does not sufficiently answer these key questions:

- What benefits does the new system offer to end users?
- What will the end users lose emotionally and psychologically in adapting to this system?
- Will the end users use the system enough to deliver a return?

If a company can't respond to these questions with the validations of a thorough business case, a robust customer model, and prototyping processes, then the project is too risky and probably should be scrapped. To have end users say they love the experience and want it launched on their desktops is not enough. For example, a trading company that builds a trading portal without sufficient validation risks failure, because the traders will have no long-term incentive to use the system. Why? Because their industry and their firm's culture are not constructed to encourage them to incorporate the trading portal into their everyday work process on an ongoing basis. No mechanism is in place to reward the behaviors that ultimately drive profitability or that produce a return on the capital invested in building the portal.

Assume that the firm goes ahead and builds the trading portal anyway. It has a great user experience that end users say they love as they see it launched on their desktops.

The portal is still going to fail because, ultimately, the traders have no long-term incentive to use the system, even though they claim at launch that they will use it.

How could such a mistake happen?

Consider if this were the case: The trading portal project is sold to the CEO who thinks the efficiencies and productivity gains sound great. The system's end users—old-school employees, whose trading relationships are closely guarded or who prefer their face-to-face transactions—see the exchange as a threat. A big conflict ensues between the CEO, with his business goals, and the end-user employees, with their needs.

Unless the CEO changes the way the trading exchange is incorporated into the traders' work flow, the employees will sing the party line about wanting to use it but will not change their established behaviors. The exchange can only be successfully integrated into the work flow if all of the old traders retire and new, younger ones—who aren't threatened by the new trading platform—take their places.

The CEO has failed to understand the broader interpretation of the user experience, to wit: The mechanics of the experience or the software or the computers are not all that's important—so are the behaviors of the people who will use it. When companies forget that a human being is at the end of the wire, projects fail to return on their massive capital investments, management gets fired, a new team comes in, and all the same mistakes get made. It's the same old story.

To avoid this problem, the planning process must include those who can contribute to the broader interpretation of user experience at the outset. Says experience strategist Deborah Frieze: "It may be a problem if the marketing people are running the user experience. They often don't have a grasp of the larger issues that are involved in designing these user experiences. The change-management people should be involved from the outset, working on ways to ensure that the end users will indeed use the system."

User Experience Demands More Cognitive Work from All Involved in the Process

The change-management part of the user experience highlights the cognitive and behavioral aspects of the experience. Specifically, management needs to understand that regardless of the strategy, the design, or technologies used, the ultimate end users are people—who don't evolve as rapidly as technology. The user experience offers the start, or the continuation, of a relationship, with significant long-term value.

The people who understand this concept best are the cognitive scientists. They specialize in the interdisciplinary study of the mind and the nature of intelligence. And they understand that the ultimate end user is a human being with well-entrenched behaviors, beliefs, goals, and needs. Far too many firms forget this fact.

Most design or marketing people do not have cognitive training in their background, but they will need it now and in the future to design ubiquitous experiences. Currently, the cognitive component of experience design in firms is too disconnected from the rest of the user-experience work. Designers sit with and collaborate with other designers, and technologists work with other technologists, but the cognitive scientists don't always talk to either one of these groups—and they need to.

In the future, a new type of hybrid environment must emerge. Experience design will have to include the following types of hybrid training:

- Hard-core formal cognitive training for designers
- Hard-core formal cognitive training for marketing people
- Design and business training for cognitive-science team members

Everybody in these distinct disciplines should also understand certain fundamentals such as how to set business goals and objectives to meet business needs. Designers should understand and keep in mind the business objective at all times. Creating an intranet page displaying the results of the experience matrix (see Table 4-4), and making this page available to designers at all times is one way of exposing designers to the business drivers. In order to accept the business goals, designers must understand them, know how to interpret them, and believe that they are important. Designers and technologists do not have to be experts in business strategy as long as they understand the objectives of the business goals and use them as essential tools—just as they do their design palettes, applications, and typefaces.

At the same time that the designers and technologists are becoming more business-aware, the project managers, product managers, and marketing managers will be under greater pressure to achieve success. The traditional methods of user-experience development (strategize, architect, design, and build) will demand better project management that can effortlessly bob and weave throughout the distinct disciplines, understanding the cognitive design issues, the design process, the challenges of technical development, and the needs of the customer—all while constantly keeping the entire process moving forward. The managers will need to understand the game plan as well as who needs to be on the playing field at any given time. Knowing who needs to be present for meetings and making sure they show up is just one way to keep the user-experience development wheel turning.

Going Forward: Hybridized Competencies and Contextual Specialists

More and more, firms will be designing user experiences for a multitude of contexts and channels: the wired desktop, wireless devices for real-time retail, voice-activated access of services over a cell phone, and intelligent broadband to the home. The emergence of new contexts will mean that we can build upon known methodologies we learned during the dot-com era. Says experience strategist Deborah Frieze: "This may be the first time that we created frameworks to transcend context. With the emergence of the Web as a platform for doing business with customers, we learned how to design in a shifting medium—for a shifting audience, and to accommodate many different types of behaviors."

We have the eservices firms and the integrators to thank for this. Under great pressure to learn quickly, to stay on the cutting edge, and to develop solutions for their clients while growing their own knowledge capital, many of them helped define formal methods for putting these constantly shifting variables—audience, medium, and behaviors—in the same sentence. Although some of them had more rigorous methodologies than others, a rich body of practices for integrating business strategy, user-centric design, cognitive methods, and technology development grew out of their work in the last few years and is now making its way into the mainstream of best practices. These firms continue to evolve these practices for new media and technologies. Their workers are now practicing experience design, either in new firms or on their own.

In the future, it will be easier to leverage this knowledge of ubiquitous computing to create experiences for a constrained medium. Although there will be experience conceptualists who understand how to create synergistic experiences across channels and thus transcend any medium, contextual specialists will also emerge who understand behavior in the wireless or appliance world. Says Alan Schell, director of product design and definition at ePrise, a Boston firm that develops content management software: "In designing for ubiquitous experiences, the contextual environment will be even more important for the designer to understand. You can be designing an experience to be used on a boat, or without power." Just as an architect who designs custom homes might not be the same architect who designs an office park or a Manhattan skyscraper, so, too, will specialists emerge who focus on the creation of wireless or appliance design, or who design for broadband consumers. Just as general-practitioner physicians are being outnumbered by clinical specialists, so user-experience design generalists will give way to specialists more and more. This field is just too complex to know about everything all at once.

The User Experience as Intellectual Property

The user experience is a new form of intellectual property that has value just like any other intangible asset such as a brand identity, a unique user-interface mechanism, or an established customer relationship.

Patents such as Amazon.com's "1-Click" buy can serve to prevent competitors from taking advantage of unique aspects of the user experience by designing experiences that are too similar and thereby gaining market share. User experiences may be covered by patents and also by copyright, which covers the expression of the idea. The icons for the Macintosh desktop are protected by copyright, for example, whereas the underlying software may be covered by one or more patents.

Intangibles such as Uniform Resource Locators are now being bought at fire-sale prices alongside computers, desks, and other hard assets. During the dot-com era, patents were thought of as less important than first-mover advantage or market share, and nobody had two months to spare to prepare patent applications, but firms today will benefit from fostering a culture of innovation that seeks to protect inventions if they are indeed novel and unique.

Valuing user experiences as intellectual property is an emerging field, and it can be a profitable one. Unique and original user experiences, often patentable, can constitute assets worth a substantial amount now and in the future. I worked for a company whose patents were sold to a competitor for tens of millions of dollars— many years after the original company had folded.

Companies can easily increase the tangible value of their user experiences by creating a culture in which intellectual property is reviewed and documented as a matter of course. They can also do so by establishing practices to help team members understand what is unique and novel about the user experiences they design and develop.

Companies can increase the tangible value of their user experiences by:

- fostering a culture in which intellectual property is reviewed and documented as part of normal practices
- having a relationship with an IP attorney, which is good practice

To do this, the process and product must be documented well enough to be delivered to an intellectual-property (IP) attorney skilled in obtaining patents. The documentation should describe the mechanics of the expression of the invention, using flowcharts and diagrams illustrating the flow of information or the completion of transactions. The clearer and more substantive the documentation, the better and faster the attorney will be able to assess the patent readiness of the user-experience design. The practices outlined in Chapters 4, 5, and 6 for defining customer and business requirements, developing prototypes, and performing competitive analysis will produce documentation, such as information architectures and storyboards, making it easier for an IP attorney to understand the invention and to produce a draft of the claims.

Having a relationship with an IP attorney who can consult on matters of patent protection is a good practice. Some firms with a high flow of inventions have in-house patent counsel. Firms in a hurry to cover their inventions file provisional patent applications to preserve the right to file formal patent applications later. In the United States, patents have value for twenty years after the application is filed. Thus, firms thinking about the longer term should put in place the best practices for capturing and processing user-experience inventions, and they should do this as part of the ongoing process of building up assets. A provisional application can often make use of documentation that already exists, and it is relatively inexpensive to prepare. However, the provisional application is not examined and must be replaced by a formal application within a year. The IP attorney will help decide if filing a provisional application in advance of the formal application makes sense. Since the provisional or formal application must be filed within one year after the first publication, public use, or sale of the system, the IP attorney should evaluate potentially patentable inventions well in advance of the one-year deadline.

I was fortunate to begin my career as a young software engineer at a firm that valued intellectual property and innovation. The CEO was an avid inventor and engineer who awarded special compensation and an award plaque for every patent produced. Young engineers were encouraged to have an ongoing dialog with the in-house patent counsel team, many of whom were engineers as well as attorneys. As a result, I learned to keep good notes about design and development process. As I became comfortable with the language of patenting, I proactively helped the attorneys prepare the claims as I went about my everyday work. Today, as the competition to develop novel and unique technology heats up, and as firms place higher value on the user experience as an asset, the designer's sketchbook will become as critical a tool as the scientist's lab notebook.

Cultural Changes in the Organization

The best user experiences are produced by teams with senior management that really "gets" user experience and thus can align the organization's culture with customers' needs. User experience will emerge as an important component of firms' strategic planning processes, and team members will play an increasingly important role in development. "User experience professionals need to bring strong persuasive skills to the table," says Alan Schell of content management software firm ePrise, "to argue on behalf of the end user but be mindful of the bottom line. Because they often don't do any code, they have to convince people to build the right product."

Aligning the functional groups around customer relationships is one way to assure that the customer is the focus of the organization. As is practiced at State Street Global Advisors' Web strategy group, design, technology, content management, compliance officers, and product management all collaborate closely in the design of the private extranets for institutional clients—and sit in one multidisciplinary group. This setup helps combat the "stovepipe" problems that plague firms that don't share product, customer-profile, and relationship information. Every project begins with rigorous business planning in which all business owners declare their business goals and work on defining the goals of their end users. Clearly articulating the end users, the tasks they need to complete to accomplish their goals, and their expectations of the experience are all critical components to define at the outset of any planning project.

As companies look to cut costs and develop and execute their Web-development strategies in-house as opposed to outsourcing, they will serve as their own integrators, or "general contractors," in the development of online customer relationships. The skills of the ecommerce integrators—cutting-edge technology, user-experience design know-how, technology integration, and execution—are being established as competencies inside of firms. Thus companies will have to foster the rich learning cultures that the ecommerce integrators have established; keeping abreast of technology, design, and user-experience methods will demand this. Management will have to make the case for usability to be part of the lifeblood of the firm, and they will have to understand the cost savings that will benefit the firm by catching usability issues early in the process, not after launch.

Measure the Overall Success of the User-Experience Strategy

The best user experience for the least capital investment is the optimum formula for profitability. In today's fast-changing business environment, companies must not invest wantonly or impulsively; instead they must allocate just enough resources to deliver what the market needs at a given moment. Rather than do "too good" a job, companies should do one that is "good enough"—although "good enough" varies from one industry to another. Cell-phone users, for example, will pay for "good enough" (that is, spotty) coverage for the sake of mobile connectivity. New-car buyers, though, won't accept a good-enough automobile that lacks attractive detailing and a high level of comfort and safety.

Creating an ROI model for new user experience means defining the business case and the business success metrics and mapping against them. The business metric must translate clearly into the user experience. For example, with Emode.com, the online personality test site with over 9 million registered users, retention is not measured by engagement. "We don't want people to stay too long; it's a cost center," says Emode CEO James Currier. Improving the interface means improving the business metrics in an ongoing fashion. Says Currier: "You are limited by what you can measure, but we look at sixteen different variables, and we do it every week. We see what people are doing, where they are going, and we gauge their response to the new features that we have added."

Emode does this analysis consistently and religiously. By measuring aspects of usability in relation to profitability, their model promotes their business strategy's success. Says CEO Currier: "Usability drives the relationship with the end users, and ultimately, our clients are paying us to build and maintain that relationship on their behalf. Usability is great brand; usability is great content."

The Web provides a leveragable platform on which Emode tests new ideas and refines the user experience by using immediate feedback and analysis of user-experience trends that impact profitability. The Emode model signals the future of how firms will develop better and more useful experiences that deliver what customers want.

part three

the future

the future of user-experience design: global, mobile, and intelligent

As we move forward into a world where microelectronics and pervasive technology begin to impact our lives in the way cell phones and beepers already have, we must keep in mind that although technology is evolving at breakneck speed, humans are not. It's a known fact that people don't evolve as quickly as technology—or businesses and investors—would like. Going forward, designing successful user experiences means that factor will have to be kept in mind. New ways will have to be devised to balance the cognitive limits of end users with the accelerated drive to develop innovative and marketable technology.

The paragraphs that follow discuss the near and far future of user experience design and its impact on creating viable businesses. Understanding how to approach creating successful user experiences in the future means first considering the past.

Shaker Experience Design

Shaker design and culture, originating from a communal utopian society in the late 1700s, embraced modern technology, and Shaker craftsmanship is known for its simplicity and admired for its excellence. Shaker culture revolved around the characteristics of devotion, thrift, humanity, and ingenuity, all in the service of applying their inventions toward enhancing their society. Today, Shakers would be considered entrepreneurial; one can only imagine the kinds of experiences possible if Shakers were now developing hardware and software.

As many of the commerce experiences become virtual in our society, the framework that the Shakers established for their work should serve as a model for companies to create successful user experiences. The Shakers embraced modern technology and dedicated themselves to continual learning, constantly reading scientific journals and applying new techniques in their work. That care and craft offers insight into how caring deeply about the end result of craft can impact the user experience, no matter if the end result is sitting in a chair or accessing the Net through a handheld wireless device. Through a deep knowledge of materials and techniques—passed down between generations by careful observation, mentoring, and trial and error—Shakers understood the problem they were trying to solve and pursued perfection relentlessly. They knew the "why" behind the "how," and they understood what it meant to design experiences in the presence of constraints. They also understood what parts of the process could leverage technology—such as new tools or devices, and what parts needed the touch of a human hand to deliver the best experience to the people who would use what they designed.

Shakers' alignment of values across their society meant that the entire organization was committed to the best possible results. They valued and shared their knowledge: Senior Shakers taught younger members the craft and techniques for solving design challenges. An even distribution of power, regardless of gender, existed in their society. Gender didn't matter; smarts, savvy ideas, and dedication to craft did. They took a deep pride in their work and a joy in the process of craft. They aimed for perfection in their designs, because they believed that any piece of handiwork should be able to stand before God. Indeed, it's been said that a Shaker designer put so much energy into the design of a chair because it was believed possible that an angel might some day sit in it.

Shaker philosophy and design offer a model for the design of successful user experiences: working in the service of helping end users of technology, people, to be better at what they do, and at how they do it, and delivering an enjoyable and highly valued experience in the process.

User-Experience Design for the Future

In the future, we can benefit by applying some of the approaches that Shakers used in designing things that produce real value. Success of the product or experience can be measured by the market and by the degree of utility and pleasure that such designs bring to the lives of those who experience them. We are approaching the limits of Moore's law: It's no longer possible to develop ever-smaller and faster silicon-based electronic chips. We'll need to come up with new ways of thinking about designing experiences that occur in a wider variety of physical locations and under more diverse and demanding conditions than we design for today.

New types of microelectronics have arrived: small-scale electronics, tiny sensors, and wireless embedded devices, for example. With them we'll have new types of user experiences that won't involve the types of interaction we have now: sitting at a desk using a machine or typing keys or speaking into a cell phone. Instead, these experiences will happen naturally, transparently. Some of these user experiences will arrive with an increase in tangibility; unlike experiences in which a graphical user interface is viewed and used, new types of experiences will be held or physically interacted with in different ways. As happens when one wears a pacemaker, these new experiences may happen without us even being aware of them. Some of these experiences will span and integrate multiple modes such as voice, gesture, and vision; others won't need to and will remain simple. "The cell phone is ubiquitous and not integrated into anything," says Maggie Orth, recent MIT Media Laboratory Ph.D. graduate and now CEO of International Fashion Machines, "and there's no compelling reason for it to change."

Designing these new kinds of experiences will be less like shaping a piece of furniture by hand and more like orchestrating an event that will occur in another environment or context, at another time. Designers will be creating rules and guidelines for behaviors that the computer will use in delivering the user experience in the appropriate context and against constraints. Because no one will be able to predict the environments and contexts in which user experiences will occur, what is truly useful must be kept in mind and a valuable experience must be designed to be delivered in many potential contexts.

In the near future, user experiences will get more translucent: We'll still be able to see them, but they may begin to be less perceptible. As computers become increasingly smaller, more mobile, more intelligent, and more autonomous, these user experiences will begin to feel more like using an E-ZPass to buy drive-through fast food. Deriving the value from the experience—the transaction completion, or the delivery of the appropriate information to the proper channel—will require little or no work on the part of the end user.

The next phase, after the near future, is the far future. This will be where it gets really interesting, and scary. It's where the integration of electronic and digital systems interface with biology.

Fixing human beings is the first branch of the far future in user-experience design. As a designer of human–machine interfaces over the last fifteen years, I have seen machines get smaller, faster, smarter—and creep closer to the human body. I know that my work will soon jump the chasm and be done at the wet/dry interface: the interstice between biology and electronics. I know I'll be designing technology and electronically delivered experiences that live inside or alongside the human body. I can't wait, although I wish I'd taken more molecular biology in college. I'm going to need it.

The evolution of the user experience in the far future presents a big ethical issue that will have to be dealt with: superhumans, whose intelligence or physical attributes have been augmented or enhanced.

This development may be the next step in human evolution. The potentially dangerous desire to control human evolution is already underway, and the ongoing debate on stem-cell research on human embryos is a glimpse of what is to come. Advertisements in the back of Ivy League alumnae magazines looking for egg donors with "blonde hair, long legs, and an Ivy degree" illustrates there's a demand out there for enhanced humans. And markets arise around demand. All of us will have to be careful about how we allow this design for living to take place.

But let's get back to thinking about user experiences in business in the near future.

Better Match Between the Business Case and the User Experience

We learned from the dot-com era that user experiences contributed in part to the value-creation equation. Sometimes, it was possible to develop businesses around these experiences. Sometimes it wasn't. Napster proved that a global conversation about music could take place on the Net and that huge demand for a user experience (in this case, a collective experience centered on a global conversation about music) could drive a new business paradigm, peer-to-peer (P2P) computing.

Yet courts ordered Napster shut down. What happened? There was a huge demand for the experience, but the business case could not be built. Copyright and intellectual-property issues got in the way—and the infrastructure and integration needed to deliver the environment for conducting commerce did not exist.[1] Record companies could have leveraged this technology to pioneer new forms of distribution for music, yet they failed to embrace this technology. We can pay for tolls without putting coins into the hands of toll takers, and we know how to implant cochlear implants into brains to enable deaf people to hear, yet we can't figure out new ways for consumers to experience music through the Internet. In the same way that video

rental did not destroy the motion-picture business (it only made consumers love movies more), the Net offers a vehicle to expose more
people to music—and to get them more actively engaged as fans. The
music industry had the perfect vehicle to deliver what consumers
want: personalized music experiences and the ability to establish
closer relationships with bands and other fans. And at the same time
the experience would have delivered exactly what the music industry
needs: loyal, retained customers. Yet, unfortunately, the industry
passed on this opportunity.

The Near Future: MultiModal and Transactional

Ubiquitous computing will move us closer to the way technology
should be integrated into our lives, without the need for abstractions
such as the desktop, mice, and icons. "The things that drive ubiquity are sensors, low-power processors, miniaturization, and wireless,"
says Joseph Paradiso, principal research scientist at the MIT Media
Laboratory. "With the blend of all that, there is no reason for the
computer to be on the desktop any more."

Ubiquitous transactions will happen invisibly, with little or no
effort on the part of the user. For firms to create value with this new
kind of computing paradigm, they'll have to figure out how to make
money from the stream of bits being delivered to the user, the relationship between the human and the bits, or the delivery vehicle—in
the underlying transactions, infrastructure, and intelligence that will
deliver ubiquitous computing.

Ubiquitous User Experiences: Like Lycra®

In a sense, a business goal for companies that want to be successful
in ubiquitous computing is to develop a business equivalent of
Lycra®, the material that shows up in all different types of apparel,
in many different guises and forms. In the same way that Lycra® has
become a ubiquitous material used for many types of clothing, new

user experiences will become part of many different objects that are part of our everyday lives, so elastic and pervasive that we won't know we're using them. Good user experiences will arise from new ventures that figure out how to create the "Lycra®" that becomes the basis for widespread and pervasive experiences. Companies that concentrate on delivering the bits and transactions to appliances and devices, the tools for managing them, and the intelligence required to get to the right place at the right time will be the winners. Similar to the way that Dolby Laboratories develops and licenses audio technologies for use in the consumer-electronics industry, the winners in ubiquitous computing will create pervasive technologies that show up everywhere, in everything, and that can be mass produced—and impact people's lives by delivering better experiences.

MetaCarta: Technology for Ubiquity

For the past several months, I have been helping an MIT startup called MetaCarta. MetaCarta makes maps more useful "by filling the previously static map with hyperlinked nuggets of local intelligence," says co-founder John Frank. The team must consider the user experience on the desktop Web, the wireless Web, and in custom applications beyond any Web browser. Maps are geographical abstractions; they reflect relationships and spatial relevance of a body of information, which can be messy and unstructured.

MetaCarta is a good example of a user experience for ubiquitous computing that can potentially drive a profitable business, similar to that of Dolby Laboratories: The back-end technology consists of patented algorithms that organize unstructured text from any source, including the Web, by placing that knowledge in context at appropriate locations in space, time, and the network of associations that make that knowledge useful. The company's vision is centered on intuitive analysis of spatial and temporal relationships among pieces of knowledge, which is clearly a highly visual, interaction intensive task.

Conscious of the changed venture-capital climate, the MetaCarta team has gone to their customers for much of their funding. Starting with early adopters in the government and focused segments inside large corporations, they have connected their development with the people most interested in buying it. This early connection is shaping the product, changing the details of the specification, helping to answer the difficult questions.

User Experiences That Deliver Real Value: Less Bloatware, More Usefulware

Ubiquitous computing will cause a higher value to be placed on the design—and it will mean the end of "bloatware." As more and more devices begin to look and behave like smart consumer devices, we'll have to focus on getting the experience just right and not more. The lousy experiences that are being handed to consumers of desktop software and called "empowering" will never pass muster in ubiquitous computing. Relevance and context will be critical, as experiences will be judged on how closely they deliver the appropriate information. The amount of pain consumers are willing to withstand won't be an indication of the value of the experience; instead, there will be more choice and opportunity for consumers to mix and match experiences using decentralized appliances and devices. They won't be tethered to the Net the way they are now. These tangible interfaces will mean that we'll have to deal with clutter more than we have before, because many of the user experiences will not be aggregated and delivered through a graphical interface. Good-enough experiences will mean basic core functionality, not lots of fancy and useless features. There won't be room for bloatware in ubiquity; there will be nowhere to hide all of the useless toolbars and buttons. Google is a great example of "usefulware"; that the firm is on its way to being profitable is no coincidence. "The central idea of ubiquity is moving to the kind of physical world that people are used to," asserts Joe Paradiso at the Media Lab. "The desktop is already an abstraction that does this to a limited extent. It's better than punched cards, but it's still an abstraction."

The marriage of physical devices with the integration of smart systems will only deliver value if the experiences have the appropriate intelligence in the underlying infrastructure—and, in turn, can drive a business case. For example, suppose the airbag deploys in my new car. The car's location is then relayed via an emergency signal sent to a twenty-four-hour premium assistance service that comes with the car. A human advisor then calls the car via the onboard cellular phone and ascertains the nature of the emergency, notifying emergency assistance in the geographical location of the car, if necessary. These multichannel user experiences will be delivering real value, and consumers will pay for them—or the manufacturers will pay for them. They will blend usefulness with business relevance.

For ubiquity to really deliver value to users, experience design for ubiquity must rest on the notion of appropriateness and the satisfaction of several key elements of the experience-design equation:

- The need for integration: an integrated underlying infrastructure
- Contextual intelligence: appropriate intelligence and sensing of the experience context
- Appropriateness: an understanding of how to fit the design of the experience to the user's needs

The hallmark of new experience architecture will be the orchestration of multiple modes and user interfaces working in concert and in new combinations; for example, one experience might combine voice recognition, biometrics measurement, gestures or eye-movement measurement, and a mobile device. Even experience architectures in use now, such as enterprise portals, will participate in ubiquity. They'll just deliver the information to other devices and appliances at the right time in the appropriate way. Ease of use will have to become more well understood. Marketers will have to know what it means to create a great experience in this new "orchestrated medium." Ease of use will be tied more closely to profitability than ever before, and usability will be factored into strategic planning the way financial services firms calculate risk into the design of new investment products and services.

Wireless Is Not Just the Web

Wireless is not just the Web. It's a constrained delivery vehicle that uses the Web. While it often offers more than the conventional desktop Web experience, it also sometimes offers less. It's less expressive than the desktop Web experience, more like MS DOS than anything else. The clicks and bits have to help the human more: They have to work harder and be more intelligent about the user's expectations. As with my colleague whose soccer scores were delivered all day to his cell phone, we'll have to be more mindful that what we design is built for use. User experiences can be measured by tracking trends about how people feel about them. One measure is how often frustrated users are smashing their computer monitors, keyboards, and mice and bringing them into computer repair shops. If we continue to see this trend in ubiquity, we'll know we're doing something wrong.

New types of licensing and partnership deals among firms will be negotiated based on the user experience. That AOL and Swatch have completed a deal to develop an Internet access watch means mobility and connectivity have reached the mainstream business. The blend of fashion and technology will result in design processes being accelerated again.

Smart phones will consolidate personal digital assistant (PDA) and beeper functionality. As we heap more functionality onto these devices, however, we'll have to carefully consider the form factor and how the user experience impacts the business case. We'll either have to file our fingernails to the size of toothpicks to use the ever-smaller keypad, or invent better approaches for people to input alphanumeric data without adding bulk to the device. Digit Wireless founder David Levy, an MIT doctoral graduate in ergonomics and former ergonomic designer at Apple Computer, has launched a company to solve this user-experience challenge. His patented Fastap keypad, intended for cellular phones and wireless devices, allows nearly three times the number of keys to fit inside the surface area of a small cell-phone keypad by use of a clever bit of ergonomic innovation. The result is a cell phone with a computer interface as easy to use as the twelve-button keypad it replaces. (see Figure 8-1). Users won't have to go through histrionics to enter a URL, write a short email, surf the Web, or buy things with a cell phone. By giving the telephone a computer interface that is powerful, quick, and intuitive, the Fastap key-

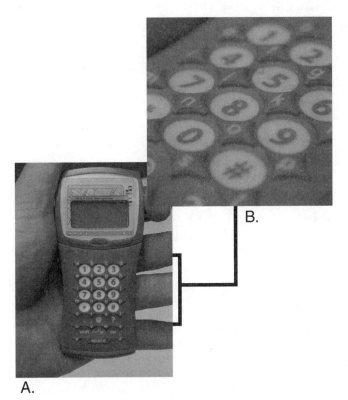

Figure 8-1. Figure A above shows the Fastap keypad, designed to make it easier to enter information into a cell phone or wireless device in a small footprint. Figure B above shows a closeup of the user interface for the keypad. Raised buttons are comfortably distant from adjacent buttons, and the valleys between them form additional keys. Pressing on any button or in any valley produces a unique output that is clearly identified—and instantly available.

pad meets all the criteria necessary to unlock the potential of the wireless Web. According to Levy: "People talk about the economic potential of ubiquitous computing and the wireless Web, but the fact is that trying to operate a computer with only twelve keys is as frustrating and slow as it sounds. The next wave of computer prosperity will come to us through relatively dumb terminals, called phones, that sit in our pockets and give us access to lots of smarts. But this next wave is not going to happen with an interface that is nearly half a century old. It can be done, but it is painful, like trying to operate a computer without a mouse." Digit Wireless's innovative, fully functional alphanumeric keypad is a step in the right direction toward making handheld wireless devices usable. More complete usability will arrive when this kind of interface is integrated with voice—specifically continuous speech recognition, allowing for a truly rich two-way experience with a handheld device.

Scenarios of the Future: What Happens to Marketing?

As we consider the future, it's impossible to consider the evolution of user experiences without looking at how the future of marketing will evolve.

SCENARIO 1:
THE NET MAKES MARKETING MORE QUALITATIVE

What happens to user experiences in the next five years if marketing becomes less and less focused on the hard numbers and more focused on the soft metrics and relationships? Qualitative measurements such as number of site visits, length of visit, number of screens and transactions completed, and user satisfaction all become a proxy for expected results.

Let's assume that all the analytics of user experience have proven not to work. Making marketing more analytical turns out to be a disaster: There are lots of clicks but no way to correlate the data to profitability. It's difficult, if not impossible, to tell from the data what is happening: The applications end up looking like big data-mining projects, and nobody has the time or the inclination to sort through the numbers. Or the tools are too difficult to use, the models too complex, too expensive, or marketers won't learn them because they don't have time. Or real-time tracking of the channel data is a disaster, because it makes the user experience too slow for the user. Perhaps consumers' privacy concerns have pushed marketers away from tracking and tracing activities of users.

In this situation, to understand the needs for the user experience, businesses will have focus on the quality of the relationship with customers and use direct observation: surveys, focus groups, and old-fashioned market research and usability tests. And all of this will take a lot of time and effort. The value will be on the relationship with the customer but measured in soft metrics, and new qualitative indices will emerge that represent the soft side of customer relationships, such as attitudes toward and feelings about the user experience. The net result is that it takes too long to develop user experiences, although they will be well-targeted to what users claim they want, if the market requirements don't change in the meantime.

Usability practice becomes a highly esteemed competency center, because it's where the business success is proven with qualitative results and it's the place where marketing managers know their products are useful and well-liked. Perhaps a new consulting industry crops up to which marketing—now solely focused on the soft metrics—outsources any of the analytics to user-experience analysts who are like actuarials at insurance agencies. Nobody wants to actually understand the models for calculating risk; they just want the qualitative answer about what to build to enhance the customer relationship, the perfect mix of features, the risk for building X versus Y. Nobody knows how to build a model for measuring the consistency of the customer relationship across channels; they just build the channels without any regard for how the overall success will be measured.

Customers who want the high-touch relationship with a firm think it's great. Those that want a more transactions, efficiency-oriented one think it's awful.

We can see where this is going. It's not going to work.

SCENARIO 2:
THE NET MAKES MARKETING MORE ANALYTICAL

Imagine that, instead of the previous scenario, analytics are proven to indeed work. New tools and analytics link the user experience to profitability in real time: marketing becomes analytical.

Marketing managers, the new owners of the user experience, become like portfolio managers, using powerful and easy-to-learn dashboard suites of tools to show them the hard numbers in real time. These tools clearly show how usability is impacting profitability. And they tell how the user experience is succeeding or failing to perform in key aspects: in initial use, in transaction initiation, in customer service across channels. Usability is tied to profitability in the real-time models, and managers can trace a 1 percent increase in usability to its impact on the bottom line. Real-time customer feedback is incorporated in the model that the manager is seeing, spawning a new practice called demand-driven design. The analytics are so good that all of the channels for communicating with customers (phone, Web, and print) are aggregated and measured in real time to see their impact on profitability. Nothing gets built unless there is a measurable demand from the channels that satisfies a specific business metric. "Kill early, kill often" is the mantra that managers live by. There's less waste, more efficiency.

The role of experience architects changes, and transactional architecture becomes a new form of dynamic information architecture. Like transportation engineers who understand how to design traffic systems to optimize the ebb and flow of traffic over the course of a commuting day—and adapt to a slower more sparse level on the weekends—these new experience architects understand how to craft the containing framework and let the experience evolve itself out of user behaviors and activities, and to maximize profitability. These experience architects report directly into marketing and are technically competent to gain the respect of development—and they can speak the language of design.

To survive, marketing managers require better analytical "chops," and they get them by being trained to analyze information, like the best Proctor & Gamble brand managers. Known as data jockeys, the younger marketers really know their numbers, but, like musical prodigies, they are sometimes criticized for being too remote from customers. They rarely, if ever, press the flesh of customers. Why should they? The numbers tell them all they need to know. And if a marketing manager can just get the board to show the right numbers, maybe up the retention rate or make the conversion rate increase by 1 percent, that big bonus will mean the purchase of a new speedboat. Nobody really knows how the customers feel about the product or service, nor does anyone actually know how users "use" it, but the numbers look good. The entire development team can see the real-time analytics on the corporate intranet and, as they would when tracing the firm's stock price all day long, they watch as their own performance is exposed to the whole company: a series of user-experience indices against which their bonuses and compensation is measured. The user experience becomes just a game of numbers.

Here the problem becomes one of passion versus technological expertise. Doesn't this marketer have to have some kind of relationship with the end user? Or does it become a game of numbers, not unlike institutional portfolio managers for large mutual funds?

Usability practice as we know it goes away. There are no more people who practice the art of testing and observing users; it's too slow and the data is too qualitative. Instead, it's all done over the Net, remotely, with sensors embedded in the devices that give real-time feedback on ease of use, usage, and even biometrics like pulse and sweat. Voice recognition registers a spoken complaint from a sweaty test subject in the field with a mobile ecommerce device—and an elevated pulse. "I can't activate my digital coupon!" he yells into the device. This is automatically recognized and translated into a critical update request that is routed to the product manager. Marketing managers know that making users' pulses race and palms sweaty—and seeing a dearth of transactions—can mean that the product is too difficult to use. Or does it mean that the user is hot because it's 98 degrees outside and he has a pre-existing health condition that elevates his heart rate? Is he shouting because he's in a noisy environment? We're not exactly sure, but the numbers pour in and the office of the marketing manager looks like the war room at the Cable News Network.

This is not going to work either.

Scenario 3: The Integrated Approach

Now imagine a scenario that harmoniously integrates the previous two scenarios. The Net makes marketing into a mix of quantitative analytics and qualitative methods, a hybrid discipline that exploits new tools that make it easier, faster, and cheaper to test and validate new designs that customers want and will use.

The practice of usability will change and, although we will still have to observe users completing tasks, we just won't be tied down to a stationary lab to collect the data. Mobility and context will impact the immediate future of usability testing, and it will become more tightly integrated into the disciplines that directly impact it: design and technology. Tying design more closely with usability testing and analysis is a good idea—and one that will greatly help deliver better and more useful experiences. Right now, a huge gap exists in the training of designers, because they aren't educated to think about usability and human factors when they are studying design at design schools. They should. And they will.

The Future of Designing User Experiences

In the future, being an expert in the design of user experiences will become more challenging. Because of the variety of skill sets that will be required, becoming a "general practitioner" of user experience will simply not be possible. Instead, practitioners will focus on specific classes of experience. Companies will emerge that focus on wireless or ubiquitous design, embedded device experiences, and wearable experiences, but it will be too difficult to master all of them, across all modes and channels. Like doctors' specialized practices, user-experience practice will become a specialty-driven one. Jeff Hawkins's skill set—entrepreneurial inventiveness resulting in the Palm Pilot and the Handspring, training in neuroscience and cognitive science, computer science, and electrical engineering—and a passion to create truly useful design—will be the profile of the experience designer of the future.

We'll also need new marketers, ones who are more technically savvy and who know how to craft valued products and brands in all of these modes and channels. They will have to work closely with technologists and designers because it will be more difficult to innovate and will require a real focus on value proposition. The Palm Pilot proved it was indeed possible to create a new market by being clear about the user experience and the product features. Features were limited to what delivered real value; at the same time the experience was constrained to leverage the strengths of the human and of technology and to minimize the weaknesses of both. This kind of efficiency will be required to deliver the killer applications for wireless, ubiquity, and beyond.

The Next Stage: Design by Darwinism

The next stages of user experiences will bring new tools that employ evolutionary techniques, such as genetic algorithms, to help remove tedium for the designer yet enable the validation of product concepts with target users earlier in the design process. The design of silicon chips is now being augmented by chemistry; indeed, soon the design of a microchip will be done in a test tube and no longer by photolithographic process. So too will experience design and prototyping processes also be influenced by new tools that help to quickly invent, evolve, and prototype user-experience concepts for testing with target users. These tools will also help designers kill bad concepts more quickly, to avoid wasting time and resources on suboptimal designs. Think of it as a form of Designer Darwinism.

New ventures such as NewcoGen Group's Affinnova, Inc., in Cambridge, Massachusetts, whose founders are engineers from MIT, are pioneering user experiences that employ a form of Darwinian evolution in product design. In effect, they give the designer a "digital workbench" on which to quickly develop and evolve new concepts. The tools and design environments Affinnova is developing will allow designers to incorporate customer feedback into the design process earlier than before and employ new types of genetic algorithms to arrive at optimal design solutions more quickly. The latter was impossible to execuse on a large scale before the advent of the Web as a collaborative medium.

In the future, instead of hand-crafting design solutions, designers will orchestrate product designs using tools that incorporate constraints about the medium and the business. They will be able to capture and employ rich user feedback in real time, in effect incorporating the customer as design partner. Affinnova's work represents the next era of product design, in which user-experience designers will employ a more hands-off approach to "breed" solutions that satisfy design challenges. As the platforms and technologies for designing experiences get more complex and demand an ever-evolving set of skills and techniques, designers of user experiences will have to employ techniques such as Affinnova's. These will help to augment processes and deliver better results to the end user more quickly.

The Far Future: Nanoscale and Biological

In the far future, user experiences will move beyond the human scale to the molecular or nanoscale. User experiences will be designed to augment broken human beings—or to create superintelligent ones. This development will mean that designers will have the same ethical dilemmas that scientists are now experiencing with human-cloning and DNA-mapping experiments. In the past ten years, the user experiences I have been asked to design are getting smaller and more intimately tied in with the human body, more mobile and global, and more intelligent. I know the next step will be to design at the interstice between biology and electronics: the wet-dry interface. I sit at a meeting at MIT and listen as a chemical engineering professor speaks about her new technique of creating microelectronics using chemicals in a test tube and cheap polymer chips that are at "nanoscale" size and that will cost less than a penny. I know this is the future of ubiquity. She mentions that these chips will soon communicate through electrical impulses with human nerves and biological systems, and I know it is only a matter of time before I begin to cross the border into designing experiences for the landscape within the human body. Asserts MIT Media Lab's Joseph Paradiso, "We'd like to make 'broken' humans better and repair disabilities—research on neural prosthetics like artificial cochlea or retinas and nerve-muscle connections is happening now and is certainly important. But the direct neural-connection 'cyberspace' interface, though, is at the edge. Right now, we have no idea of how to do it."

I'm nervous. And I can see the ethicists revving their engines.

**If technology doesn't seem like magic,
it's probably obsolete.**

The photo above is from 1960 and shows technology for producing audio stimuli for a deaf child. The rabbits' ears have been placed on the headphones to allay his fear of the machine.

Photo credit: Hulton Archive by Getty Images
Composition and caption credit from a card by: The Borealis Press, Inc. 207 667 3700

conclusion

Technology is evolving at breakneck speed. Humans
are not.

Going forward, designing successful user experiences means we will
have to find new ways to balance the cognitive limits of end users
with our accelerated drive to develop innovative technology.
Humans are not evolving as rapidly as businesses, and investors,
would like them to be. We will have to balance the need for profitability and accountability with the desire to innovate and create
new experiences that are truly exciting and unique and novel:
Napster taught us that.

The user experience now bridges the increasingly narrow gap
between humans and technology. Delivering an experience that gives
the end user something of true value is the ultimate goal. Perhaps the
goal might be to give users more time to do what is important to
them, which would mean giving them better tools to work more
effectively so that they have more time to themselves, to be outdoors,
to be with their friends and loved ones. Perhaps what is valued is getting hourly updates on an obscure European soccer team's scores
during the championship—silently sent to a pager held during a long
and boring meeting. Perhaps, for someone who is deaf, what is wanted is to hear music for the first time. That experience is possible now,
with cochlear implants directly into the brain, and we'll be able to do

much more in the next twenty years. All these are user experiences that deliver value.

We will have to work hard, and be willing to make mistakes, to learn about what it means to create relationships that are built—or severed—based on the click. As new forms of technology and connectivity enable us to escape the limitations of being tethered to bulky equipment, we'll go beyond clicks and have new units of interaction: the look, the wink of an eye, the wave of a hand, or the wiggle of a finger. All of these have the opportunity to serve as possible interfaces and input devices to technology. The automobile will soon be considered a mobile wireless device, just as the cell phone is considered to be one now. To make progress, we will have a few serious design accidents. Do we really need real-time interaction to trade equities from our cars? If someone at a particular moment needs to trade from his or her car, and if that person has a portfolio that is already in trouble, other drivers on the road could be in trouble, too. As if cell phones don't cause enough accidents!

As science, medicine, and technology move toward practices that exist on the molecular level, we no longer consider the whole human being anymore. We're way below that, at the molecular scale now. Nanotechnology gets us down to the "tiny science" of molecular microelectronics, and stem-cell research and human cloning make us think about cells, DNA, and laboratory techniques, not people. And as experience designers, we will undoubtedly have to wrestle with these same issues, in a different way. What about the human? Is human scale gone? We need to consider the human in the experience, not to get so focused on the subhuman level that we forget that the end users are people.

Among the finalists at the MIT $50k Business Plan competition in 2001, not one of them was a dot-com organization. The winners? Angstrom Medica, a firm founded by two Ph.D. chemical engineers and a medical doctor who is also a business school student. Angstrom Media uses a nanotechnology platform to make hydroxyapatite, a material identical in composition to synthetic bone. Angstrom's products will be used to reconstruct fractures with implantations of the material at the fracture site. Once the material is inserted at the fracture site, it gets incorporated with the natural bone, allowing faster and more uniform healing. Drug delivery is a future possibility. Remember the wet-dry interface mentioned in the last chapter? It's already here.

Pervasive technology will become even more a part of the fabric of our lives: The warp and weave will be the sensors and chips and biometric devices that we will wear and use every day. To win in this new world of microelectronics and mobile technology, companies will need to understand what user experiences will be valued by end users. And they will have to do this more quickly, more cost effectively, and for increasingly more complex technology with lots of constraints. New evolutions of technology—in new combinations that span multiple modes and allow users to engage with technology through multiple senses and with new mobility—will offer endless business opportunities to those companies that can figure out how to add value in the transactions, the delivery, the infrastructure—or all three. Delivering the killer app will mean leveraging and combining these new technologies into experiences that add value. Firms will have to think entrepreneurially, with vision tethered to sound business models, to learn rapidly and kill bad ideas early. We will see new configurations of development teams—molecular biologists and chemists—working with technologists and designers.

User-centric design coupled with business relevance is what customer-experience architecture should be about, now and in the future. Driven by a solid business model and mindful of the needs of the customer, the best experiences will leverage both motivators to develop user experiences that deliver value in new markets.

Keeping the human in control will be key. If I choose to shut off my beeper or pager or cell phone, I can. I can't shut off my cochlear implant or my pacemaker. Human-centric means that the human is still in control and that humans' needs are at the core of the design. The difference between a world that lets technology and innovation run amok and one that is careful about its evolution is like a city that grows too large too fast to ever afford a comfortable stroll around the neighborhood—it goes beyond the human scale. Amsterdam, with its concentric rings of canals, is an example of a city that is built for use, at the human scale. One strength of desktop computing is that the technology is still on a scale that we can see and feel. Soon, we won't even have that.

Like DNA sequencing, once computing goes beyond the human scale—to the nanoscale—we won't be able to see it, we may not trust it, and we may lose control of it. Control is one of the most critical aspects to creating user experiences. If we lose this, or if we take it away from the user, we lose the trust of the human at the other end of the wire.

To keep it from all spinning out of control, recall the quiet Shaker hand on wood, planing the chair until it's perfect, smooth, built for use—good enough for an angel to sit on.

appendix:
tying profitability to usability

Firms should consider these guidelines in planning and developing user experiences.

1. Drive the design and development closely by the business case.

2. Make sure all team members—business, technology, design—clearly understand the business goals and how usability impacts these goals.

3. Connect financial metrics to customer satisfaction and usability metrics, and measure them in an ongoing fashion.

4. Make the success measurement the responsibility of one person. Share this information with the team as an index (or set of indices) of usability.

5. Share knowledge among the development team and create a learning culture so each team member understands what other team members contribute to the user experience.

6. Architect for scalability, and make capital investments in architecture before look and feel.

7. Know the customer's needs, tasks, and goals—and make sure the user experience satisfies them.

8. Only add features and functionality that blend value for the customer with value for the firm.

endnotes

CHAPTER 1

1. S. Rajgopal, et al., *Does the Quality of Online Customer Experience Create a Sustainable Competitive Advantage for E-Commerce Firms?*, Stanford University Graduate School of Business, December 2000.

2. Randy Souza, Ronald Shevlin, and Emily H. Boynton, "Next Generation Financial Sites," *Forrester Research,* March 2001.

3. "Only the Ubiquitous Will Survive," *Extraprise Report,* Vol. 3 No. 5, June 2000.

4. Timothy J. Dolan, "eCRM: The Difference Between Winners and Losers in the E-Business World of the Twenty-First Century," *Deutsche Banc Alex. Brown Research Report,* September 1999.

5. The research used scorecards of online customer experience provided by Gomez Associates.

6. For a detailed discussion about issues surrounding business strategy for wireless technologies, see Bryan Bergeron, *The Wireless Web,* McGraw-Hill, 2001.

7. The author compares the process of rearchitecting a site experience to doing structural work on a home, as opposed to doing just cosmetic adjustments.

8. "Turning Browsers into Buyers," *MIT Sloan Management Review,* Winter 2001, 8.

9. "Absurd Valuations in the New Economy," *The New York Times,* March 18, 2001. Sources include Bond & Pecaro, Morgan Stanley Dean Witter, Media Metrix, Bloomberg Financial Markets.

10. Customer acquisition costs for retail sites increased by 15 percent in 1999, from $33 per customer in 1998 to $38 in 1999, according to the *State of Online Retailing 3.0* research report by Shop.org and Boston Consulting Group.

CHAPTER 2

1. Michael Schrage, *Serious Play,* Harvard Business School Press, 2000.

2. For an excellent resource on prototyping and simulation, see *Serious Play.*

3. A. MacCormack, "Product Development Practices That Work: How Internet Companies Build Software," *MIT Sloan Management Review,* Winter 2001, 75–84.

4. Randy Souza, Ronald Shevlin, and Emily H. Boyton, "Next Generation Financial Sites," *Forrester Research,* March 2001.

5. This is also related to Metcalfe's Law.

6. Michael Peltz, "The Voice of the Future," *Worth Magazine,* February 2001, 70.

CHAPTER 3

1. "Turning Browsers into Buyers," *MIT Sloan Management Review,* Winter 2001, 8.

2. J. Nielsen, et al, "E-Commerce User Experience Trust," January 2001, 9.

3. M. Venkatachalam, S. Rajgopal, and S. Kotha, *Assessing an E-Commerce Firm's Value: Customer Service vs. the Bottom Line,* Stanford University Graduate School of Business, February 2001.

4. G. Urban, F. Sultan, and W. Qualls, "Placing Trust at the Center of Your Internet Strategy," *MIT Sloan Management Review,* Fall 2000, 39–48.

5. This notion was suggested to the author by management consultants Hollie Schmidt and Peter Schmidt, partners at Lifting Mind in Lexington, Massachusetts.

6. Malcom Gladwell, *The Tipping Point: How Little Things Can Make a Big Difference,* Little, Brown & Company, 2000

7. Urban, Sultan, and Qualls, "Placing Trust at the Center of Your Internet Strategy," 39–48.

8. Emode.com features a complete Privacy Statement at www.emode .com/emode/privacy/.

9. See the work of Professor Roz Picard at the MIT Media Laboratory: www.media.mit.edu/affect.

10. Ernst & Young site for *Trust, Nielsen Norman Group Report on Trust.*

CHAPTER 4

1. Alan MacCormack, "Product-Development Practices That Work: How Internet Companies Build Software," *MIT Sloan Management Review,* Winter 2001, 75–84.

2. *Forrester Research* recommends segmenting customers by attitude. For more information, see Mary Modahl, *Now or Never: How Companies Must Change Today to Win the Battle for Internet Consumers,* HarperCollins 2000.

3. For more information, see Modahl, *Now or Never.*

4. For a thorough analysis about online marketing research methods, see Joshua Grossnickle and Oliver Raskin, *The Handbook of Online Marketing Research: Knowing Your Customer Using the Net,* McGraw-Hill, 2001.

CHAPTER 5

1. For an excellent source on the process of defining information architectures, see Louis Rosenfeld and Peter Morville, *Information Architecture for the World Wide Web,* O'Reilly, 1998.

2. Information architectures can also be used to satisfy nonbusiness goals.

3. Hans Peter Brondmo, *The Engaged Customer: The New Rules of Interest Direct Marketing,* HarperCollins, 2001.

4. Trellix and Trellix Web are registered trademarks. WebGems is a registered trademark of Trellix Corporation.

CHAPTER 6

1. Tom Gilb, *Principles of Software Engineering Management,* Addison Wesley Longman, 1988, 84–114.

2. Alan MacCormack, "Product Development Practices That Work: How Internet Companies Build Software," *MIT Sloan Management Review,* Winter 2001, 75–84.

3. For more on the topic of integration in B2B systems, refer to M. Davydov, *Corporate Portals and e-Business Integration,* McGraw-Hill, 2001.

4. For more information about the work of the Affective Computing Group at the MIT Media Laboratory, under the direction of Professor Rosalind Picard, visit www.media.mit.edu/affect.

CHAPTER 8

1. A new Napster membership service is set to launch in early 2002. As of the time this book went to press, the firm reached a preliminary agreement with the National Music Publishers' Association (NMPA), in which songwriters will get paid when their works are shared.

glossary

3G: Third-generation communications infrastructure, with the ability to deliver information to hand-held wireless devices at speeds of up to 2 Megabytes per second.

B2B: Stands for Business-to-Business

bots: An abbreviation for "robot," typically meaning software robots, or software agents that can be either autonomous and perform tasks on behalf of the user or serve to perform tasks that might be tedious for a human, such as answering basic customer service questions.

brand: An expectation on the part of a customer that a firm will deliver on its value proposition. For many firms whose business is transacted primarily online, the user experience of the Web site is the brand.

broadband experience: Currently an ill-defined term in the technology industry, but generally representing an ability to consistently transmit more than 1 megabit per second (Mbps) of data to a user through a cable modem or other connection. Broadband can be characterized as either one-way communication (transmitting to the user at high data rates but not allowing the user to transmit back at similar speeds). Newer digital subscriber line (DSL) connections enable full two-way communication at speeds of 1+ Mbps and would be considered full broadband.

browser: A software program that interprets Web-based documents and displays them on a machine such as a desktop computer or wireless device. Internet Explorer and Netscape Navigator are the two most popular browsers used today.

browser conversion: A relationship metric that reflects when a customer actively purchases or transacts, as opposed to just looking or "browsing" for products and services (typically on a Web site).

channel: A medium for communication with customers such as phone, Web, email, or print.

channel harmonization: An effort to deliver a single, seamless relationship to the customer across all channels.

cognitive science: The formal study of the relationship between the brain and intelligence.

compliance: Adherence to a set of guidelines and procedures that govern site content and functionality to ensure that the content meets regulatory and legal requirements, business policy, and appropriateness. In the design of Web sites and online financial experiences, compliance is also a part of content management, as it includes authoring and approvals processes.

conversion: A relationship metric that reflects the point at which a customer furthers his or her relationship with a firm, such as moving from being a browser to a purchaser.

cookie: A small piece of code that is stored on the user's machine that identifies him or her to the Web site. Cookies can help to streamline the user experience by storing such identifiers as account name and password, making it faster for users to log in to a site. At the same time, the use of cookies opens up a potential for privacy invasion because the information stored in the cookie is personal.

corporate portal: A secure and private Web site that delivers aggregated enterprise or corporate information through a user interface that aggregates information into one screen and allows for searching.

DSL: Digital subscriber line, a connection enabling full two-way communication from a digital subscriber line at speeds of 1+ Mbps.

CRM: Customer relationship management, a set of business strategies designed to manage and optimize customer relationships.

eCI: Ecommerce integrator. Firms that specialize in the delivery of business solutions that incorporate business strategy, design and technology development, and integration.

ecommerce: The buying and selling of goods and services through the Internet, especially the World Wide Web.

eCRM: Electronically mediated customer relationship management.

empathy: Being sensitive to the point of view of another. In the case of the design of user experiences, empathy for the end user means that the design considers the goals, needs, and tasks that the user must be able to complete and proactively addresses the concerns and challenges that users will face in using the system.

extranet: A secure and private Web site that delivers enterprise information to the firm's partners or clients.

experience strategist: A practitioner who synthesizes business strategy, design, and technology knowledge into a strategic plan to deliver customer experiences across one or more channels.

first use: The initial experience a user has when seeing or engaging with a site or application for the first time. First use is a critical part of the user experience, because it can greatly affect the ongoing customer relationship.

genetic algorithms: A method of developing software that uses an evolutionary or adaptive approach to solving a problem, such as finding an optimal solution among many options.

HTML: Hypertext Markup Language, the language that browsers interpret to display Web pages.

information architect: A professional practitioner who understands the design of information and how to construct a blueprint for the user experience that satisfies both business and customer goals.

integration: Allowing disparate sources of information, data, or software applications to communicate and exchange data with one another.

intranet: A secure and private Web site that delivers enterprise information to the company.

IP: Intellectual property, such as patents or copyrights.

mobile devices: Devices such as cell phones and hand-held personal-information devices, which may or not be wireless.

navigation: A component of the user experience that enables purposeful action on the part of the user toward satisfying goals and tasks. Navigation can also serve to further the business goals by presenting information designed to upsell or encourage exploration of other products and services to which the user might not otherwise be exposed. Mistakes in navigation impact usability, which in turn impacts customer relationships.

P2P: Peer-to-peer, a decentralized system of networked computers that communicate and share information without a central server.

PDA: Personal digital assistant, a handheld electronic device that serves as an organizer for scheduling, contacts, and email. May have email or connection capability and can also be wireless.

pervasive computing: A new paradigm in computing where embedded microelectronics and underlying network connectivity enable communications among small, cheap devices that may be embedded in appliances and other technologies.

portal: An experience architecture that has been employed successfully in the B2B and consumer spaces, featuring a single aggregated interface to many types of disparate data, typically featuring a search-engine tool.

retention: Maintaining a relationship with a customer. Retention rate is considered a metric of success for online experiences where loyalty is the measure of business success.

ROI: Return on investment, a business measure of success.

ubiquitous computing: The post-desktop computing environment, where intelligent, networked devices and appliances will offer increased mobility and accessibility. Ubiquitous computing is being enabled by the blend of miniaturization, new sensors, low-power processors, and wireless technologies.

UEXP: User experience, one of several abbreviations for this term.

URL: Uniform Resource Locator, the address for a Web site on the Internet.

usability testing: A formal practice of testing users with specific tasks for the purpose of validating that Web sites or applications are usable and enable the successful completion of tasks, and that they satisfy both end-user and business goals.

usage log: The data log that reflects the activities of users on a site, including clicks and transaction completions.

user experience: Describes the customer relationship and underlying enabling mechanisms, including the physical user interface, the engagement and interaction processes, and the feedback system. At a broader level, the user experience also encompasses the business goals and success metrics, the behaviors of end users, and the change management required to drive adoption and usage.

user interface: A component of the overall user experience. Includes the processes and mechanisms that enable a human being to communicate and engage in a dialog with a technology or set of technologies.

WAP: Wireless Application Protocol, a standard for delivering information to cell phones and Internet appliances.

index